THE GRISSIM BUYER'S GUIDE TO MANUFACTURED HOMES & LAND

How to find a reputable dealer and negotiate a fair price on the best kept secret in American housing

Second Edition

By John Grissim

Previously titled:
The Complete Buyer's Guide to Manufactured Homes & Land

RAINSHADOW PUBLICATIONS

Published by: Rainshadow Publications,
a division of Rainshadow Ventures, LLC
7456 Old Olympic Highway, Sequim Washington 98382
Phone (360) 683-1458 Fax (360) 683-1108
www.grissimguides.com Email: publisher@grissimguides.com

This book may be purchased online at the above web site
or by calling toll-free 1-800-304-6650

Images on the cover:
Top: Life Stages home by Fleetwood Homes
Courtesy of Fleetwood Homes, Inc.
Middle: Fairmont home
Courtesy of Fairmont Homes, Inc.
Bottom: Palm Harbor Discovery series, Buckeye model
Courtesy of Palm Harbor Homes, Inc.

Inside photographs: by the author unless otherwise indicated

ISBN   0-9725436-2-7

Printed in the United States of America by McNaughton & Gunn
Cover design: Diedra Steirle, Three-Sixty Graphics

SECOND EDITION

2 3 4 5 6 7 8

Contents

Preface to the second edition

It is a special pleasure to bring this, the second edition of the *Buyer's Guide*, into the manufactured home shopper's marketplace. Not only does this edition contain many revisions, updates and new material, it embodies the helpful comments and suggestions submitted by many of the thousands of home buyers who purchased the guide's first edition. The title has also been revised slightly—from *The Complete Buyer's Guide...* to *The Grissim Buyer's Guide....* and here an explanation is in order:

Within a few months following the book's first publication, a deluge of questions from readers about different manufacturers and brands persuaded me that the chapter I had devoted to brief descriptions of the 25 largest builders was woefully inadequate. In the absence of any guide that described and rated all U.S. builders (79 at last count), I resolved to tackle the project, one that ended up taking nearly 18 months.

The result was a second consumer guide, *The Grissim Ratings Guide to Manufactured Homes*, published in early 2006, designed to be an essential companion resource to this book. Thus, in a real sense, the two books together now properly comprise the *complete* buyer's guide for informed home shoppers. Hence the title change. For more about the *Ratings Guide*, please see the last page of this book.

This new edition has a major expansion on the topic of selecting the right home, including a new three-page Construction Rating Table with 56 criteria that enables you not only to identify what features are associated with different levels of quality, but also to determine the construction quality of any home you are evaluating. This table is by far the most comprehensive listing of construction features ever made available to consumers.

Two other topics are given more attention in this new edition. The installation (or set-up) process—including the role of the set-up contractor—receives an expanded discussion. The reason: many, if not most, major problems that new home owners encounter are caused by improper or negligent installation, not by factory defects. Elsewhere, warranty issues and how best to deal with them are given stronger focus, particularly given the poor ratings that consumers have given the industry in customer satisfaction surveys.

With best wishes for every success in your search for the home of your dreams.

John Grissim

Introduction

Until quite recently, if anyone had told me that early in the 21st century my wife and I would buy a manufactured home and be telling anyone who would listen how thrilled we were, I would have smiled politely and asked them if they were still taking their medication. After all, while the industry strives earnestly to upgrade its product's image, aren't we really talking here about a mobile home? An instant house-in-a-box, built in a factory and then trucked in and dropped off in a trailer park, or plopped down in a field in some rural backwater county to become an attractive nuisance, or tornado bait, or both? Surely you jest.

However, if this same person had predicted that early in the new millennium we would buy property and put on it a 1500 square foot two-bedroom, two-bath, factory-built home with vaulted ceilings, lots of sky lights, a den, a retreat room, a large master bath, a spacious kitchen with Whirlpool appliances and solid oak cabinetry, and that sliding doors would open onto an expansive 300 square foot sun deck, and that the total cost, including a detached two-car garage, well and septic system would be a whopping 25 percent less than the cost of a site-built home with the same features—plus, we would move into that home a mere 73 days after we inked the purchase agreement—well, I still might have given the same skeptical response. But I would have been intrigued.

And intrigued we were when, not long ago, we decided to sell our home in California's Bay Area and move north to a semi-rural community in Washington State. Soon after arriving here we began looking at homes for sale. We found many in our price range but nothing really excited us. Moreover, many homes needed repairs. After a decade of doing our own upkeep and improvements to our last home, we were ready for something less demanding. That's when we decided one morning to check out one or two of the manufactured home dealerships in the area.

Walking through one of the double-wide lot models that was sticker-priced in the mid-range, around $55,000, we were amazed to find ourselves in surroundings that were indistinguishable from a custom site-built home: double-pane insulated windows, high ceilings, solid construction throughout, quality doors and fixtures and a great floor plan.

Before the day was out we had visited several dealerships, looked at a dozen models and collected a stack of brochures. In the process we got a strong first impression that dealers can vary considerably. At one lot, when we walked into the sales offices, the stench and haze of cigarette smoke was so overpowering we had to rush back outside. The salesman on duty probably sensed that our behavior was not a good sign. He was right—we soon left.

By that evening, for the first time since we had arrived, we were excited by a new possibility: buy some undeveloped land and put a new manufactured home on it, get exactly what we want and save a bundle. Could this be done?

Yes, it was possible. And we did it. But in the process we had to deal with a great many issues apart from selecting a home and land—everything from finding a reputable dealer, interpreting well water analyses, working with septic system design engineers and applying for permits, to researching habitat boundaries, building codes, covenants and restrictions and dealing with general contractors, subcontractors, escrow officers, bankers, inspectors and utility districts.

We were fortunate in that our backgrounds were a great help. My wife in earlier years had learned carpentry and had helped build a house, while I had once been active in an environmental group and was familiar with dealing with local government planning and building departments. Still, we often asked ourselves, What about buyers who don't know what's involved, and who don't have the knowledge they need to make important decisions, and to protect themselves from being misled or defrauded and to avoid costly mistakes? What resources do they have?

Very few, we learned. And from that discovery grew the idea for this guide. As our own home project proceeded, we used the experience to learn as much as we could. We took notes and photographs and asked questions, and did a lot of listening. My reporter's instincts were piqued as I learned more about the manufactured housing industry, how it works, and, unfortunately, how its reputation has been sullied by predatory operators, primarily unscrupulous dealers and lenders, who have used fraud and deceit to swindle unwary buyers, especially the most vulnerable—those with limited means such as young families and the elderly .

In the pages that follow you will learn more about these scam tactics, and how to protect yourself, but rest assured the majority of manufactured home dealers are decent reputable professionals whose success and longevity owes to their honesty and commitment to fair dealing and to providing great service, before and after a home sale. This guide shows you how to find them. Indeed, these same dealers were anxious to offer invaluable tips on how to quickly spot the sleazeballs who are simply out to take you.

Likewise, the Arlington, Virgina-based, Manufactured Housing Institute (which ably represents the industry) is acutely aware of the challenge it faces in weeding out the less reputable segments of the industry. The MHI and other industry advocates may be less than happy with some of my opinions and characterizations, but I hasten to add I have no axe to grind. Indeed, without the cooperation and good will of many in the industry, a guide this comprehensive would not have been possible. If I have erred, I have done so on the side of the consumer.

This guide is designed specifically for the first-time buyer of a manufactured home, whether it be a single-wide starter home or a four-section retirement palace, and whether sited on purchased land or in a land-lease community (otherwise widely called a mobile home park).

The recommendations are drawn from interviews over a year's time with scores of people, both inside and outside the industry. They include retailers, installers, retired sales people, home owners, loan officers, county officials, realtors, contractors, warranty repair techs, transport drivers, attorneys, escrow officers, park managers, government officials, consumer advocates, lobbyists, manufacturers, and many buyers and homeowners.

In the pages that follow you will learn how the industry developed, how it markets these homes, especially how they're financed, and what the dealers (even the good guys) don't want you to know. You'll find here ways to calculate your buying power and to determine the true total costs of a home purchase.

The goal is to help you become an informed, pro-active, swindle-proof buyer who knows how to identify and select a reputable dealer, how to determine the fairest and best price, and who can confidently negotiate a square deal.

There are tips and strategies in here designed to save you thousands of dollars and avoid costly problems. But if this guide does nothing more than give you the peace of mind that comes from knowing you made the right decisions at each step on the path to acquiring your new home, its purpose will have been served.

Good luck!

John Grissim

Would you like some expert assistance at a modest cost?

Shopping for and buying a manufactured home, and purchasing or leasing the land that goes with it, can be a daunting process, especially for first-time buyers. There are many decisions to be made, everything from checking out dealerships, to selecting a home and options and negotiating a sales price, to finding reputable lenders with the best loan packages and working with contractors and sub-contractors.

If you would like some personal assistance, I'm here to help. With years of experience dealing with the manufactured home industry, and with a trusted network of experts and professionals I can call on, I can help guide you through the process, providing the no-nonsense advice and clear honest answers you need to help ensure a successful outcome at a significant savings in time, frustration and worry. In short, I'll be your personal consultant. The fee: $60 per hour.

Not sure if I can help in your particular situation? Call me toll-free (800-304-6650) during business hours (Pacific time) and I'll give you ten minutes at no charge to discuss possibilities. Or email me. The address: john@grissimguides.com

Here's how it works:
Order one, two or three hours of my time—your choice. You can call direct to the office or order online—www.grissimguides.com—click on the Home & Land Advisor tile. I'll put you on the clock each time I consult with you. You choose how best to spend your time, either a few minutes at a time as needed, or we can block out much longer blocks of time.

You set up a consultation schedule that works best for you. Should you desire a review and consultation of documents such as purchase contracts or construction bids, we'll arrange for you to provide them by fax, email or mail.

I will do my best to be available to you during crucial periods of the process to ensure you have access to my input and recommendations in a prompt, timely manner.

Once you have purchased assistance, you may take advantage of my services at any time for up to 12 months.

Chapter 1

Great Product, Checkered Past, Flawed System

If you are a prospective buyer of a manufactured home, understandably you are more interested in learning about this kind of housing than its history. However, a brief description of the origins and evolution of today's manufactured home—in particular the 1990s boom and bust—offers insights that smart home buyers should know concerning how the industry operates.

During the 1920s, following World War I, a great pent-up restlessness created by the war swept the country, finding expression in America's growing love affair with the automobile, and with traveling. The growth in car ownership in that decade alone was breathtaking—from 9.2 million in 1920 to a staggering 23 million by 1930. By the mid-1920s, with family auto camping trips a new and popular pastime, some car campers began building their own tent trailers, little more than folding canvas tents on a wooden platform mounted on a single axle. The idea caught on and within a few years a number of companies were marketing recreational tent trailers.

Soon the race was on to design and produce improved trailers with more amenities for camping families. Manufacturers began building solid body trailers with framing and plywood sides, some large enough for sleeping bunks, folding chairs and tables. Luxury models included a camp-size stove, cold water storage and fold-down bathroom fixtures. Called travel trailers (or trailer coaches) by the fledgling industry, they were affordable to many, popular and just in time.

The Great Depression in the early 1930s generated enormous population shifts throughout the country as hundreds of thousands of people moved to other regions to escape poverty and to start new lives. From the drought-stricken Dustbowl alone thousands of families headed west to California. With little or no housing available to the new arrivals, many turned to travel trailers as full-time living accommodations. It wasn't long before campgrounds that accepted these semi-permanent tenants were dubbed trailer parks (their concrete urban counterparts were trailer courts). By 1938, the American Automobile Association put the total number of travel trailers at 300,000 and estimated perhaps 10 percent of them were being used for extended or full-time housing, not recreational travel.

It was this 10 percent of the so-called "trailerite" population that became the focus of some municipalities around the country. Irate citizens, shocked by what they regarded as unsightly "trailer slums" peopled by transients of questionable character, demanded their abatement. Before the end of the decade many towns and cities passed exclusionary zoning and ordinances that prohibited the use of trailers as housing, banished them from the city limits, or to commercial trailer courts, or required occupied trailers to be moved every few days. For its part, the industry, fearing government regulation, steered clear of promoting trailers for housing, and instead focused on trailers as recreational accessories for vacationers.

World War II and the first house trailer

These controversies were all but forgotten as World War II triggered a huge immediate demand for temporary wartime housing for workers at defense plants, in mines and elsewhere. The travel trailer industry responded quickly by designing for government use a spartan 22-foot-long, eight-foot-wide trailer with a canvas top that included a kitchen and bathroom—the first true house trailer. The government ended up buying 35,000 of these units at $750 per trailer, and constructing 8,500 trailer parks to site them.

The government also authorized two more wartime housing designs, one consisting of a factory-built single housing unit that could be trucked to a site, hooked to utilities and immediately occupied. The second design was comprised of two sections that were towed to a site and joined together to form a single two-story home. In an astonishingly short 90 days, a thousand of these two-section homes—precursors of today's manufactured home—were built and sited at Oak Ridge, Tennessee, for workers at the Manhattan Project.

Ironically, after the war, the innovative, multi-section home construction typified by Oak Ridge, was abandoned by the industry as it geared up to meet a new opportunity. In the immediate postwar years entire populations were once again on the move to new regions of the country where housing shortages were common, triggering a huge demand for house trailers that could be pulled by the family car, and used for year-round living.

The industry, freed from wartime restrictions on the use of strategic materials and less concerned about the possibility of regulation, responded with a torrent of new models, featuring stronger framing, metal siding, full-size bathrooms and kitchens, and home-like appointments. With these models, designed for long-term or permanent siting, the house trailer was history. The mobile home era had begun.

WWII defense plant trailer park. Uncle Sam bought 35,000 of these fully equipped canvas-roofed units for housing. They performed admirably. (Manufactured Housing Institute photo)

Mobile home parks and the rise of snob zoning

There to accommodate these new dwellings were the first true mobile home parks, renting cheek-by-jowl sites, sewer connections and utility hookups for the benefit of permanent residents. Thousands of mobile home parks sprung up throughout the country. The manufacturers, realizing their continued success depended on the availability of parks (and high-quality ones at that) formed a manufacturers group that provided developers with trailer park designs and issued an annual ratings guide for consumers. During a span of more than 20 years, the group helped create thousands of mobile home parks, always striving for their acceptance as respectable housing within the larger community.

In the 1950s, lengthy luxurious travel trailers looked great going down the road behind the family Buick (above), but when these behemoths were unhitched, put on blocks and used as permanent housing (below), the old bugaboo of "trailer camp slums" surfaced. Snob-zoning soon followed. (MHI photos)

The industry's well-intentioned effort was generally successful, but in the postwar years the old bugaboo of "trailer-camp-slums" re-emerged. This time some municipalities tried a new tactic: classifying mobile homes as buildings, then outlawing them because they failed to meet local building codes that had been quietly changed to render compliance impossible. In many cases, the ploy withstood court challenges, but

on other occasions the courts sided with the industry's claim that because a mobile home had a chassis (frame) and wheels, it was legally a vehicle, not a building. The truth was somewhere in the middle.

Many municipalities skirted the building-versus-vehicle issue by "snob-zoning," declaring trailer parks commercial businesses and relegating them to nonresidential zones, i.e. on the other side of the tracks, in industrial areas, and alongside highway corridors outside of town. Needless to explain, trailer parks in seedy neighborhoods inevitably tended to take on like characteristics. In response, many developers chose less restrictive unincorporated areas to build their parks.

By 1950, as the postwar housing shortage neared its end, mobile homes increasingly were being embraced more for their affordability as good, fully functioning permanent housing than as mobile dwellings that would be regularly towed. Accordingly, the exterior appearance and trim became less like a coach in motion and more house-like as manufacturers equipped models with standard doors, windows and trimmings similar to those of a conventional home.

But the biggest changes were in the length: up to 38 feet, then 40, then 50, and finally 55 feet. The longest lengths required a special driver's permit, and highway laws had to be changed to accommodate these behemoths, but nonetheless, the law in many states still allowed them to be towed by that all-important determinant: the family car. Parenthetically, America's craze for the automobile showed no sign of slowing. From 1945 to 1950, the number of cars increased from 26,000,000 to 40,000,000.

Manufacturers also continued to turn out lines of recreational travel trailers in the same factories that made mobile homes because the width of each was the industry standard eight feet, the maximum allowed to be legally towed as a trailer. But all that changed in 1954 when a Wisconsin mobile home builder and inventor, Elmer Frye, broke the mold by building the first ten-foot-wide model, proclaiming that buyers wanted more space. No longer a trailer but rather an oversize load, Frye's "ten-wides" would be towed by commercial trucks on the nation's highways, with special transport permits, just like other oversize freight.

Early 10-wide. It won no beauty contests but looked more like a home instead of a railway dining car. (MHI photo)

The invention made perfect sense but when Frye, who was also a tireless promoter (he was credited with coining the term "mobile home") began campaigning with state legislatures to allow ten-wides on the highways, he initially caused an industry uproar, in part because leading manufacturers at the time were lobbying for longer trailer lengths, and felt threatened. But as Frye's state-by-state campaign gained momentum, other manufacturers followed suit marketing their own ten-wides. Consumers loved them.

By 1960, the ten-wide had grabbed a 90 percent share of all mobile home sales to become the industry standard. Three years later, the industry had essentially split into two components: mobile homes and recreational travel trailers (soon to be known collectively as RVs, or recreational vehicles). Thereafter, manufacturers generally followed one path or the other, but a few companies, notably California–based Fleetwood Enterprises, Inc., continued to produce both mobile homes and RVs and became a dominant player in both sectors.

In the mid-1960s, mobile home production really began to take off. Manufacturers were early adopters of new technologies such as pneumatic-powered hand tools for nailing, stapling and cutting; automated machinery for manufacturing windows, doors and drawers; new and stronger adhesives, and panel construction machines. These advances greatly reduced the hand labor involved in the construction process and drove down the costs, making mobile homes better and more affordable. During this time, the first two-section homes (double-wides) came onto the market, offering floor plans akin to conventional homes, but their significantly higher cost initially slowed their acceptance. Meanwhile, the sections themselves kept getting wider—from 10 feet to 12, then 14, for the first time making possible a hallway down the length of one side, eliminating the need to go through one room to get to another. The result was dramatic, sustained growth. In 1965, just under 300,000 mobile home units were shipped. By 1972, the industry shipped an astonishing

575,000 units, amounting to one-third of all new single family housing constructed that year in the United States, a remarkable achievement and the high-water mark for the mobile home industry that has not been equaled since.

Early double-wide, c. 1960 The concept was a winner. By now the industry had split in two: those who built RVs and those who built mobile homes. (MHI photo)

One of the regions where mobile homes garnered strong acceptance was the Sunbelt, in particular the Gulf Coast of Florida, which had become a prime destination for thousands of "snowbirds" (retirees who each winter escape from the cold north). In contrast to the less than open-armed reception experienced in other regions, these newcomers were welcomed, largely because they were generally more affluent than the average mobile home owner, were less of a drain on public services and their spending boosted the economy.

There for them were a multitude of quality parks that offered community amenities such as swimming pools, tennis courts and club houses. Some parks were built around golf courses. It was in Florida that the first mobile home subdivision, where the residents own the land beneath their home, was established.

Tarnished image—abuses, defects and disasters

But the industry's impressive record was accompanied by a dark side. As the boom developed, dozens of companies jumped into the business. In the absence of any meaningful regulation or standards, many greedy upstart manufacturers began churning out poorly engineered, shoddily constructed mobile homes made of the cheapest possible materials, particularly plastic products that were highly flammable. Many models were dangerously unsafe and full of plumbing, electrical and structural defects.

Hollywood and the house trailer

In 1954 Lucille Ball and Dezi Arnez, whose I Love Lucy TV show was at the time a huge success, teamed up for the feature movie, *The Long, Long Trailer.* Story line: the couple buys an incredibly long (40-foot plus) house trailer that they tow across country with their two-door roadster while Arnez, playing his real-life role as a Cuban band leader, is on a road tour. The movie remains a small comic gem, providing a fascinating glimpse at the 50s era of trailer courts and "trailerite" communities and convincingly depicts everything that can go wrong when towing a trailer. Still widely available on video, and worth watching.

There to market them were unscrupulous dealers who used high-pressure sales tactics and practices to push them on unsuspecting consumers. Less than reputable finance companies preyed on naive borrowers who could least afford it, snaring them in retail installment contracts at near-extortionate interest rates. Little attention was given to proper installation and siting of these homes and warranties were either weak, ignored or nonexistent. Today some state Housing and Urban Development regulators claim they still are.

It wasn't long before mobile home tragedies became a staple of the daily papers and television news. The media was permeated with images of the charred remains of a mobile home in which children or elderly victims had died; stories of electrocutions, gas explosions, plumbing failures; and panoramas of scattered and wrecked mobile homes in the wake of storms.

So frequent were the photos of damaged and destroyed mobile homes after violent weather that even industry insiders (not to mention late night talk show hosts) joked that tornadoes and hurricanes were attracted to them. The continuing adverse publicity was a huge black eye for the industry, undercutting its deserved achievements and further stigmatizing the reputation of its products.

Responding to a growing public outcry for regulation, the Mobile Home Manufacturers Association pointed to a construction standard that it had developed in the 60s and that had been accepted in 43 states. But the standards were voluntary and useless against the worst offenders. Instead, the states began laying down their own laws, notably Texas and California, both of which enacted codes and regulations to curtail abuses. Others followed suit. Soon, observers predicted the MHMA's worst nightmare: conflicting codes would prevent mobile homes built in one state from being shipped to another. In the midst of all this, Congress held hearings. Many testified. Even Ralph Nader's Center for Automotive Safety weighed in with horror stories (*Mobile Homes—The Low Cost Housing Hoax*).

The Magna Carta of manufactured housing

In 1974, Congress passed watershed legislation, the National Mobile Home Construction and Safety Standards Act, which formally recognized mobile home manufacturing as a major industry, and directed the Department of Housing and Urban Development to develop uniform mobile home building standards and a federal program for their nationwide enforcement. Two years later, in June 1976, on what some proclaimed Magna Carta Day for manufactured homes, the Federal Manufactured Home Construction and Safety Standards, which quickly became known as the "HUD Code", became law.

The provisions defined the manufactured home as distinct from all other types of housing, principally owing to the requirement that it be built on a chassis with its own wheels and axles and be towed from the factory of origin. The law set mandatory minimum standards for construction (e.g., structural, plumbing, electrical, safety and insulation) and encouraged the states to establish enforcement offices (currently 37 states have such offices). As important, the HUD code pre-empted all state and local building codes, ensuring that manufactured homes were legal in every state, and preventing local governments from adopting their own codes to discriminate against them.

Initially the industry grumbled; notable complaints were that government inspections and higher construction standards would drive up the product's cost, which in fact occurred. But the HUD code turned out to be the best thing that could have happened to the industry. For starters, the benefits of better construction, increased safety, and protection

A basic, no frills "14 by 70" single-wide. These leviathans, retailing for $22,000-$28,000 are popular in the Southwest and still comprise about 25% of all US manufactured home sales. If sited properly and well cared for, they can be fine affordable housing. Photo: Consumers Union, SW Regional office.

from discriminatory building codes soon became clear. The industry was now building homes, not vehicles, and these higher quality, more durable dwellings were embraced by consumers who, in turn, discovered that lenders, equally impressed, were extending better loan terms at lower interest.

Despite these positive developments, the manufactured housing industry continued to lurch through cycles of boom and bust. Home sales fell from the historic high of 575,000 in 1972, when a huge number of baby boomers entered the housing market, to 230,000 in 1979 before stabilizing, then growing again. Nationally, many local governments still used restrictive zoning to ban or limit mobile home parks. A manufactured home by any other name still evoked images of seedy trailer parks inhabited by transients, burned out single-wides, and tornado-tossed wreckage. Today, the stigma endures.

"In the popular mind," writes University of Minnesota professor of geography John Frazer Hart in his new book, *The Unknown World of the Mobile Home*, "trailers are synonymous with violence and sex. If a crime happens anywhere else, nothing is said, but when one is committed in a trailer, the media let you know."

In fairness, that image is outdated and no longer deserved. Unfortunately, one other stigma remains very much alive. The industry, despite wonderful advances in its products, continues to be flawed by a largely unregulated system of selling and financing its products that invites abuses—collusion, misrepresentation and fraud, to name a few. These ongoing abuses, which have victimized thousands of unwary home buyers, in some cases leaving families literally homeless, are the manufactured home industry's 21st century stigma and one that continues to taint its reputation.

Historically, the manufactured home industry, like the auto industry from which it grew, has been a rough and tumble business with its share of boom and bust cycles. Like the auto industry, it relies on a system of dealerships, most of them independent, that sell the homes very much the way car dealers do: fast turnaround with quick loan application processing (approval often in hours or less), and retail installment contracts that subject the buyer to repossession of the product in the event of default. Buying a conventional home, in comparison, is glacial. Even a cash transaction takes at least 30 days.

Unlike the auto makers, the manufactured home builders have never fostered a strong cradle-to-the-grave system to protect the buyer after the sale. There is no unified chain-of-accountability or unified oversight of a home's site preparation, its installation, delivery inspection, follow-up warranty work, or 24/7 customer support. Instead, the system relies on dealers, installers, contractors and sub-contractors—each an independent operator—to work together by informal agreement. Most of the time this system works, as long as everything goes smoothly. But as later chapters illustrate, the consumer can get burned when things go wrong.

There is one other key member of the industry: the manufactured home financial sector. These are the finance companies, S&Ls, banks and credit unions that provide the money to borrowers, which in turn fuels the industry. How easy (or hard) these lenders make it for would-be home buyers to obtain loans has a direct bearing on the health of the industry as a whole. Which is why you may hear people remark that the manufactured housing industry is finance driven. Here, too, if this financial sector gets out of whack, the result can be serious disruption.

By the 1980s, even modest double-wide homes like this one could be rendered very close in appearance to a site-built home, and often at much less cost. (MHI photo)

Recent history—the great boom and bust of the 1990s

A good illustration of what can happen occurred during the 1990s when the industry went on what some observers called its "latest suicide binge."

In the early 1990s, in the wake of a regional recession in Texas, Louisiana and other oil patch states, several major lenders involved in financing manufactured home purchases pulled out of that market. Their departure left the field wide open to the few remaining lenders, but not for long. With the national economy starting to boom again, new lenders who saw the hefty profits that long term high interest chattel mortgages generated stepped in. Because these new lenders did not have well-established relationships with manufactured home dealerships, they offered them easier credit terms in order to gain a foothold in the market.

By the mid-1990s, with half a dozen new players competing for manufactured housing loans, lenders everywhere began weakening their underwriting requirements, expanding programs for higher risk applicants, reducing down payments to five percent, even expanding the length of purchase contracts out to 25 and 30 years to provide buyers with a lower monthly payment they could afford. Extending the contract length was intended to help buyers, but its ultimate effect was negative: a great many buyers who should never have qualified, were able to get into a home they could not afford to keep.

At the height of the irrational easy-credit frenzy, as one Louisiana dealer quipped, "If you could make an X you could get a loan." Not surprisingly, sales in manufactured homes boomed.

Contributing to higher sales were great improvements in the quality and design of manufactured homes that gave them a much closer appearance to site-built homes, and at better prices. Along with the flood of easy credit pouring into the marketplace, other developments were happening that helped fuel the boom.

Early in that decade two of the industry's largest manufacturers, Oakwood Homes and Clayton Homes, independently of each other, established their own retailer networks. The objective was to control all phases of the manufacturing, distribution and sales process. They continued to supply independent retailers as well, but the emphasis was on company-owned retail centers. By 1993 Oakwood had 120 company-owned retail outlets, while Clayton had 143 locations. To meet the rising demand, the two companies continued to open new dealerships and factories to provide homes for them.

Other manufacturers also expanded their distribution by signing up independent dealerships to carry their lines, often providing generous terms on lot models and factory rebates. In this hot market, hundreds, indeed thousands, of new dealerships sprung up, many of them run by fast-buck operators with limited capital and dicey track records.

Then, in 1997, Fleetwood Enterprises announced a partnership with Pulte Homes, one of the nation's largest site-built home builders, to establish a large chain of retail sales centers. Shortly thereafter, Champion Industries, by far the industry's biggest manufactured home builder, announced it was acquiring Home USA, a chain of 91 retail locations (with more to come), triggering an industry stampede. Many other manufacturers soon followed, including Cavalier, Palm Harbor and Southern Homes. Some did so defensively in order to prevent their retail distribution networks from being bought out from beneath them, but all touted the virtues of so-called vertical integration.

Reaping the rewards of this buy-up frenzy were many established retailers. Dealerships with hard assets of $50,000 handily sold for up to 10 times that amount. Fleetwood alone poured an astonishing $200 million into its dealership purchase program. All told, perhaps $500,000 million was collectively sucked out of the coffers of major manufacturers to purchase dealerships.

More plants continued to pump out more homes for more dealerships. No one was keeping score, but there were indications the industry was turning out a great many more homes than there were customers—not a good sign.

Enter Wall Street

Several of the manufacturers—Oakwood, for example—also owned subsidiary financing companies that made consumer loans to manufactured home buyers, mostly through their own dealership chains. Like the other lenders during this free-for-all scramble for market share, these subsidiaries loosened their borrowing requirements for less credit-worthy consumers. Everyone knew that the result would be an increase in loan defaults, but many lenders figured the substantial profits from the higher-interest subprime loans (averaging 12 percent to 15 percent) would more than offset the losses. A major exception to these practices was Clayton Homes, whose home financing subsidiary, Vanderbilt, took a conservative path, maintaining higher loan standards for which only the most creditworthy home buyers qualified. Palm Harbor Homes steered a similarly conservative course.

With hundreds of millions of dollars in new loans flowing out of their coffers, and business continuing to boom, many of the big lenders turned to Wall Street to restock their money supply and continue making more loans. The fresh capital was obtained by selling the loans already made. For example, Carmel, Indiana-based Conseco, the industry's largest lender, with $25 billion in mobile home/manufactured home loans, periodically bundled large chunks of these loans and sold them at a discount to eager Wall Street investment banks. They in turn sold them to institutional investors. Such a deal is called an asset backed securitization, a well-established, legitimate undertaking in the financial community.

Back on Main Street, with dealers demanding a fast turnaround approval time, bank and finance company loan officers, themselves under pressure to meet monthly quotas, didn't have enough time to properly check out an applicant's credit worthiness, and OK'd questionable loans. To top it off, many dealers, unbeknownst (and never disclosed) to the consumer, were getting healthy kick-backs from lenders for sending them borrowers. In short, there was a lot of questionable dealings between dealers and finance companies. For awhile there, a case could be made that what was really being sold were not homes, but loans.

Meanwhile, although many manufacturers were now running their own retail dealership networks, the principal day-to-day concern was maintaining the factories at a constant rate of production, essential to sustaining profitability. So they continued to crank out the boxes and ship them to dealer lots.

Lenders were falling over themselves to lend money to the dealers to pay for their lot inventory because the manufacturers co-signed for these "flooring" loans, agreeing to repurchase the homes if the loans defaulted. Home shipments rose from 170,000 in 1991 to 353,000 in 1997. At one point, one out of every four new single-family homes was a manufactured home.

With the national economy now booming, the race was on to grab and keep market share. Of least concern were the needs of the home buyer, let alone his or her creditworthiness. As far as the manufacturers were concerned, they couldn't live without the dealerships; to them the retailers were their end-users, not the actual home buyers.

The bust—and the aftermath

In early 1999 things began to unravel: the pipeline was full, dealerships were stuffed with lot models—and they weren't selling. Analysts at one point estimated the industry had cranked out 166,000 homes of excess inventory. Factory assembly lines were forced to slow or halt. Buyers were suddenly scarce. Not only had the market been pretty well tapped during the go-go years, but the economy was faltering.

Some observers believe the unraveling actually began two years previously when

Oakwood Homes went to Wall Street to report a much higher than expected number of loan defaults, which subsequently escalated, resulting in a $1 billion write-down of Oakwood's market value, not to mention its credibility on Wall Street. The binge was over.

Then the second shoe dropped: not only at Oakwood but everywhere, all those risky loans began defaulting, first by the tens of thousands, then by the hundreds of thousands. As recession loomed, and lay-offs mounted, loan defaults turned into a torrent, burying banks and finance companies in an avalanche of foreclosures. Many borrowers, with no equity in their just-purchased homes, simply walked away from them. The rate of repossessions, which normally averaged 10 to 12 percent, rose to as high as 27 percent. The industry headed toward the brink of collapse.

By the end of 2000, repossessed manufactured homes numbered in the hundreds of thousands. The lenders who were stuck with them refurbished and began gradually re-selling them, usually through retailers, many for less than half the original price. However, these so-called re-marketed homes competed with new homes, which in turn stalled the industry's recovery.

In 2002, while early industry projections indicated that the demand for manufactured homes would top 290,000, one third of that total, 96,000, would be served by the re-sale of repossessed homes. By the fall of that year, the revised projection of actual new homes built barely topped 175,000, less than half the number produced in 1997.

Elsewhere, early that same year, one of the largest lenders in the manufactured home industry, Green Point Financial, citing a forecast of huge losses from bad loans (about $630 million), announced it was exiting the business and taking a loss. Some Wall Street observers wondered if Conseco, with its $25 billion in loans, would be next, or whether it would even survive. Others questioned whether Oakwood Homes, whose subsidiary finance company was being buried under an avalanche of defaulting loans, might be headed for a similar fate.

The answers came that fall. In November, 2002 Oakwood Homes filed for Chapter 11 bankruptcy. A month later Conseco, after defaulting on loan payments on $6 billion of debt, followed suit. For this $52 billion company, the failure was stunning—the third-largest bankruptcy in U.S. history, behind only WorldCom and Enron.

In retrospect, it would appear that the principal cause of Conseco's eventual demise stemmed from its 1998 acquisition of Green Tree Financial, at the time the largest lender in the manufactured home/mobile home industry. Not only did Conseco wildly over-pay for the acquisition (critics say) but its timing could not have been worse. As one industry observer quipped: "Yup. Got too close to the trailer rattlers. Got bit."

In the aftermath of the binge came plenty of finger-pointing, but there was more than enough blame to go around. True, the banks and finance companies were the principal drivers, but they could not have caused the havoc they did without the cooperation of the street dealers, many of whom knew they were making bad loans, putting people in homes they knew they could not afford. The lenders tracked all their loans and thus knew who the crooked dealers were, but failed to stop them—and vice versa. So did many of the manufacturers, several who own subsidiary finance companies, but they, too, failed to curb the abuse. The prevailing view was, "Well, everyone else is doing it, so it must be OK." Some outside observers saw it differently: "Nearly everyone in the manufactured home industry got greedy, looked the other way and took the money." It's worth noting that during this time of wretched excess, a number of small, reputable, privately-held manufacturers and their dealerships foresaw the problems, made corrections, and quietly steered clear of the train wreck.

Entering the 21st Century

One can debate whether or not the manufactured home industry had only itself to blame, but what is not arguable is that the industry often ignored the needs and concerns of the home buyer, the true end-user. Many consumers were victimized, pressured, lied-to and manipulated by less than reputable dealers and lenders, and many buyers suffered terribly.

From 1999 through 2004 the industry suffered a whopping 65% contraction, which at least squeezed out a great many of the crooks and the fast buck operators. Many reputable companies barely hung on. Not surprisingly, bargain hunters appeared, notably Berkshire Hathaway, Inc., the huge holding company managed by billionaire investor Warren Buffet, purchasing industry leader Clayton Homes, Inc., for $1.7 billion, triggering a wave of consolidations. The "Berkshire effect" included a much needed infusion of new capital into the lending market, particularly for chattel loans, a welcome development for both the industry and its home buyers.

By early 2006 the industry had largely regained its health. The surviving companies were stronger and wiser, but clearly a sea change had taken place. No one is predicting robust growth, let alone a return to a boom cycle. A chastened industry seemes resolved to settle down for the long haul, showing a new willingness to reform itself.

The flaws in the system remain, as you'll soon see. The abuses have lessened, but the shenanigans are still there. The pity is, while construction quality varies widely, the fact remains that quality manufactured homes can be a wonderful product, and there are a lot of decent people out there selling it. The chapters that follow will help you find both.

Chapter 2

Today's Manufactured Home—a Quick Look

Simply defined, a manufactured home is a complete dwelling unit designed for year-round-living, and substantially constructed in a factory in conformance with a national building code developed by HUD (the Department of Housing and Urban Development). The home can consist of one or more transportable sections, each constructed on an integral permanent steel chassis to which are attached axles, wheels, brakes and a hitch. Each section displays a manufacturer's red metal certification label on the exterior. (**Note**: don't ever paint over the label or remove it.) The complete home, with a central heating system and/or air conditioning system and usually factory-installed kitchen appliances, rugs, and sometimes, even furniture, is then transported in one or more sections by specially permitted commercial truck(s) from the factory to a dealership, or to a home site. Once placed on the latter, more than 95 percent of the homes will never again be moved. **Note**: according to HUD code, the home is not completely constructed until it is properly installed on the site.

Most homes these days (about three-quarters) consist of two sections, each averaging 14 feet wide and a little under 60 feet in length, which are bolted together length-to-length. Prior to transport, thick plastic sheets, usually emblazoned with the company's logo, are stapled across each section's exposed side to protect the interior during the move. A two-section home (commonly called a double-wide) provides about 1450 square feet of interior floor space. Homes with three and four sections are available in the top-of-the-line models.

Although two-section homes are the most popular, single-section homes still make up about 25 percent of homes sold since they are by far the cheapest instant-house available (as low as $22,000). Most single-wides are 14 feet wide and 70 to 80 feet long. Compared to their double-wide brethren, they're humble but quality models can be fine starter homes, providing about 1200 square feet of living space. Some states allow models 16 feet, even 18 feet wide. Travelers who have encountered these behemoths coming at them down a two-lane Texas road strongly recommend pulling over, and ducking.

Typically, manufacturers locate their factories no farther than 250 miles from the markets they serve, this being close to the maximum distance the transport trucks can travel during a day's drive (the law in almost all states restricts transportation of oversize loads to daylight hours).

On arrival at the home site, the transport driver will most often position the towed section directly on a previously prepared foundation, usually poured concrete piers, a concrete slab, or slabs. Some states require only a graded land, but all require underfloor support systems such as precut concrete piers, steel piers or blocks. Many states also require tiedown systems: metal straps and ground anchors that tie the home securely to the earth (or concrete foundation). These metal strips, one or two inches wide and called hurricane straps in the trade, are informally known in some quarters as banker's knots (which can be easily untied in the event of a repossession). According to some HUD code regulators, all homes should be anchored to the ground to meet minimum compliance standards, but enforcement varies widely.

The installation process, also called the set-up, involves connecting the sections together (if the home is multi-section); leveling the home and securing it to its foundation; removing the axles, wheels and hitches; connecting the utilities; and finishing the interior. The latter task involves disguising the marriage line, that is, the point along which the home's sections are joined (a single-wide, of course, has no marriage line), repairing any cracks, flaws or incidental damage from the moving process, often applying a final coat of interior paint and/or texturing, hooking up all appliances, laying down carpeting, and, finally, scheduling a cleaning crew for a thorough pre-inspection cleaning.

Other elements of the set-up include the installation of gutters and downspouts, and adding skirting around the exterior foundation perimeter, usually made of vinyl, but cinder blocks or treated plywood panels are also common. The entire process, from delivery to final cleaning, averages 30 days. In general, it takes on average 75 days from the time a home is ordered from a factory until the owner takes possession. But, in hot markets, it can take up to six to nine months.

Note: Most of the major problems that owners of new homes experience are not caused by factory errors but, rather by mistakes made by the set-up contractor (a.k.a., the installer). A reputable dealer will make sure that the set-up crew is fully qualified, professional and stands behind the installation.

On-site additions to a manufactured home—such as decks, porches, covered entry ways and attached garages—are allowed by the HUD code (but must comply with the local building codes), and can go a long way to adding to the home's attractiveness, often rendering it indistinguishable from a site-built home. However, additions may not be permanently attached to the house unless the manufacturer has designed the home for such add-ons (with HUD signing off on the design).

Manufactured homes fall in the category of factory-built homes, which also include:

> **Modular houses**—Homes constructed of prefabricated three-dimensional modules, entire rooms and larger, then transported to a site and assembled, using a crane for placement. Built to local building codes, not HUD.

> **Pre-cut homes**—Essentially kit homes in which all the lumber and other materials are measured and precut at the factory, then transported to the site and assembled by the builder. Packages may include many more building materials such as pre-hung windows and plumbing. Homes in this category can be very high-end. Also included here are log homes, A-frames and domes. Built to local codes.

Panelized homes—Homes that are constructed of largely complete (or closed) panel sections. For example, a wall panel could consist of windows, a door, all inside wiring, and insulation, its interior side covered with gypsum, its outside with exterior siding. The finished panels are then transported to the building site, together with floor and roof panels, and assembled, usually with the help of a crane. An alternative system uses open panels in which the interior is left open for on-site installation of wiring, insulation, etc. Built to local codes.

Mobile homes—A rose by any other name, these are officially defined as manufactured homes built prior to June 15, 1976, the day HUD construction code became effective on all manufactured homes produced thereafter.

Two other terms you will hear frequently are stick-built and site-built, often used interchangeably when speaking of a home built on-site. Actually, manufactured homes are also stick-built (in the factory), so it's more accurate to use the terms site-built and factory-built when making the distinction between the two.

Is a manufactured home right for you?

A great many people live in manufactured homes and love them. In 1999, the latest year for which statistics are available, 21.4 million Americans were living year-round in 8.9 million manufactured homes. That's about 7.6 percent of the U.S. population. Moreover, 68 percent of the new homes were being placed on private property rather than on leased land communities, reflecting their growing acceptance as a popular option in the mainstream single family detached housing market. In 2000, one out of every six new single-family homes built was a manufactured home. By 2006, that percentage has slipped slightly due to the '99-'04 manufactured home industry slump and the contrasting record growth rate of new single-family site-built housing.

Still, the question remains, Is a manufactured home right for you? To help you decide, here is a listing of the pros and cons of a manufactured home. Most are discussed in detail elsewhere in these pages, but the list provides a quick overview and reference. Bear in mind that some points to consider have less to do with the physical qualities of the product than they do with lending practices, financing, re-sale value and related issues.

Pros

In general, significantly less costly than new or used site-built homes. Perhaps the biggest selling point. This is especially true of a single-section home which, including typical installation costs, sells for around $33,000, excluding land. A typical double-section home with 1,675 square feet averages $54,000 (without land). In comparison, in 2006 the median cost of a new single-family site-built home (with about the same square footage, including land) had risen to $238,000.

In this factory frame shop (above), walls are constructed horizontally, then raised to vertical and rolled through the door at right into an adjacent building to be secured to the main body. The framed section is readied for the next phase: roof construction. Below: a single-wide home during exterior siding phase. With factory construction even elaborate high-end homes can be built in as little as three days using assembly line techniques. A climate-controlled environment, little waste, frequent inspections, and a well-coordinated work force provide additional advantages that can mean a cost savings over site-built homes without any sacrifice in quality. (MHI photos)

Rolling on eight tires, a section of a double-wide home leaves the factory, window drapes and all. HUD code requires industrial strength home construction to ensure safe highway transport. How tough? Ask "How well would a comparable site-built home fare screaming down the Interstate at 55 mph with breezy cross winds? Note ultra-wide rear-view mirror holders. (MHI photo)

To be fair, the site-built home's cost includes site preparation, basement, garage, air conditioning and other items that are added on later to the manufactured home's cost. In fact, high-end manufactured homes are quite close in cost to comparable site-built dwellings. (**Note**: just about every manufactured home sold south of the Mason-Dixon Line comes with central air conditioning, typically costing $1,500-$1,600). But even with these added onto the manufactured home's base price, the total represents a price advantage.

Can be purchased with a retail installment contract, similar to a car or RV. This is both a pro and a con. Credit-worthy buyers who don't qualify for a conventional home loan can still get into a new home with financing obtained through the dealer, involving a low down payment and much higher interest rates than conventional home loans. Often this is the only option available, and it can make sense; however, this method of financing is risky, expensive and fraught with abuses—and it can lead to ruined credit, bankruptcy and the loss of the home.

Factory-constructed and government-inspected. Modern assembly line construction in a climate controlled environment provides many advantages over site-built construction than simply a large cost savings. The structure is safe from any weather damage (wet weather on a site-built home can soak lumber and is a major factor in the formation of mold that can cause serious health problems). It's also subject to frequent inspections, and is built by professional teams with constant oversight. State-of-the-industry design, engineering and fabrication techniques are employed. Inspections are conducted by third-party agencies approved by HUD.

Quality construction. While many low-end models exhibit marginal or poor quality materials and construction—they still have to meet HUD code requirements, however— homes in the mid-range and above generally score high in both categories, as good or better than site-built dwellings. The typical manufactured home has superior rough-construction characteristics—framing in particular. The lumber is cut much more accurately; assembly is done with pneumatic nail guns and there is much more use of bonding adhesives (they are really strong). But finish workmanship is another story (see Cons).

Wide selection of options. A wide range of buyer options are available, generally at competitive prices; choose from sliding glass doors, sky lights, fireplaces and tiled entry

Palm Harbor Homes' Mesquite model, shown here at one of its sales centers in Texas. Beautifully landscaped lots and fully furnished and decorated home models are a hallmark of Palm Harbor-owned dealerships. (Photo courtesy of Palm Harbor Homes)

ways, to upgrades of carpeting, vinyl flooring, counter tops, sinks, and brand name kitchen appliance packages.

Fast construction and/or delivery. Homes purchased off the lot at a retail sales center can be disassembled and delivered to a site within a week or two, sometimes sooner. A custom-ordered home is usually ready for delivery from the factory in 30 days, but most of that is waiting-in-the-backlog time. Once all the materials and customer-ordered options are dialed into the system, the actual construction of the home on the factory assembly line averages three days.

Can be similar in appearance to a site-built home. True, many homes still look like manufactured homes (see photo above), but some home buyers don't mind this. With modest changes such as higher roof pitch and an attached garage, many brands can be indistinguishable from site-built homes. Three examples are on this book's cover.

Excellent model selection. Despite all the brand names, the truth is there is not all that much difference between models in each price range. With a little research, a consumer can find roughly the same attractive home model in the desired price range offered by several area dealers, important when shopping for the best price.

Accessibility. Manufactured homes, with their mostly single-story layout, floor plans, and entry ways near-to-ground-level (ideal for wheelchair ramps) are very accessible for people with disabilities.

Low-maintenance. Upkeep cost for even the low end models is on par with many entry-level site-built homes. Many manufactured homes feature high-quality, durable synthetic materials, particularly on exterior siding and surfaces, that are long-lasting and require less maintenance than comparable site-built homes.

A good option for leased-land communities. Siting a home in a good manufactured home community and leasing, rather than purchasing the land, can save a bundle on the initial dollar investment, and, in addition, provide a spacious home with a yard and parking space, superior to an apartment or condo.

Appreciation. Manufactured homes on private property and deeded as such, can appreciate in value right along with neighboring conventional homes.

Cons

You're on your own. Buying any home is complex, and there is no trained, licensed real estate agent by your side. A manufactured home has its own peculiarities that a first time buyer may never learn about until it's too late. You need to do your own research, ask questions, and learn a lot on your own just to protect yourself in a buyer-beware environment.

Predatory lending and abuse is common. For many buyers, the only option is financing the purchase with a retail installment contract, also called a personal property loan or chattel mortgage. Here is where most misrepresentation, fraud and abuse occurs in the industry. Extreme vigilance must be exercised. Such contracts are very expensive and should not be considered a reasonable alternative for low-income buyers.

Lenders reluctant to write loans on used homes a threat to resale. When you try to sell your home, buyers needing a home loan may not be able to find willing lenders. Banks are quite adverse to writing loans on what they perceive as "used mobile homes."

Looks like a manufactured home. With its low-angle roof, no roof eves on the backyard side, and long boxy shape, the average model projects a utilitarian, plain, cookie-cutter look that is not especially appealing. For those to whom appearance is a big factor, the budget will need to be increased for the cost of on-site additions to give the home the appearance of a conventional site-built home.

Quality of finish workmanship less than site-built homes. Excluding high-end models, the finish work has always trailed that found in site-built homes: interior carpentry, cabinetry, door-hanging, sheetrock finishing, painting, etc.

No attic or basement. Although a basement can be constructed with the foundation. A number of manufacturers feature homes with inside basement access, a popular feature with a great many homes in the Midwest and Northeast.

No alterations, changes without permits and inspections. Aside from putting in a cat door (and even that may require a permit), many, but not all states require permits and inspections for almost any alteration to your home. Examples: add a door or window, install a gas stove, replace a roof, install an air conditioner, make any change to the plumbing or electrical system, or make any structural change. The permits cost money and the inspection standards may discourage do-it-yourselfers. Enforcement varies widely state-to-state. Plus, any alteration or remodel made without a permit (even when made years previously) can stop

This gives you an idea what can be done with a HUD code home. Some builders are now offering two-story dwellings such as this one. Hardwood floors are a factory option with many builders. Working with a local contractor and an architect, a home buyer can do a great deal to give a manufactured home the look and feel of a site-built residence, often at less cost, and certainly in a lot less time. (MHI photo)

or delay the sale, rental, or refinancing of a manufactured home. Often corrections require the owner to hire a licensed contractor to do any required work.

Limit on where home can be placed. The home site itself may be perfect with a lovely view, but the access way may be too steep, too narrow, too twisting and/or the vertical clearances too low to accommodate the home.

Limited availability of good home sites. Manufactured homes still carry a stigma in many regions. Many fear they contribute to lower neighborhood property values and the covenants and restrictions of many subdivisions, in-fill lots and single parcels specify site-built homes only. Such restrictions are legal. Many counties and municipalities have zoning laws that prevent any "mobile homes."

Depreciation. A manufactured home in a land-lease community generally depreciates, but there are growing exceptions. Homes in upscale land-lease communities with many life style amenities do just fine. But in some states government regulations actually mandate that such homes be depreciated automatically.

Social stigma. There is no denying it, there are some people who simply would never be caught dead in a manufactured home, and others who would feel stigmatized living in one. That's their loss. The mistaken public perception is that these homes are not as well constructed as site-built homes and that all depreciate in value.

That's a brief overview of the product. Now for a look at how manufactured homes are marketed and sold. Hang onto your checkbook (at least for the next chapter).

Chapter 3

Your Piece of the American Dream—
Just Across That Pressure Pit

The manufactured home has a rich and honorable connection with the automotive industry, but in the decades since the development of the HUD Code, the industry has more properly belonged within the arena of home construction where it continues to mature as a major industrial enterprise with a bright future. Nonetheless, because both manufactured homes and cars are marketed and financed nearly the same way, and because dealerships for both products are often found in the same locales, a good percentage of people working at manufactured home dealerships have backgrounds in car sales. As one sales manager of a manufactured home dealership in the Pacific Northwest remarked, "There's a lot of back and forth. People get burned out selling cars and come over to this market and vice versa. Very few have backgrounds in home construction or related skills."

One legacy from the manufactured home industry's automotive past, however, continues to taint its reputation: the culture and mentality of the slick, unscrupulous used car dealer. It's not hard to see why.

For many years, when most manufactured homes sold were plain-looking single-wides designed to meet basic housing needs, the customer base was largely comprised of the newly wed and the nearly dead: young families with marginal credit, the elderly with limited incomes, and lower income consumers, all of whom tended to be more trusting, less educated, less sophisticated and less able to defend themselves against high-pressure, deceit, manipulation and misleading claims. They were—and still are—easy pickings for the industry's bottom feeders: ruthless operators committed to extracting as much money as possible from buyers by any means possible. Because the sale of manufactured homes is significantly less regulated than that of the auto or real estate industries, the opportunities for fraud and abuse are greater. Add the fact that the purchase and siting of a manufactured home is much more complicated than a car purchase, and thus provides more ways to conceal rip-offs, and there is little wonder that the abuses continue.

Some who speak for the industry counter that there are crooks in every line of business and it is unfair to single out the manufactured home industry. Perhaps. There is no reason to doubt the majority of retailers are on the up and up—but virtually every dealer and industry insider interviewed for this guide agreed that, historically, the manufactured home sales and lending sector has attracted more than its share of less-than-reputable operators. This particularly occurred during the boom of 1990s when the number of dealerships grew to more than 8,000, roughly twice the number still open today, and a lot of fast-buck operators set up shop.

In the absence of evidence to the contrary, the prudent shopper must take pains to find a trustworthy dealer before talking in earnest about any home purchase. For these reasons

A showcase concept home (MHI photo)

The Buckeye by Palm Harbor is available in both modular and HUD-code standards, about $145,000 delivered to your site.

Home sweet single-wide. Fleetwood Homes

These photos show the wonderful diversity of home designs based on the HUD code. There is great potential for manufactured homes in the mainstream housing market but the irony is the distribution and retailing system is still largely limited to street dealerships that sell the homes like cars. As this chapter demonstrates, this environment can be daunting and dangerous for the uninformed home shopper.

Designed for Sunbelt living and indistinguishable from a site-built home. (MHI photo)

A small two-story gem by Silvercrest Homes

A classic, cozy double-wide. (MHI photo)

this guide devotes what may seem a disproportionate amount of time to the retail shopping and purchasing experience.

The heavenly deal from hell

To help you understand the many ways an unwary home buyer can be seriously fleeced, let's take a walk on the shady side of manufactured home retailing and examine a hypothetical worst-case scenario that illustrates just about every predatory abuse and fraudulent practice that in recent years was reported to the Better Business Bureau, government regulators, investigative reporters and consumer groups. While it would be truly remarkable to find an actual purchase transaction that contained all of the rip-off moves described here—and while a few items such as hefty "origination fees" are history—it would also be fair to say that some of these abuses occur regularly somewhere around the country.

The hapless buyers in our hypothetical example are a couple in their early 30s—we'll call them Brenda and Tom Miller—who have long dreamed of owning their own home. They hold steady jobs; Tom works in a furniture warehouse and Brenda is the office manager for a painting contractor. They have $4,000 in a joint savings account and modest credit card debt.

One Sunday morning they decide to look at some display models at the HeavenSent Homes dealership in their area, the one with the flags and the sign reading "Your new home is here! Low, low down!" Getting out of their car, they're met by a salesman who introduces himself as Andy, and after a moment of pleasant chat, he invites them to take a look at a few homes.

The couple are surprised and impressed, especially by a three-bedroom model that features a master bath with his and hers sinks, and a spacious kitchen with lots of cabinet space. When asked its price, Andy replies, "Probably somewhere between forty-five and fifty thousand dollars. I'll have to check. This model has quite a few extras."

When Tom replies that's out of their league, Andy smiles pleasantly. "Well, actually, you might be surprised. We've been able to come up with some pretty creative financial solutions for folks." Then, after a pause, "If you don't mind my asking, how much rent are you paying right now for where you live?" Tom answers they pay $720 a month for their three bedroom apartment.

"Gosh, " the salesman replies. "Now, don't hold me to this, but I wouldn't be surprised if we were able to get you into this home, or something close to it, for about what you're paying now." Already that rosy glow has begun to show on Brenda's face as she steps back into the kitchen for another long look. "How about we go back to the office and throw a few numbers together and see what we come up with."

The Millers agree and soon are seated at a table in a comfortable room in the dealership's sales center. Its walls are covered with photos of HeavenSent Homes in beautiful settings. A shelf on one wall contains samples of rugs and cabinetry and tiles and vinyl floor patterns. They accept an offer of coffee which they sip as they listen to Andy sing the praises of HeavenSent Homes, a national brand name with an outstanding reputation and a full range of services including financing and insurance through the company's own lending bank, HeavenSent Financial Services. They even offer home sites and site preparation, a major reason, he explains, why they are able to provide such high quality homes at the lowest cost.

Andy guides the conversation back to the house model the Millers saw, mentions a few more aspects of its quality construction, then says, "I checked the price on it and it's listed at forty-eight-five, as is."

The Millers look at each other, crestfallen.

"Hang on a moment," Andy grins, holding up a hand. "Let's not give up just yet." He invites them to tell him more about their financial situation, "to help me research the best deal for you." The Millers answer they earn together about $3,400 a month, and pay about $600 a month in combined credit card and car payments. Tom explains he went through a bankruptcy before his marriage, and that the couple are "sometimes a little late" in making monthly payments, adding "we don't know how good our credit is these days."

Andy nods and writes down the figures and uses his calculator for a moment, then beams.

"I was right. You two are in a lot better shape than you thought." He pauses briefly. "Here's what I've been thinking. The home sites that we have for sale as part of our land-home packages run about twenty-five thousand. In addition, you can expect to spend that much or more for the foundation, garage, septic system and a well. That would push the total beyond what you qualify for. But if you were to place your home on a rented site, like in the new Cascade Meadows park over near the mall, that would definitely be in your range. It's a very nice development, all manufactured homes, lots of families moving in, a real community. Later on, as your earnings go up, as I'm sure they will, you'll be in a great position to move up to a land-home deal."

Brenda and Tom brighten. A land-lease deal in a park would be the smart move, and it would get them into their dream home now at an affordable price.

"What's the monthly rent out there," Tom asks.

"I believe it's three-fifty. That includes the costs of your garbage, water and sewer. What did you say you were currently paying? About thirty-four dollars a month in addition to your apartment rent? Tom nods.

"OK," Tom continues. "What are we talking about in terms of the whole package, the interest and monthly payments. How does that work out?"

"I can't give you an exact total just yet until we send your credit info to HeavenSent and they approve your loan and give us the interest rate," Andy replies. "But the down payment will be five percent. As it stands now we'll be providing you our special Park Package which covers everything for twenty-four thousand-five hundred. That includes all the siting work, government fees and permits, a foundation, the home's installation, the skirting, hookup to sewer and utilities, landscaping, and an attached garage, all done by excellent local contractors we know and have worked with. Aside from that, there'll be some one time costs for insurance, tax and other fees.

"Let me suggest this, if I may," Andy continues amiably. "If it turns out that the three-fifty a month, on top of your monthly house payment is too much of a reach for you right now, we can work out something with our lender to pay the first year's rent for you and include it in your loan. Plus, to keep the monthly payments to a minimum, we can go out to a full thirty years."

"Sounds good," Tom smiles, then turns to his wife. "Honey, what do you think?"

"Until I walked in here, I didn't believe something like this was in any way possible for us," she beams. "It's wonderful."

"One more thing I should add," Andy says. "You happen to have come in during our May Sales Incentive month, which allows me to take as much as fifteen hundred off the price of that model if needed to make a deal affordable, but to do that, and to lock in that price for thirty days, we would need a modest deposit.

"So let's do this: Let's write up a purchase contract and get an earnest money deposit from you. Say, five hundred dollars. This way we can get a good preliminary look at the numbers and guarantee the home price for a month. And I'll need twenty five dollars to run a credit check on you. If I am unable to get your loan approved, we will certainly refund your deposit—and that promise will be in writing, of course."

By this point the Millers are—to borrow a familiar phrase from the auto industry—in the ether. Their eagerness is palpable, their faces radiating hope and joy. They are giddy with the prospect of owning their piece of the American dream. After one more "What d'ya think, Honey?" They turn to their salesman and nod. "Let's go for it," Tom says.

"Great!" Andy replies, pulling out a folder with a sheaf of forms. During the next 45 minutes, Andy goes through the purchase contract, filling in numbers where possible and writing "to be determined" in the remaining spaces. He explains that HeavenSent Financial requires its borrowers to be properly insured. To this end he sells the couple a two-year homeowner's insurance policy ($2,000), and a five-year extended warranty homeowners plan and a seven-year joint credit life insurance policy ($7,000 for both), all bundled into the loan. Together with the $24,000 special Park Package, the total comes to $80,000.

"There will be some origination costs, finance charges and tax added to this," Andy says breezily, "but we're getting close." He turns the purchase contract around and slides it over to the Millers, deftly placing a pen on top of it. "We should have a definitive reply from our lender by the end of tomorrow."

Tom writes two checks, for $20 and $500, and hands them to Andy. For a long minute the Millers look over the document, taking note of the dollar amounts. All looks in order. They each sign, then shake Andy's hand.

"Alriiight," Andy laughs. "It's too early to say congratulations, but you're on your way. I'll get started on this right now. In the meantime, feel free to look around all you want in the home while I call Cascade Meadows and tell them to expect to hear from you."

Tom and Brenda leave the HeavenSent Homes lot in a state of exhilaration. Later that afternoon, they visit Cascade Meadows, a manufactured home community with more than 100 sites, about half of them developed. Andy was right, the place has a great neighborhood feel. They meet with Dave, the park manager who provides them with a brochure and a copy of the park's guidelines and restrictions, plus an application that they fill out and sign. Before leaving they chose a couple of possible home sites from the wall map in Dave's office.

That evening doubt and fear begins to dampen the Miller's excitement as they wonder if their credit rating would be good enough to get the loan, and if the monthly payments will be within their reach. As it stands now, the loan total is already up to $80,000, meaning a five percent down payment would come to $4,000. That they can handle but they worry about having to wipe out their whole nest egg if the total goes much higher. Brenda wonders if maybe they should have taken time to look around at a few other dealers before they signed anything. Tom assures her he can't imagine how anyone can beat Andy's deal because it's such a competitive market and the margins are so thin. And besides, he adds, they're depending on him to swing the loan.

The following day Andy calls Brenda at work to give her the good news, adding "We really had to go to bat for you but they finally came through. You've got the loan. Come on in after work and we'll put it all together."

Late that afternoon a noticeably excited Tom and Brenda are once more seated at the table in the HeavenSent Homes dealership as Andy removes a typed purchase order and more forms. He explains that the couple's marginally satisfactory credit rating, combined with Tom's previous bankruptcy was initially a real problem, "but I was able to convince them that all that was history and you both have good steady jobs and are now excellent credit risks. So we've put together something that I think is going to work for you."

Andy begins by noting that because HeavenSent Financial evaluated the Millers as higher risk borrowers, the interest rate would normally be at least 15 percent or more for a 30 year loan. But that rate could be reduced if the Millers would agree to add to their loan "pre-paid financed points" that would enable HeavenSent to lower their interest rate to 13.99 percent.

"A point," he explains, "is equal to one percent of the amount you're borrowing. HeavenSent will loan you the amount of those points to get that interest rate down. It'll amount to several thousand dollars but you'll have 30 years to pay it off. This has become a pretty popular way in our industry for lenders to help first-time home owners."

The Millers nod agreement, and Andy moves on to "another accommodation" he has been able to work out. To help the Millers get into their new home with lower initial monthly payments, the lender has not only agreed to pay the Millers' first year's rent to Cascade Meadows and add it to the loan, but they will also reduce their interest rate in the early going, charging them only 10.5%, with annual step increases over the following three years—to 11.5%, 12.99%, and then 13.99%

"This way," Andy continues. "You have a full three years before you will start paying the thirteen-nine-nine, and by that time you'll both be earning more money so your budget should be able to comfortably handle the increase. Plus, at that point the interest rates could be down, and with your improved credit rating you could refinance your home and lock in a lower rate."

"What's the first year's monthly payment?" Tom and Brenda ask, speaking almost simultaneously.

Andy smiles triumphantly. "Eight-hundred-thirty-nine dollars and sixty cents a month." He pauses a beat. "If I've done the math right, that's only eighty-five dollars more than you're now paying for your apartment and utilities. And it's all money that's going into your home purchase, not some landlord's pocket."

The Millers let out a sigh of relief, grinning at each other.

"How about the down payment? How much is that?" Tom asks.

Andy looks down at his papers. "They're going to need five percent down, and that comes to....let's see....four-thousand-eight-fifty-seven."

The couple grimace with disappointment, their faces clearly reflecting the stress of an emotional roller coaster ride. Tom heaves a sigh of resignation. And here they were so close to their dream.

"I was afraid of that," Tom sighs. "That's just too much of a stretch for us."

"I had a feeling it would be." Andy answers brightly. "And I think I've come up with a work-around strategy that just might solve our problem."

Tom and Brenda, on the very brink of failure, give Andy their rapt attention.

"Our dealership has a lot of experience helping families get into their first homes, and, believe me, it's not at all unusual for borrowers to be unable to come up with the five percent in cash needed to close a deal. In looking around for help, we were fortunate to connect with a service called the DownAssist Fund. They're set up specifically to offer down payment assistance to folks like you. Now, they don't lend the money directly to the borrower in these cases. Instead, they lend it to a family member with good credit—any of your parents, for example— and then they in turn give the money to you as a gift towards the down payment. You would co-sign the DownAssist agreement.

"These are basically small one-time consumer loans for borrowers with your credit standing, and they allow family members to help without having to be a party in any way to the home loan, so they're protected. And the monthly payments are modest. In fact, you could even help him on his payments as your earnings improve.

The Millers jump at the suggestion, mentioning that Brenda's father Ken had recently told them he might be able to help them out a little if they needed it, and that they were sure he had good credit.

They quickly decide they will put $2,000 towards the down payment, and ask Brenda's father to agree to borrow the remaining $2,830.

"Well, I think that clinches the deal!" Andy says. "Folks, you're about to become new homeowners."

That evening the Millers call Brenda's father who, after listening to their story and their promise to pay him at least $50 a month toward the monthly payments, agrees to borrow the additional money needed for their down payment. He even offers to write them a check from his savings so that they can close the deal without having to wait for the money from DownAssist. The Millers accept.

The next morning they phone Andy to give him Ken's social security number for a credit check. That afternoon they return to the HeavenSent Homes dealership where the Millers proudly show her father the home they are purchasing before entering the office to sign the papers.

There is a lot to sign, including various waivers and Truth in Landing notices that Andy breezily describes as "routine boiler plate stuff" that retailers are required to provide. Once Brenda's father signs the Down Assist loan contract, Andy produces the retyped purchase contract, and rather quickly, reviews the main points, asking Tom and Brenda to "Sign here," Initial there," as he reviews the line item numbers.

This nice-looking entry level home is very similar to the one purchased by the Millers in our fictional example, except they were talked into a detatched two-car garage. The carport with this home costs far less. As the Millers would learn, the home was a little slice of heaven, but the deal was from hell. (MHI photo)

The purchase contract—description

$47,000	Price of the Heavenly Home, 3-bedroom Prestige model (incl. installation)
$24,000	Park package (site prep, landscaping, garage, utilities, skirting, gutters and spouts
$2,450	Documentation and loan origination fee
$3,290	Tax (at 7%) on purchase price of home
$2,000	Two year fire and property insurance, incl. personal property
$2,000	Homeowners Extended warranty protection (5 years)
$5,000	Joint credit life insurance policy (7 years)
$7,195	Prepaid financed points
$4,200	First year's rent, Cascade Meadows
$97,135	Total
$4,857	Less cash down payment
$92,278	Total amount financed

The payment schedule lists the step-increases:

1st year: Interest rate: 10.5% Monthly payment: $839.60
2nd year: Interest rate: 11.5% Monthly payment: $908.94
3rd year: Interest rate: 12.5% Monthly payment: $979.59
4th year and following: 13.99% Monthly payment: $1086.81

The $2,830 consumer credit loan from the DownAssist Fund carried an annual percentage rate of 23.6% and required a pre-payment fee of $210.17. Brenda Miller's father Ken was surprised by the high rate and the up-front fee but in the euphoria of the moment, signed anyway.

As Brenda and John sign the final formal purchase agreement, Ken hands Andy a personal check for $4,357 (reflecting the $500 deposit previously given), followed by congratulations and handshaking all around. Andy assembles a copy of all the documents and hands them to the Millers. The deal was done.

The grim slide

Tom and Brenda's cherished dream of home ownership was officially doomed the moment they signed the purchase agreement, but it would be close to a year before they were forced to confront the nightmare their dream had become. First came the excitement of watching the work: the construction of the concrete slab on the lot they had chosen, followed by the arrival of the home, then the trench work for utility connections. As soon as the house was tied to the foundation, work started on the driveway and the adjacent post-and-pole two-car garage.

The home was ready for occupancy in just over 30 days. A week later the Millers, with the help of friends and a U-Haul truck, moved in. A few days later, still in a state of exuberance, they went to Sears, received on-the-spot approval for a Sears credit card, and bought a new washing machine and clothes dryer (both clearance sale models) for the small utility room just off the kitchen. Cost: $520 delivered, no payments due for six months. It was their one extravagance.

The Millers loved their new community, and their home. For the first seven months the total $890 they paid monthly ($840 + $50 to Brenda's father) was barely a stretch (they dipped into their savings to cover extras). Then came a letter from the County Assessor notifying them that $200 in personal property tax was due by year's end, based on their home's $40,000 valuation (at $10 per $1,000 of assessed valuation prorated for six months). They could pay that out of their diminishing savings, they agreed, but neither had thought about budgeting $400 a year for property taxes.

By the end of their eighth month, they received a second notice, this one from Cascade Meadows management announcing a five percent increase in rent due to various cost increases for park services—$17.50—to take effect in 30 days. The grim slide had begun.

One evening Tom took out a calculator and the Millers' copy of the HeavenSent Homes purchase agreement, and with a sinking feeling, calculated what the couple would be looking at in less than four months when the second year of the contract kicked in:

> $909.00 Year Two monthly payment at 11.5% interest
> $50.00 Monthly payment to Brenda's father
> $367.50 Monthly space rent
> $1,326.50 Monthly total

His anxiety growing, he saw the monthly total was $436.50 more than they were now paying, or $5,238 more for Year two. Adding $400 in Year Two property taxes, and the Millers would need to earn an additional $5,638 next year just to keep their home. Year three would require $847 more due to still higher interest, plus they would have to take out a new property insurance policy which could make it over $1,000 more. Tom could not bring himself to look at the Year Four increases in what had become the deal from hell.

The couple were numb with the realization. Even if Brenda's father suspended their $50 a month obligation, the Millers would still need to earn an additional $5,038 to stay afloat in Year Two. Determined to hold on to their home, the Millers took part-time second jobs. Tom worked four nights a week as a pizza delivery driver. Brenda found a part-time clerical job with a bookkeeping service. Tom, an avid fisherman, with great sadness sold his cherished aluminum fishing skiff and outboard motor for $975 cash. The Millers' frantic work schedules kept them from seeing much of each other, or enjoying their new home. Fear and anxiety took their toll. Tempers flared. Their marriage was getting shaky.

The Millers were desperate. Tom called the HeavenSent Homes dealership to see if Andy might help them, but was told the salesman no longer worked there, and the manager said the matter was out of his hands. Tom called HeavenSent Financial's out of state number and was informed that no change could be made to the purchase contract's payment terms. When the Millers considered selling their home, they quickly realized they owed far more than the home's market value. In fact, they had no equity in their home at all, and would not have any for years.

One month into year two, the Millers, exhausted and demoralized, realized they simply could not keep up with the payments. Only one viable option remained: rent a small apartment while their credit rating was still acceptable, using the last of their savings for the first and last month's rent, then pack up and move out — and declare bankruptcy. This they did. It was their one smart move.

The post mortem—what happened and why

Reading the above account, you could see the disaster coming, and yet the Millers' story illustrates typical abuses that many consumer advocates say are widespread in the industry (see side bar p. 46), nor is the degree of deception and misdirection in our story exaggerated.

Buying a home under the best of circumstances is a complex, often confusing process, much more so for lower income buyers who can easily become overwhelmed. Young buyers with limited or no experience in the marketplace of big ticket items like homes tend to be more trusting and more easily manipulated. Dishonest dealers will pounce on them like piranhas on a capsized cattle barge.

What follows is an analysis of what occurred. Keep in mind that many elements of the deal the Millers signed are legitimate and appropriate to most any purchase transaction, and dealers are right in offering them. However, these combined with the predatory terms amounted to a death of a thousand paper cuts:

First visit to HeavenSent Homes.

Good old Andy was right there to meet and greet the Millers as soon as they climbed out of their car. His objective was to completely control their experience at the dealership, and to do whatever it took to get a first visit "write-up" in which they sign a purchase contract and give him a small deposit. Doing so would establish their dependency on him and strongly dissuade them from looking at competing homes or other lenders.

Andy played a hunch and showed Tom and Brenda several lot models first to get the juices flowing before going inside "to look at some numbers." A common alternative is to usher the shopper into the office first for a short sales pitch and to pry loose enough financial

Our story's fictional new land-lease community of Cascade Meadows is like this one: modest new homes in a subdivision with cul-de-sacs and street lighting, a far cry from the much less spacious mobile home parks of years past. (MHI photo)

information to determine if it's worth the sales person's time to show the models. Had Andy done so, he would have explained his questions were merely to determine what models best fitted the price range they could comfortably afford. To prevent casual browsing unattended by a sales person, some dealerships go so far as to lock all their lot models "to ensure this home is protected for its future owner." Some post a sign reading, "Our insurance policy won't let us allow people in the homes unaccompanied."

Lot model price range.

Very few states currently require a Manufacturers Suggested Retail Price (MSRP) sticker on new manufactured homes, as is universally required for new cars. The state in which the Millers live has no such requirement, and Andy avoided stating a specific MSRP that might have scared the Millers away.

"If you don't mind my asking..."

Getting the Millers to reveal their current monthly housing cost gives Andy a powerful sales tool. The $720 a month figure provides a benchmark for what they can pay each month on a home, plus it identifies the Millers as likely "payment buyers," i.e., people who are far less concerned about the total price of a home purchase than they are about monthly payments. Less than reputable dealers love payment buyers because on a 25- to 30-year chattel loan they can pile on thousands of dollars in profitable extras without putting the monthly installment out of the buyer's reach.

To be fair, there's certainly nothing wrong about a dealer or salesperson attempting to get an idea of what the Millers think they can afford in a home during their first visit, especially if the sales center has 30 lot models, some with six-figure price tags. But a salesperson's attempt to extract too much financial information at this point should be regarded as a warning sign. For their part, if the Millers were informed shoppers, during that first visit they would have disclosed only the price range of the homes they were interested in seeing.

When the Millers happily agreed to adjourn to Andy's office, he knew all he needed to do was focus on giving them a down payment and a first year monthly installment the couple could afford.

"It's listed at forty-eight-five, as is."

This model had been on the HeavenSent Homes lot for nearly six months, and the dealership had been making monthly payments to a so-called flooring lender that underwrote the cost of buying the home and putting it on the lot. Manufacturers run a tight ship: they demand full payment for their houses, usually within 15 business days. With the dealer's payments eating into the home's potential profit, Andy knew his boss would accept $43,500, or at the very least $42,000. But the Millers had no idea of the home's fair market value, nor how much home they can reasonably afford, nor did they understand that price is negotiable or even how to negotiate.

The small comfortable room in which the Millers were seated is known in both the auto the manufactured home industries as "the closing room," a relatively private enclosure where a sales person (or persons) can more effectively apply tactics to clinch a sale and close a deal.

The Millers disclose their financial situation.

Providing Andy detailed information about their finances during this first meeting gave him all the cards. The Millers trusted Andy to get them into the best possible home for an affordable low down and a monthly payment. Andy's goal was quite different: to qualify them with his lender for the largest possible loan on terms that seemed affordable for the first year. In short, get them into a deal, any deal.

Had the Millers a good credit rating, which would have allowed Andy to estimate with near certainty the interest rate for which they would qualify, he could have used an alternative approach and calculated how much money they could borrow on a 30-year loan. Then he would deduct all the line-item expenses, except the cost of the home, from a hypothetical purchase contract. The amount remaining would represent how much money the Millers could afford to spend on a home.

Needless to predict, Andy would somehow find the couple a home to their liking for exactly that price, and not a dime less. Either way, Andy maintains control over the Millers' experience, presenting them options they never question.

Land-home sale v. land-lease

It has been said that the most powerful lies begin with small modifications of the truth. Buying a home and siting it on a rented site makes sense for some buyers, particularly retired seniors, if the monthly rental costs are reasonable and stable. But had the Millers done a little research, they may have concluded a land-lease deal has too many negatives for them, particularly as it affects resale value. Here again, Andy's objective was to get the Millers into something, anything, and close a deal.

"Can't give an exact total just yet....some one time costs..."

Andy truthfully claims he doesn't know the exact total, but he deftly steers clear of offering even a rough estimate. He knows the Millers will be hit with sales tax, overpriced insurance premiums and hefty lender "points." As for the $24,500 Park Package, "which covers everything," the Millers are unaware and are never told, that 1. The package has been worked out by agreement with the corporate owner of the manufactured home community (the park), which, in turn, hires its own contractors, including two relatives of the park's resident manager, all of whom are paid very generously; 2. Bundled into the total is a portion of the cost of local government permitting fees that the Park, as developer, should properly be paying for; and 3. The park is paying the HeavenSent Homes $1,000 for every new customer who sites a home there (Guess where that comes from. Right, the Park Package construction cost, which is part of the loan package.)

While many, if not most, land-lease communities routinely hire their own contractors to do park improvements for new sites, the Millers still have the right to review the line items of the park package, even to confer with a knowledgeable outside contractor and to negotiate prices. For example, had the Millers been properly informed, they could have ordered a very serviceable carport instead of a more expensive garage, for a revised total of $18,000, a savings of $6,500.

Note: Park Packages in the $12,000-$14,000 range are fairly standard around the country for existing land-lease communities, but during the late 1990s many buyers were sold packages that easily topped $20,000 in new land-lease communities.

Lender to pay the first year's rent.

This offer is so dangerous—and so expensive. The total rent, in this case $4,200, gets tacked onto the loan. Over a 30-year period the cost of a that year's rent, including the interest paid on it, would be more than $14,000. Had the Millers been aware that many land-lease communities waive the first six months rent as a premium to attract new residents, they might have been able to negotiate a substantial reduction.

$1500 off for Sales Incentive Month

This is a simple ploy to demonstrate Andy's willingness to help the Millers, but the actual hook is Andy must have a signed purchase agreement "to lock in that price for 30 days." Once the Millers fork over their $500 deposit and sign the contract, HeavenSent Homes can assert the Millers are committed to a legally binding contract, regardless of how many blanks are filled in with the phrase "to be determined." True, it's almost impossible for a dealership to keep a deposit, and should the Millers walk away from the deal, HeavenSent Homes is not likely to press its claim in court, but the dealership could be slow in returning their money, which would be at the very least an inconvenience.

HeavenSent Financial requires borrowers to be properly insured.

This may be true but the Millers don't know, and are not told, the property, not the borrower, must be insured against loss (from fire, weather, etc.), and they can shop for insurance elsewhere and save hundreds of dollars. As for credit life insurance, this type of policy pays the surviving spouse or family member off in the event of the borrowers' death, from which amount the surviving member can pay off the home. Few lenders require this because such policies are expensive and their addition to the loan amount may discourage borrowers from signing the deal. (Note: term life insurance would have accomplished the same purpose and been far cheaper.) In failing to disclose that the lender required only property insurance, Andy misled the Millers into believing they had to purchase all coverages that were offered.

The homeowners two-year extended warranty for $2,000 is a high profit extra for the dealership. Moreover, if the Millers had looked at the date of commencement, they would have noted the warranty started the day the home was purchased, thus running concurrently with the automatic one-year warranty required by HUD.

Extended warranties can be a good deal depending on their cost, coverage and duration. For example, a five-year warranty costing $895, which also covers all the homes appliances, can pay off for many home buyers. But the Millers were egregiously overcharged.

"So we've put together something that I think is going to work for you."

Andy should have added, "Well, for the first twelve months, anyway. After that, you're probably screwed." The year's "free" park rent, the step-increases in interest, and the loan extension out to 30 years are merely devices to make the Millers' first year affordable.

To be sure, there is nothing inherently evil about step-increases in interest. Banks routinely offer them for conventional loans and many borrowers prefer knowing exactly what their future mortgage costs will be rather than face the uncertainties of an adjustable rate mortgage (see next chapter). But the Millers, caught up in the euphoria of buying their first home, didn't take time to do the math and understand the burden they faced down the road.

Why, you may wonder, would a lender deliberately go to such lengths to approve and fund a loan that is sure to put the borrower under a great deal of financial pressure after the first or second year, and thus increase the likelihood the borrower will default?

Part of the answer, as the review of recent history in Chapter 1 described, is that the profits pouring in from the high-interest loans that don't default are so large that lenders can write off the bad loans and still make a lot of money. The rest of the answer has to do with that all-important minimum required down payment the Millers must pay to close the deal.

"They're going to need five percent down."

The purchase agreement must show that the Millers' down payment was at least five percent of the total loan amount because the lender, HeavenSent Financial, intends to sell the loan, along with thousands of others it has made, to other financial institutions. HeavenSent needs to show its bankers that the borrower has made at least a five percent down payment to qualify the loan to be sold. There's nothing unusual about a lender selling to another financial institution he loans it has made. Banks routinely sell a good percentage of their home mortgage loans on the secondary market. The bank gets back immediately all the money it lent, plus a percentage of the interest that would be earned during the life of the loan, and can use the money to make new loans to consumers. The buyer often takes over the loan and services it, eventually recovering the principal, plus interest, assuming the loan doesn't default.

In the manufactured home arena, however, where dealer financing with high- interest consumer loans is common, the lure of quick profits from selling loans on the secondary market has helped foster an atmosphere of collusion between dealers and lenders that encourages "creative solutions" that victimize borrowers.

In the Millers' case, for example, the salesman and the dealership quickly profit from the deal and have no further responsibility or liability. The same is true if HeavenSent Financial sells the loan.

Down payments: funny, phony, false and phantom

The *Portland Oregonion*, in a major 2000 investigative series on fraud and misrepresentation in the Oregon manufactured home retailing industry, uncovered many of the abuses that Consumers Union found in Texas. Hundreds of home buyers found themselves trapped in bad deals, many taken in by the lure of low down payments—some requiring no actual money. When lenders lowered the minimum down payment to as little as 5%, dealers devised ways to get around even paying that. Examples:
• Dealers would offer their own commissions to cover the down payment (which they in turn tacked onto the loan amount).
• A salesman "gave" a couple his roommate's Jet Ski which the buyers then "sold" to the dealership for the amount of the down payment (the couple never saw the Jet Ski).
• Dealers suggested customers buy a home with a furniture package, then sell the furniture to pay for the down payment.
• Dealers would offer "rebates" on the home which would then be used as down payments; the rebate was quietly tacked onto the total amount financed.
The *Oregonian's* investigation found that Oregon has virtually no regulatory authority over personal property loans greater than $50,000 for homes in land-lease communities and that manufactured home dealers are regulated far less than car dealers.

The DownAssist Fund

This "fund" is nothing more than a very high interest consumer loan that defines the term "predatory." The reason Andy does not offer the "assistance" directly to the Millers is because the purchase agreement, in order to qualify for sale on the secondary market as a so-called conforming loan, must reflect the money came through the Miller's bank account and that no side loan contract was made with the Millers to enable them to meet the minimum down payment.

During the boom in the late 1990s, it was not uncommon for some purchase agreements to show phantom down payments, in which the amount shown on the down payment made line was either never paid, or was actually borrowed from the lender but disguised as some other line item (see sidebar).

The line items of the purchase contract. Otherwise known as the devil in the details:

The documentation and loan origination fee of $2,450.

This goes straight to the dealership. The figure is based on a percentage of the loan, and amounts to a finder's fee from the lender for bringing in a customer. Given that the

Consumers Union Study of Texas:
Fraud and misrepresentation all too common in sale of manufactured homes

In February, 2002, the Southwest Regional Office of Consumers Union, the publisher of Consumer Reports magazine, released a scathing report claiming "the manufactured home buying experience in Texas often resembles an old-fashioned, high pressure auto deal and may be tainted by allegations of dealer fraud and misrepresentation."

The study analyzed more than 400 consumer complaints filed primarily in 1999 and 2000. Dealer fraud and misrepresentation (46 percent) and consumers upset about the condition of the home (41 percent) were the two largest complaint categories. Here are some excerpts from the press release:

Dealer problems included falsified down payment information on credit applications and misrepresentations about the terms, the price or the home itself.

Consumers also reported loans packed with insurance, financed "points" and other charges that left them "underwater"—or with negative equity—for several years following their purchase. The terms or conditions of the sale worsened, including additional costs for items consumers thought they had already covered....

Dealers discourage shopping around in various ways. Some charge $25 or more for a credit check—or "application fee"—and warn consumers against getting credit checks at multiple dealerships, saying it will damage their credit score.

Some families start off owing more than the home is worth. Dealers offer expensive extras like trips, rebates, insurance or even offer to pay off credit cards. They add thousands of dollars to a consumer loan to pay for these extras....

...Fraud and predatory loan practices that strip families of equity are responsible for many of these problems, which have led to a recent downturn in the manufactured home market.

While some of these complaints relate to highly individualized incidents, most reveal a pattern of problems shared among many consumers that should be addressed through a stronger and more coherent regulatory system.

NOTE: The full report is available on the Web at www.consumersunion.org/other/mh/overinfo.htm

dealership and the lender are subsidiaries of the same corporation, this fee is questionable at best. Lenders who have close connections to dealerships—providing flooring loans for lot models, for example—often provide rebates to dealers who bring borrowers to them, usually around two percent of the amount loaned. Perfectly legitimate, but that amount is paid by the lender, not tacked onto the loan.

State tax of $3,290.

Borrowers are often not told early on that they'll have pay sales tax on their home (in those states with sales tax), and the amount will be in the thousands. Just another unpleasant shocker hidden in the details.

Prepaid financed points of $7,195.

This equals 8% of the loan value, a big chunk. If asked for an explanation HeavenSent Financial would say it calculated the amount as follows: "Based on the Millers borderline credit rating, we would have to charge them 15.99% interest. But we will reduce the interest rate by one quarter of a percent for each point the Millers purchase, in this instance eight points, to yield a 13.99% interest rate. We are allowing them to borrow the money to buy those points."

With conventional home loans, banks often give borrowers the option of lowering their loan interest rate by paying for a portion of that interest, referred to as prepaid points, in cash up front. This can be a good deal for both parties. The bank gets the cash value right away of the amount the interest would have generated over time, while the borrower enjoys lower monthly payments while reducing the overall cost of the loan.

Alternatively, some conventional home loan banks, just as HeavenSent Financial did, will tack the cost of the buy-down onto the loan principal, in effect lending the buyers the money. Again, perfectly legitimate.

In the Millers' case, however, the advantage is decidedly in favor of HeavenSent Financial which appears to have picked the 15.99% starting rate to justify an add-on of $7,195 to the loan package. Over the 30-year life of the loan the financed points provide only a tiny savings while significantly slowing the rate of the Millers' equity build-up in their home.

In fact, the couple would have no equity in their home for years. In essence, HeavenSent's imposition of prepaid financed points as a *fait accompli* without prior discussion is tantamount to charging the Millers a hefty fee for giving them a loan.

Andy, the salesman, had a professional obligation (that he ignored) to explain the pros and cons of a buy-down and to leave the decision up to them.

Buying down points makes no sense if the Millers anticipated selling their home in five to ten years. While they may have saved $60-$70 on their monthly payment, when they resell their home, they would need to raise the asking price by more than $7,000 to pay off the additional loan cost.

However, if the Millers intended living in their home for more than 20 years, a buy down would be prudent, saving money on the monthly mortgage payment while their equity in the home increased over the long run.

The current lending environment

And that's how Tom and Brenda Miller got caught in the pressure pit on their way to their piece of the American dream. It's worth noting here that no party to the transactions did anything unlawful. Rather, ethics aside, those in a position to do so simply pushed the envelope here and there to their best advantage. Several deal terms of the Millers' purchase contract (hefty loan origination fees, step-increases on chattel mortgages, and credit life insurance) are far less common now compared to the anything-goes boom of the 1990s. But this is not to say that they have vanished. And if history is any indication, they could easily reappear during the next upturn.

One unfortunate result of the industry's near collapse was that many major lenders exited the market, and for several years chattel mortgage financing was very difficult to find. Still, there was, and is, a substantial market for this type of loan. The good news is that, as of 2006. new players have stepped into this arena.   But these new lenders are employing stricter standards for creditworthiness. The days of easy credit are probably gone forever.

The dangers remain: while these days the big industry players have corrected many of their excesses, there still remain finance companies out there that will not hesitate to take advantage of the unwary.

As this chapter has illustrated, the process of buying a manufactured home—or any home for that matter—is a complex business, even with the most upstanding honest dealer. But if you will keep the Millers' story in mind as you continue reading, that process will become clear and straightforward.

Chapter 4

Getting Started—Calculating Your Buying Power

As the misfortune that befell our hypothetical couple, Tom and Brenda Miller, illustrates, the sale, financing and installation of manufactured homes offers abundant opportunities for unwary buyers to get taken. We will be referring to the Millers' experience as we examine more closely each phase of the buying process. But first, here are three ground rules to follow:

Ground rule #1: *Go slow.*

Buying any home is a serious, quite complex process. It is not at all unusual for a conventional home purchase to take months. First time buyers must learn a lot, so take all the time you need to understand everything, particularly contracts.

Ground rule #2: *Take it one step at a time and in the following order:*

1. Do a little research, obtain your credit rating and calculate your buying power.

2. Shop for the money and, if possible, get pre-approved for a loan.

3. Purchase or lease your home site before you buy your home.

4. Shop for, and purchase, your home.

The order of these steps is crucial. Calculating your buying power makes you knowledgeable, and puts you in control. Shopping for a loan and, if possible, getting pre-approved, before you shop the dealerships, will always give you better terms than dealer financing. As for purchasing or leasing your home site, depending upon the circumstances—buying land as part of a construction loan, for example—the purchase of the land and your home may happen at the same time, such as at the close of an escrow. But the point is to make absolutely sure you've got a site for your manufactured home nailed down—including assurances it is legally entitled to be placed there and that it can physically be brought to that site—before you legally commit to the purchase of that home. Stories abound of land purchases that fell through, leaving the buyer not only paying monthly house payments, but also hefty storage fees on a factory-ordered new home sitting in pieces on a dealer's back lot.

Does this mean you shouldn't set foot on a dealer's front lot until you have done your research and lined up your financing? Not at all. By all means, visit a few dealerships and look through their models, dream a little, get excited, collect brochures, but be defensive. Recommendations:

Reveal nothing useful. Be polite but firmly vague: "Just looking, thanks..." Be prepared to repeat this more than once when responding to questions. The reply puts up a boundary that most sales people quickly detect and generally respect. But don't hesitate to ask questions as long as you don't disclose personal information. Keep it friendly. The first sales person you meet may turn out to be the one from whom you buy your home.

Don't sign any "guest books," fill out tickets for prize drawings or respond to similar other information-gathering ploys, unless you want to be contacted (at this stage you don't). Exception: Some dealers ask you to sign a guest book before they give you keys to the lot models. This is reasonable. Use your judgement.

Consider a personal advocate

Here's a strategy that can really help: If you, like many, are inclined to feel intimidated by the shopping experience involving major purchases such as a car or a home, if you find it difficult to ask hard questions or hold your ground in the presence of smooth-talking pressure merchants, then consider taking along with you on your visits your own personal advocate. He or she can be your spouse or partner, a friend or relative or someone in business or the professions—anyone you trust who can play the role of dispassionate observer and polite skeptic.

Your advocate need not be knowledgeable about manufactured homes but should be someone who doesn't rattle easily, who can ask probing questions, make requests on your behalf, and protect you from disclosing information before doing so is warranted.

One benefit you will experience is a feeling of being guarded, free to browse without having to speak or be distracted (or feel intimidated) by anyone. In fact, if two people are visiting a dealership, they can agree in advance that one will do the talking while the other remains silent. Not only does this tactic work, it can be fun.

As the purchasing process moves along, an advocate can play an effective role whether representing your interests during face-to-face negotiations, or just being available for a phone call to serve as a sounding board and to offer suggestions.

Now, for the rest of this chapter, let's take a closer look at the first two steps of the buying process for buyers who will need a loan to purchase their home (that amounts to 91% of all manufactured home buyers.:

Step 1. Research, get your own credit rating, and calculate your buying power

Research. According to the Manufactured Housing Institute, the majority of manufactured home purchases continue to be financed through loans made available through dealers. The principal reason for this is that many, if not most of those who buy their homes this way, would not otherwise qualify for conventional home mortgage loans. Another reason is many buyers simply don't know many other choices may be available to them. Here's where your doing a little research can really pay off.

Financing your purchase through a dealership may make sense, especially if you're looking for a "home only" loan (i.e. with no land purchase), which is financed through a retail installment contract, also known as a chattel mortgage ("chattel" meaning personal property such as a car or an RV). A reputable dealer will share your interest in getting a square deal that you can handle financially over the long haul. There are reputable industry lenders out there providing loans only through manufactured home dealerships to good credit buyers—and reputable dealers know who these lenders are.

But here is a major rule:

Financing through a dealer should be considered only as a last resort and only after you have researched all the loan programs available to you.

Here's why:

It used to be that conventional banks would turn you down if your credit history was even slightly tainted, let alone showed a past bankruptcy. But that has changed in this era of banking deregulation. These days more banks are willing to give loans to people with a history of some credit problems, often at interest rates lower than those offered by the finance companies that work through the dealers. Yes, you will pay a higher interest rate than conventional borrowers because statistically people with troubled credit histories have a higher rate of loan defaults, so the banks charge more interest to cover their anticipated losses and still make a profit.

These loans are called subprime loans, a term that is a bit misleading. Subprime refers not to the loan, but to a borrower who is considered less than a prime credit risk. Depending on your credit history, your interest rate may be anywhere from two to five interest points higher than a prime credit risk borrower, sometimes much higher. But some subprime loans allow the borrower to pay as little as 5% down on a manufactured home purchase.

If your credit problems have been cleared up and your future income prospects are steady, a subprime loan may allow you to get into a manufactured home and begin to build equity. After a few years, you might qualify to refinance at a lower rate. If you don't own the land under your home, you will have little chance of getting a conventional mortgage loan, but those chances may be improving (see below and in Chapter 6).

With the near collapse of the manufactured housing industry at the end of the 1990s, chattel loans from conventional banks virtually dried up. But as of 2006, with the industry largely recovered, chattel loans are once again available, but mostly only to borrowers with good credit (think FICO scores of 690 and above). Take time to check with the banks in your area to learn what new loan programs may be available.

Get your own credit report and credit score. Until recently, the three national credit bureaus that together compile and rate the credit worthiness of the nation's consumers provided that information only to banks and businesses, credit card providers and other subscribers who paid for such information. But thanks to Congress' passage in 2001 of the Fair Credit Reporting Act, everyone is entitled to receive annually a free copy of their credit report. The fastest way is to request and download your report from the Internet. The official (and only authorized) web site for doing this www.annualcreditreport.com. (For more information, go to http://www.ftc.gov/bcp/conline/pubs/credit/freereports.htm). This web page also gives direction for obtaining your report by phone or mail. If you do so online, within about ten minutes you can download and print out your report, complete with full explanations and comparisons, including instructions for correcting errors.

Note: Each bureau has the same, or close to the same, information and credit rating for you so you only need to request the information from one, although some credit advisors suggest you get your credit history from all three on an annual basis just to eliminate the possibility of reporting errors.

Here are the three big bureaus:

Equifax. http://www.equifax.com Phone: (800) 685-1111

TransUnion. http://www.transunion.com Phone: (800) 88804213

Experian. http://www.experian.com Phone: (888) 397-3742

In addition to your credit report, for a nominal fee (around $25), you can obtain your credit score—a three-digit number variously called a bureau score, or a FICO score or a Beacon score—based on an analysis of your credit card payment history as well as other transaction activities such as mortgage and car payments. The great majority of consumers score between 300 and 850, with the lowest score representing the highest risk and the highest score the lowest risk. Your score shows how you compare with the rest of the population. For example, a score of 710 would put you in the 43rd percentile, which means about 43% of consumers have credit scores that are the same or lower than yours. A score of 725 would put you at the 50th percentile, the national average.

Generally, lenders consider any score over 700 to be good—and consumers with 700-plus scores to be an acceptable credit risk. For example, statistically, only 5% of consumers with scores in the 700-749 range become delinquent payers (i.e., more than 90 days past due or worse on any account over a two year period). Forty-nine percent of consumers have scores between 700 and 800, with 11% above 800.

Here's the distribution of scores below 700 and their delinquency rates:

Score	Percentile	Delinquency rate
up 499	1 percent	87 percent
500-549	5 percent	71 percent
550-599	7 percent	51 percent
600-649	11 percent	31 percent
650-699	16 percent	15 percent

Historically, the average credit score of those who purchase a manufactured home through a dealer financed loan is between 635 and 650. During the 1990s' boom, lenders competing for market share set the stage for disaster by greatly increasing loan approvals for borrowers with credit scores under 600.

Thus, a rule:

Obtain your credit score before you begin shopping for a loan.

If you ask a dealer to work up an informal estimate on the price of a home and the loan terms, you need only provide your credit score, your estimated down payment and a monthly mortgage payment with which you would be comfortable. You do not need to provide your social security number or sign any document to obtain this information.

This rule applies when you are shopping for so-called good faith estimates, and reputable dealers should not have any problem agreeing to your request. But keep in mind that if you decide to make a formal application for a loan through a dealership—again, only after you have considered all the alternatives—you're signaling that you're serious and ready to buy, and that dealer may require that you also sign a purchase agreement and put up an earnest money deposit.

Doing so can be OK but you must be sure the agreement contains language that specifically allows you to walk away from the deal, with your deposit, if you determine that the loan terms offered you are unacceptable.

Many dealers have boilerplate purchase agreements with language that in effect says you're stuck with the contract if they can secure financing for you, even at sky-high interest rates and predatory terms over which you have no say (See Chapter 7).

Calculate your buying power—Here is where a bit of simple math and some research can answer the all-important questions:

1. How big a loan can I really afford?
2. How much of a down payment can I make?
3. What will my monthly payment be?

These days, especially with the help of a personal computer and the Internet, you can research and answer these questions, and many more, before you talk to any lender, broker or dealer. Here's how to determine your buying power:

The debt-to-income ratio

When you apply for a loan, one of the first things every loan officer in the known universe looks at is the percentage of your gross monthly income that you currently spend for your housing costs whether you rent or own your dwelling. For you to qualify for a conventional home loan, that figure should be 28 percent or less of your monthly income. This number is sometimes called the front-end ratio or housing-cost ratio.

They also want your total monthly debt, which is your housing costs plus your consumer debt, to be no more than 36 percent of your gross monthly income, called the total-debt ratio. For chattel loans—that is, personal property loans that don't involve a land purchase—many lenders will accept a higher total: 40 to 41 percent. Consumer debt consists of one's monthly payments on credit cards, car payments, student loans and/or child support, but does not include costs such as those for food, clothing, medical expenses, entertainment and miscellaneous expenses. You can also subtract from the total debt periodic payments such as car insurance and life insurance.

To illustrate, let's calculate these percentages for Tom and Brenda Miller before they began shopping for their manufactured home. The Millers' combined monthly income was $3,400 and their monthly housing cost was $755 (rent $720, plus $35 utilities), which yields a housing-cost ratio of 22% (755 ÷ 3400 = 22). That's very good.

But when we add their $600 per month consumer debt to the housing costs ($755+$600 = $1,355), to calculate their total debt as a percentage of income, the result is 40% (1,355 ÷

3400 = .40). That's 4 percentage points over the 36% maximum that lenders usually allow for conventional loans, but OK for a chattel loan.

The watch-word here is "usually." Some conventional home lenders are comfortable with a total debt percentage two or three points higher while others may require the percentage be as low as 33 percent if the borrower intends to put less than ten percent down. Lenders often have leeway in decision-making, and the Millers' score alone does not mean they won't qualify for a conventional loan.

The scoring formula also suggests a way in which the Millers could improve their score: 36% of their monthly income amounts to $1,224, or $131 less than their current total monthly debt. If the Millers could reduce their monthly consumer debt by $131, they would be right on target. Conceivably, had the Millers known about debt ratios (and done the math), they may have wisely decided to hold off their home purchase until they met that goal, which in turn could have qualified them for a conventional loan at a significantly lower interest rate than a chattel loan.

Loan amount, amount down, payments

Aside from the amount you have saved (or need to save) for a down payment, the amount you can comfortably afford to pay each month as a house payment is the biggest factor determining how much money you can borrow. The key word here is "comfortably." Only you can be the judge of that.

One recommended way to calculate that number is to take a good honest look at the past two years of your income and expenses. A two year look-back will give you a more realistic picture to determine how much of your total monthly income, after subtracting all other expenses and set-asides (such as a monthly deposit into your savings account, for example) is available to pay for a home mortgage or a loan.

Once you have that monthly figure, you can use the Mortgage Table in this chapter to calculate approximately how large a 30-year loan you can afford at various interest rates.

To illustrate, let's suppose Tom and Brenda Miller calculated they could afford $850 a month in house payments and wanted to know how much they could borrow with a 30-year loan at 9.50% interest. Using the chart, find the amount of their monthly payment, then read across the row to the column beneath the 9.5% interest. The figure where the two cross is the total dollar amount the couple can borrow, in this case $101,088.

Actually, this amount is only technically correct. The amount is accurate only if all of the Miller's $850 were put towards paying down that amount (i.e. the principal), but in their case this is not likely.

With conventional home loans (as opposed to the retail installment contract the Millers signed), lenders often require borrowers who are putting less than 20% down to make monthly payments into what's called an impound account for things like property insurance, property taxes and mortgage insurance which, together, can easily total $175-$200 a month. Deducting that amount, let's say $200, from the Millers' $850, leaves only $650 a month to go towards paying down the interest. Using that figure on the mortgage chart, the true amount the Millers can borrow is $77,302.

But wait....there's more (to borrow from the late night VegeMatic TV commercials). Don't forget the state sales tax the Millers will have to pay. If the sales tax in their state is 5%, their tax hit will be $3,865, further reducing the actual amount they can borrow to $73,437.

Finding answers on the Internet

If you have access to the Internet (most public libraries now have computer terminals that the public can use at no charge), a number of Web sites provide a variety of mortgage calculators that allow you to explore all kinds of "what if" scenarios. The Fannie Mae site (the Federal National Mortgage Association (www. homepath.com) has a wealth of information about home buying in general that is applicable to manufactured home/land purchases. Click on "Calculators" on the top bar of the home page and you will be presented with a half dozen calculators that enable you to answer queries such as: What monthly payment do I need for a house with a specific sales price? What monthly payment can I afford? and How much can I borrow? You'll also find calculators to determine your 28/36 percent debt ratios.

Other helpful Web sites with calculators:

HSH Financial Publishers   www.hsh.com

Interest.com   www.interest.com.

Step 2. Shop for the money and, if possible, get pre-approved for a loan

These days most people who are about to begin looking for a new or used conventional site-built home will first sit down with their local banker, credit union loan officer or a mortgage broker and calculate how large a home loan they can get. Sometimes a real estate agent will assist in this process. There are several advantages in doing so:

- The buyer knows before starting the home search exactly how much he or she can afford in a home.
- Being pre-approved (or pre-qualified) by a lender, the buyer knows that after a purchase offer is accepted, he or she will not be faced with the time-consuming task of securing a favorable loan under the pressure of a deadline.

Often the lender or mortgage broker will provide a "To whom it may concern" letter that the home buyer can include with a purchase offer that states the buyer has been pre-approved for the amount of the loan needed to purchase the home. In the case of a home being sold through a Realtor, such a letter, by providing assurance that the money is there and waiting, can make a difference in persuading a seller to accept the offer, especially if multiple offers are being considered. You should do the same.

A note on mortgage brokers

These professionals don't themselves make loans, but instead they're in touch with scores of banks around the country that pay them a fee for sending them qualified borrowers. You, too, may be charged a fee. A broker will assemble all your financial and credit information, then send it to several banks whose lending qualifications you meet, to see which can give you the most competitive loan terms. For this reason homeowners typically turn to mortgage brokers when the time comes to refinance their homes. But be careful in selecting a broker.

Unfortunately this arena of business has its share of predatory smooth-talkers. Avoid brokers who try to extract fees and/or contract signatures from you before they do any work. They're trying to lock you in, just like the fast-buck dealers. Ask friends and associates for referrals. You want a broker with whom you feel comfortable, who will happily, patiently answer your questions. Don't hesitate to ask a broker about the fees he or she will receive.

How conventional home loans differ from dealer-financed purchase contracts

When shopping for a conventional home loan or a home-construction loan, one quickly sees a basic difference between these types of loans and the retail installment contracts that finance companies offer borrowers through manufactured home dealerships. The latter are structured so that all costs associated with the loan, apart from the down payment, are included as part of the loan. With Tom and Brenda Miller, for example, these costs included the loan origination fee, points and the premiums for creditor insurance, property insurance and their extended warranty. In contrast, a conventional home loan—and this is mandated by federal law—requires all these costs to be paid by the borrower at the time of closing, or settlement. These expenses, together with the down payment, are called closing costs.

This carefully structured purchase process reflects the many decades of legislation on both state and federal levels to ensure that home sale transactions are clear and understandable, and that the money being borrowed will be used only to purchase the home and the land on which it sits. In addition, the transaction between the buyer, the seller and the buyer's lender, is handled by a disinterested fourth party, usually a title insurance company that holds all the funds in an escrow account, releasing them according to instructions agreed upon by all parties. In the broadest sense, the settlement procedure is designed to be as free of misunderstandings and as swindle-proof as possible.

Most brokers and loan officers use software applications that contain the standardized settlement form (or settlement sheet), which allows them to easily look at various loan terms and costs. Brokers often provide their clients with good faith estimates in the form of the settlement sheet, together with the federal truth-in-lending disclosure statement that will accompany the finalized settlement.

Rescuing Tom and Brenda

To illustrate, let's rescue Tom and Brenda Miller from their nightmare and put them once more on the starting line of their original dream: a manufactured home on their own land. Only this time they've done their homework and have concluded they should try for a less expensive, but still very nice, two-bedroom manufactured home for $40,000. Let's give them one more plus: they've reduced their monthly consumer debt by $131 and thus have an acceptable debt-to-income ratio.

Through a realtor they have found several buildable lots, each selling for $25,000, and a contractor they interviewed has agreed to do the site preparation, including a septic system, water hookup and construction of a car port, for $18,000. Adding $2,000 of sales tax (which is 5% in their state), the Millers need $85,000, not including the closing costs. They have saved $4,000 toward a down payment.

MORTGAGE TABLE — Calculate how much home you can afford

This table shows roughly how much home you can afford for the monthly house payment you pay, based on a 30-year mortgage at a fixed interest rate. From the far left column select the monthly payment you can afford, then read across to the interest rate nearest the current rate. The intersection of the two lines shows approximately the loan amount your monthly house payment will buy.

Monthly Payment	6.00%	6.50%	7.00%	7.50%	8.00%	8.50%	9.00%	9.50%	10.00%	10.50%	11.00%
$300	$50,040	$47,460	$45,092	$42,905	$40,885	$39,016	$37,285	$35,678	$34,185	$32,796	$31,502
$350	58,380	55,370	52,608	50,056	47,669	45,519	43,499	41,624	39,883	38,262	36,752
$400	66,720	63,280	60,123	57,207	54,513	52,022	49,713	47,571	45,580	43,728	42,003
$450	75,050	71,190	67,638	64,358	61,328	58,524	55,927	53,517	51,278	49,194	47,253
$500	83,400	79,100	75,154	71,509	68,142	65,027	62,141	59,463	56,975	54,660	52,503
$550	91,730	87,010	82,669	78,660	74,956	71,529	68,355	65,410	62,673	60,126	57,753
$600	100,075	94,925	90,185	85,811	81,770	78,032	74,569	71,356	68,370	65,592	63,004
$650	108,415	102,840	97,700	92,961	88,584	84,535	80,783	77,302	74,068	71,059	68,254
$700	116,755	110,850	105,215	100,112	95,398	91,038	86,997	83,249	79,766	76,525	73,504
$750	125,095	118,660	112,731	107,263	102,213	97,540	93,211	89,195	85,463	81,991	78,755
$800	133,435	126,570	120,246	114,414	109,027	104,043	99,425	95,141	91,161	87,457	84,005
$850	141,770	134,480	127,761	121,565	115,841	110,546	105,640	101,088	96,858	92,923	89,255
$900	150,110	142,390	135,277	128,716	122,655	117,048	111,854	107,034	102,566	98,389	94,506
$950	158,450	150,300	142,792	135,867	129,469	123,551	118,068	112,980	108,253	103,854	99,756
$1,000	166,790	158,210	150,308	143,018	136,283	130,054	124,282	118,927	113,951	109,321	105,006
$1,050	175,130	166,120	157,823	150,169	143,098	136,556	130,496	124,873	119,648	114,786	110,256
$1,100	183,470	174,030	165,338	157,320	149,912	143,058	136,710	130,820	125,346	120,252	115,506
$1,150	191,810	191,940	172,854	164,571	156,726	149,561	142,924	136,766	131,043	125,718	120,757
$1,200	200,150	189,850	180,369	171,621	163,540	156,064	149,138	142,712	136,741	131,185	126,007
$1,250	208,590	197,760	187,884	178,772	170,354	162,567	155,352	148,659	142,439	136,651	131,257
$1,300	216,830	205,670	195,400	185,923	177,168	169,070	161,567	154,605	148,136	142,117	136,508
$1,350	225,170	213,580	202,916	193,074	183,982	175,573	167,781	160,551	153,854	147,583	141,758
$1,400	233,510	221,490	210,431	200,225	190,796	182,076	173,995	166,498	159,531	153,049	147,009
$1,450	241,850	229,400	217,946	207,376	197,611	188,578	180,209	172,444	165,229	158,515	152,259
$1,500	250,190	237,310	225,462	214,527	204,425	195,081	186,423	178,390	170,926	163,981	157,509
$1,550	258,530	245,230	232,977	221,678	211,239	201,583	192,637	184,337	176,624	169,447	162,759
$1,600	266,870	253,140	240,493	228,829	218,053	208,086	198,851	190,283	182,321	174,913	168,010

The Millers meet with Cathy, a local mortgage broker recommended by friends, who tells them she works with several area banks that regularly provide construction loans for new manufactured homes as part of land-home deals.

She recommends the Millers look at a 30 year adjustable rate mortgage that features a low fixed rate of 6.125% interest for the first three years. After that the interest rate would be periodically adjusted in relation to an index rate, but the adjustment would not exceed 2% during any adjustment period.

The Millers agree and Cathy, in less than ten minutes at her computer, works up the following estimate, based upon a settlement form:

Good Faith Estimate

Items payable in connection with loan:

$382.50	Loan discount of 0.5% (a one time fee charged by the lender)
$400.00	Appraisal fee (to inspect and appraise property and home)
$18.00	Credit report
$66.00	Tax-related service fee
$65.00	Processing fee
$200.00	Underwriting fee (a one time fee charged by the lender)
$20.00	Flood certification
$100.00	Reappraisal after home is installed and ready for occupancy

Title company charges:

$220.00	Title company's escrow fee
$271.00	Title insurance (one time expense to insure clear title to the property)

Government recording and transfer fees:

$30.00	Recording fee (to record transaction with the county clerk)
$1,772.50	Total estimated closing costs

Items required by lender to be paid in advance:

$480.00	Mortgage insurance premium

Reserves deposited with the lender:

$80.00	Two months of property/hazard insurance (at $40/month)
$56.10	Mortgage insurance premium reserve
$170.00	Taxes and Assessment Reserves (2 months at $85/mo)
$730.00	Estimated prepaid items/Reserves
$2,502.50	Total Estimated settlement charges

Total Estimated Funds needed to close:

$85,000.00	(+)	Purchase price of home-land
$76,500.00	(-)	Loan amount
$1,772.50	(+)	Estimated closing costs
$730.00	(+)	Estimated prepaid items/reserves
$8,500.00	(+)	Amount paid by Seller (down payment, 10% of purchase price)
$11,002.50		Total Estimated Funds needed to close.

Total estimated monthly payment:

$ 464.82	Principal & Interest
$40.00	Hazard insurance
$85.00	Real Estate taxes
$56.10	Mortgage Insurance
$645.92	Total monthly payment

Tom and Brenda take one look at the $11,002 in cash needed to close the deal, and sigh. Brenda says they were hoping they could get in with only five percent down, "but we still have to pay an extra two-thousand-five-hundred-and-two dollars in settlement costs."

Cathy nods. "OK, right now your cash position isn't strong enough for this loan. But you're close, don't give up. Here's some points to consider: Yes, the bank needs ten percent down but the buyers only need to be able to document that they are paying five percent themselves. The rest can be in the form of a gift, say from a relative.

"You mentioned Brenda's father might be able to help, maybe with up to three thousand of the down. That gives you seven thousand of the eleven thousand you need. If you can put aside an additional four thousand, say, over the next year or two, you'll be in great shape.

"Plus, think about the advantages you'll have once you get in with that loan," she continues. "If the starting interest rate is the same, your house payment of six-forty-six will be seventy-five dollars less than you're now paying for your rent. And your yearly mortgage interest, which will be around five thousand dollars, will be tax deductible. Plus, you'll be building equity in your home from the get-go and will have a locked-in rate for three years, after which you can refinance into a thirty-year fixed rate."

The Millers came away from their meeting with Cathy feeling a mixture of disappointment and excitement. They accepted the broker's assessment that it was a bit too early to try for a home purchase, but they were excited to learn how close they were to their goal. That evening they sat together and drew up an 18-month plan to scrimp, save and find extra work here and there to pull together the needed $4,000. During the months that followed, as their efforts showed results, the Millers felt great satisfaction and pride in the sacrifice they were making. A little more than a year later, they returned to see Cathy and to announce that they had the money at last. This time they got the loan.

The happy ending versus the nightmare

When you hold up the HeavenSent Homes' predatory deal from hell for comparison with the adjustable rate mortgage (ARM) just described, the differences are huge:

With the HeavenSent Homes loan, the Millers, after their $4,857 down payment, owed $92,278, of which $47,000 was for a home on land they didn't own, only rented. The remaining $45,278 owed was fees, tax, financed points, insurance, a garage and site development. Significantly, the garage and site development package ($25,000) was not only overpriced, but in effect the Millers had paid for improvements on land owned by Cascade Meadows—improvements they could not take with them if they ever decided to move their home. That's a sweet deal indeed for the park, which additionally made a profit as the general contractor on the park installation package.

In contrast, with the adjustable rate mortgage, the Millers owed only $76,500 after their $11,002 down payment ($15,778 less than Heavenly Homes loan), yet owned both the home and the land it was placed, and started out with ten percent equity in their property. Plus, their monthly payment of $649.92 was $189.68 less than their first year payment under the HeavenSent contract (in Years Two and Three it would be $259.02 less and $329.67 less, respectively).

Most of the closing fees listed on the ARM settlement form are self-explanatory. Some notes on the others:

$382.50 Loan discount of 0.5%. The bank (lender) is requiring you to pay them at closing a fee equal to one-half a percent (or one-half a point) of the money it's lending you. Seems odd, doesn't it? In short, you're paying interest on 100% of the loan but actually you're getting only 99.5% of the money. Many banks charge more, in the 1 to 2 percent range.

$200.00 underwriting fee and $65.00 processing fee. These go to the bank to cover processing your loan application. Separately, the bank will pay a referral fee to the broker for bringing in a qualified borrower. These and the loan discount fee total $647.50, compared to the $2,450.00 "Documentation and loan fee" on the HeavenSent purchase agreement.

$480 Mortgage Insurance Premium. Banks routinely require borrowers who are putting up less than 20% as a down payment to buy Private Mortgage Insurance (PMI). In the event that the borrower defaults, the policy pays off the mortgage. Once the borrower has accumulated 20 percent or more equity in the home, PMI is no longer required, and the monthly payment can be decreased accordingly.

Note: Don't confuse PMI with Credit Life Insurance. The former protects the lender, not the consumer, paying off the bank directly. On the HeavenSent agreement, the $5,000 premium for the Joint Credit Life Insurance Policy, the beneficiary is the surviving spouse, not the lender.

$730 estimated reserves deposited with the lender. Typically, lenders want a couple of months of taxes and insurance payments in-hand to cover costs in the event that the borrower falls behind in payments.

Do what many dealers won't do

As you may gather from the above, banks and traditional lenders tend to be cautious types who carefully screen applicants and require various guarantees, reserves and insurance before they spring for the money. They also require a great deal of documentation on everything, such as: salary payment stubs, tax returns, bank account records, work history, credit card statements and proof of ownership of assets (e.g., car, home, securities). Processing your application can take weeks, drive you a little nuts and require you to make regular calls to your loan officer to nudge the process along.

Returning to the realm of dealer-financed loans for a moment, the consequences of a bad decision on borrowing are far more serious for the buyer than for the dealer. So, it's really important for you as a buyer to do the things a dealer won't do: take the time to make a serious effort to get a good loan, and be prepared to work for it. When you divide the money saved over the years by the hours invested to get a good loan, you can bet the hourly rate will be in the many hundreds of dollars—it will be well worth it.

In sum, when you compare dealer-arranged purchase contracts (often also called chattel mortgages) with conventional home mortgages, sadly, the message is: "The poor pay more." Or, more correctly, "Those with poor credit pay more." This can be said even of square deals provided through reputable dealers.

Buying a home, whether new or used, site-built or factory-made, is a complicated business, especially the first time around, but it's not rocket science. By first doing a bit of research, getting your own credit rating and calculating your true buying power before you start shopping in earnest for your home, you will not only be much more savvy and confident, you will be well on your way to being swindle-proof.

Remember, too, that there are a lot of good, reputable dealers out there who are willing to help—and with the help of this guide, you will find them.

Chapter 5

Finding and Buying Land for Your Home

Although precise figures are hard to come by, an estimated 75 percent of all manufactured homes in the United States are currently located in rural, or semi-rural areas. This percentage is expected to decrease in the coming years as more buyers who prefer living in urban or suburban neighborhoods recognize manufactured homes' terrific quality and competitive value. In many regions, notably in California, small scale developers and home buyers are saving a bundle buying individual lots inside city limits (called infill lots) and placing manufactured homes on them, often adding components such as garages, porches and covered entry ways that render the dwellings indistinguishable from more expensive site-built homes next door. In what is perhaps the strongest indicator that the manufactured home has become a part of mainstream housing, the U.S. Census Bureau figures for 1999 show that 68% of new manufactured homes, whether in the city or the country, were located on private property. In the northwest 85 to 90 percent of manufactured home purchases currently involve a land/home deal of some kind. The remaining 32% were located on leased land, mostly in parks that the industry nowadays calls manufactured home land-lease communities.

Whether to buy or to lease, searching for a site for a manufactured home has its own challenges, but doing so is certainly a lot more fun than crunching numbers and talking to loan officers.

For starters, while renting a home site can make sense for some homeowners (retired seniors on fixed incomes and with a fair lease, for example), owning your home and the land on which it sits is by far the more desirable option. The advantages are many: the home qualifies for conventional home loans which have much lower interest rates than consumer loans or chattel mortgages, thus saving you thousands of dollars; your monthly payments, unlike rent, build equity in your home; your home may appreciate in value, sometimes at a rate exceeding other types of investments; your home will always be saleable at the current market value, and to whomever you choose to sell it; you are not subject to uncontrolled rent increases, or changes in park management, or, worst case scenario, a demand that you take your home elsewhere due to the sale of the park and its planned conversion to other commercial use; you don't have to abide by a long list of rules and regulations typical of leased land communities; you will enjoy the freedom to do as you chose around your property, and build what you want. True, unlike park residents, you have to pay property taxes (the taxes park tenants pay is buried somewhere in their rent but they can't deduct them), but this negative is more than offset by the many positives. Note: The interest portion of your mortgage payment is tax deductible, but so, too, is the interest a park tenant pays on the purchase contract for his or her home as long as it is used as a primary residence.

Finally, just when you're starting to feel discouraged, you find this lovely piece of land—sunny, plenty of room, a splendid view of the mountains, good well water, not too far from town and the price is right. Now things begin to get really exciting.

Seventy-three days after this land was purchased, the owners moved into this spacious double-wide. The detached garage was completed by move-in day. A comparable site-built home would have taken at least six months, weather permitting, and cost 25 percent more. Examples like this are why many mainstream home buyers are starting to look at manufactured homes as an attractive housing option.

In sum, your home is truly your castle and likely your biggest wealth builder. This said, the task you face as a prospective manufactured home buyer differs in a few ways from that of someone looking at land on which to put a site-built home.

Welcome to "No mobiles" land

Philosopher-humorist Will Rogers once quipped, "Last time I looked they weren't making any more land in these parts." One is tempted to add, "And these days there's less of it." In many regions of the country, prospective buyers of manufactured homes shopping for home sites soon discover that a good percentage of the lots for sale come with a "no mobile home" deed restriction, spelled out in an accompanying document called Covenants, Conditions and Restrictions (CC&Rs). The constraint is a carryover from the days of widespread community zoning codes that were established to keep neighborhoods safe from the blight of seedy 10-wide trailer homes and the galvanized ghettos that, among other perceived nuisances, lead to lower property values. A lot of those zoning codes are still found in many regions of the country, particularly in the East. This is why you may encounter fewer lots for sale than you expected.

Manufactured homes, zoning and covenants—what the courts are saying

Generally, courts around the country have sided with manufactured home owners when the latter have challenged old zoning laws originally designed to prohibit house trailers and trailer courts (snob zoning). However, the rulings involving challenges to private property restrictions have been mixed.

In a lengthy article for the American Law Review, published in 2000, attorney Kurtis Kemper reviewed recent court cases around the country, mostly involving residents of subdivisions who sought to prevent manufactured homes. Plaintifs argued they violated the subdivision's restriction on house trailers. The courts have struggled with the terms "mobile home," "trailer house," and "manufactured home" in applying the law.

In a majority of cases, Kemper reported, the courts have held for the subdivision, concluding the manner in which the structures are brought to the property (i.e., on their own wheels) is the determining factor.

"Nevertheless," the author continues, "the courts in a large number of cases have arrived at the opposite conclusion, usually finding that the appearance or permanence of double-wide mobile homes or modular homes distinguished such structures from those intended to be restricted by covenants using the terms "mobile home," "house trailer," "trailer house" or "trailer."

As one industry wag described helpfully, "We don't make house trailers any more; we make manufactured trailers."

In fact, in many communities, the single greatest factor limiting the sale of manufactured homes is the limited inventory of available land for sale on which manufactured homes may be placed. Or, as one old-time dealer complained, "They ain't no place to put 'em."

You would think that today's manufactured home, by virtue of its very similar appearance to a site-built home, and the fact that Congress in 1980 officially recognized it as a dwelling type distinct from a mobile home, that this deed restriction does not, and should not, apply.

If recent court rulings against municipalities around the country are any indication, your thinking is correct (see side bar), but that assumption is not yet universally recognized. In short, while your chances are excellent that you would win in court, the time and legal costs involved would be prohibitive. **Note**: Should you decide to challenge the restriction in court, be sure to contact your state or regional manufactured housing association. They can be a great help with legal advice and resources.

This predicament is vexing, but sometimes the dilemma can be resolved informally when a private property owner, not local government zoning, is responsible for the deed restriction. For example, in the case of a lot that is not part of a subdivision and whose owner wrote the restriction, consider contacting the owner and describing the home you are buying; as likely as not he or she will agree to remove the deed restriction at the time of sale.

On the other hand, if the lot is in a subdivision for which there is a set of CC&Rs that apply to the whole development, the power to waive them (or any portion) does not lie with the seller of an individual lot, because such a waiver would affect other property owners who have purchased lots, or houses on lots, in reliance of those restrictions. In fact, even the developer who created the CC&Rs may not arbitrarily waive them because others have already bought lots in reliance of the legally enforceable restrictions. It is not unusual for these affected property owners to file suit to get a court order to stop any waiver of the CC&Rs. Avoid any such court battles. Not only are they very expensive and protracted, but if you win, you get to move in and live among your "loser neighbors."

In most states it may take a unanimous action of the property owners, in the form of a recorded amendment to the CC&Rs, to change them. In principle this hurdle may not be insurmountable if you're looking at a small rural subdivision (say, eight to ten lots) that has a homeowners committee that meets from time to time as needed. You could request a meeting and make a presentation. But the process will take time, and even one negative vote will sink your effort, plus, you may be asked to pay all attorneys fees. This being the case, other than making an earnest inquiry into the status of CC&Rs on a property within a subdivision, you're generally better off simply moving on to look at other locations.

Land-home packages

Some dealers, in an effort to eliminate the buyer's time-consuming hassle of looking for a home site, will contact the owners of suitable parcels of land and obtain agreements to be the owners' exclusive representative for a fixed period of time (usually a year) during which the dealer offers the home sites at an agreed upon price as part of a land-home package.

At the close of the deal, the purchase of the home and the land are separate transactions. With this arrangement the dealer benefits through increased sales (and often a rebate from the landowner), while the landowner profits from a locked-in sale price on which he or she does not have to pay a sales commission (usually ten percent) that would be required had the property been listed through a real estate agent.

One dealer interviewed for this guide described how he would find a property for sale for, say, $10,000, and ask if the owner would be willing to give him the right of first refusal to sell the property for $11,000, for a period of six months to a year. He often found willing

takers. Said the dealer, "I was able to line up a lot of property that way, at a cost of a dollar apiece, and put together quite a few sales at the higher price, so everyone was happy."

Land-home packages can be good for all parties involved, and can be creative, legitimate strategies. But be wary. Dishonest dealers may offer what appear to be attractive packages that are really rip-offs.

Examples: the sites themselves may be priced much higher than their true market value; the site is in a subdivision in a remote or unattractive location with undisclosed negatives such as periodic industrial odors or a near-by, busy railroad crossing; the subdivision itself is unfinished (e.g., no surfaced road or street lighting) with no written guarantee when or if the work will be completed; the accompanying site work and installation charges are tied to the land-home package, are nonnegotiable, and contain hidden overcharges. See the discussion on manufactured home subdivisions at the end of this chapter.

Even landowners can be victimized. One dealer in a western state shopped for a number of suitable home sites in his area, each for sale at around $30,000. He made offers on all of them, putting down $100 earnest money on each, but included in the offers was some vaguely worded contingency language and "subject to's" that gave him six months before each deal closed, in Realtor parlance, "tying up the property." **Note**: the terms Realtor, broker and real estate agent are often used interchangeably in conversation, but there are distinct differences—see sidebar.

The dealer, unbeknownst to the landowners, then proceeded to promote the properties in land-home packages. When he failed to sell the packages before the end of the contingency period, he turned to the fine print to weasel out of the deals. The landowners, who had in effect optioned their properties for six months for $100 each, were outraged.

Dishonest? Some would say no, arguing that the dealer was using his noggin and that the sellers had a responsibility to read and understand the fine print, and that "flipping" properties is a ubiquitous practice. In real estate slang, a flipper is someone who buys a piece of real estate and immediately turns around and sells it for a profit (a perfectly honorable business practice).

Others would disagree, saying this was not an instance of flipping because the dealer never intended to take title and possession of the property, only assign the purchase contracts to incoming buyers, if they materialized. They would argue the buyer has an ethical obligation to tell the seller his intentions and that the dealer's failure to do so amounted to defrauding the seller.

Ethical debates aside, guess who can get caught in the middle? What you need to know is that these loosey-goosey contingency deals are out there and you, the prospective buyer, may have no clue that you're walking into one of them. It may turn out that everything will work out fine, but then, too, there may be problems with the property that the dealer has not discovered or disclosed. So, once again, it's buyer beware.

Rule: Give any land-home package the same critical scrutiny you would a land-only offering, including your own research of county records, and insist on full disclosure on the land ownership and a clear intelligible line-item breakdown of all costs. Don't hesitate to negotiate the cost of any items you believe are out of line.

Working with a real estate agent

Simply put, if you're looking to buy land get a good real estate agent and stick with him or her. Doing so won't cost you a dime (the seller pays the commission) and can save you an enormous amount of grief. Even if you have found a reputable dealer who is offering an attractive land-home package, don't make a decision without checking out the current inventory of available home sites from a local Realtor.

For one, you may find something much better for the same price, and for another, you'll get a good feel for local land values that may enable you to negotiate a lower price on the land part of a land-home package.

Some dealers may recommend a real estate agent with whom they have dealt. Fine, but interview one or two others before you choose. Understand that not all agents will be thrilled to help you look for vacant land. Here's why:

- The commissions are smaller than those on home sales. For example, a lot that sells for $30,000 with a 10% sales commission yields a fee of $3,000. In most states half of that fee, or $1,500, goes to the broker representing the seller and half to the broker representing the buyer. Typically each broker in turn splits the commission with his or her agent, each earning $750. In contrast, a home on that same lot selling for $130,000 with a 6% commission, will generate a $7,800 commission, yielding $3,900 each for the two brokers, and thus $1,950 for each broker's agent—more than two-and-a-half times greater for roughly the same amount of work. For this reason, the agents you interview may try to convince you to buy a site built home. Resist their temptations, stay the course.

  An agreement to have your Realtor represent you on a "fizbo" land purchase can be a prudent strategy to ensure your interests are fully protected.

- The agent often has to work harder. The sale of vacant land exposes a Realtor to a greater risk of lawsuits than a home because, unlike a home, the seller of undeveloped land is not legally required to disclose much of anything about the land. It's up to the buyer to conduct tests, evaluate hazards and otherwise sniff around, and the buyer's real estate agent must exercise a greater standard of care in helping assess the property for site feasibility, including the absence of hazards (such as being on an old landfill containing asbestos) or the presence of negatives such as being near a gun range or a busy road or being subject to periodic strong winds. This due diligence process also generally takes longer than a home sale, delaying the close of escrow and the payment of the agent's commission.
- Buyers not infrequently decide to buy unlisted property For-Sale-by-Owner (called a "fizbo" in Realtor slang), leaving the agent with whom they have been working completely out of the deal.

Here's a good way to remedy the above concerns: Offer to sign an agreement with your broker to have him or her exclusively represent you in your property search for a specified period, plus, in the event that you buy land that is unlisted, you agree to pay a buyer's commission of, say, five percent of the purchase price. This exclusive buyer agency agreement will: assure your broker that you will not suddenly ditch him or her for someone else at another brokerage (which can happen when nothing is in writing); it locks in your agent's commission and thus provides an incentive for your agent to work harder in your behalf, and; you will be able to drive around looking for For-Sale-by-Owner signs—which you should do—knowing your agent will be there to protect your interests. You should also check the local newspaper classifieds for unlisted properties under land/acreage for sale headings. And because of your agreement, your agent will be happy to discuss with you any promising ads you come across.

Tip: Don't overlook vacant lots that are not on the market. Some very good properties can suddenly become available if the price is right.

Another tip: Consider running a classified ad in the local paper under Manufactured Homes that reads to the effect "Private party looking for property to buy on which to place a manufactured home."

Don't worry about paying a 5% commission. You will almost certainly cover that cost by offering at least 5% less than the landowner's asking price, and it's well worth that expense to have a pro working with you on your behalf. Keep in mind that the only party benefiting from a For-Sale-by-Owner transaction is the seller, who avoids paying that 10% sales commission. In fact, you as buyer could find yourself at a distinct disadvantage if you don't have a real estate agent representing your interest. Consider that a good agent:

- knows the local history and gossip about properties for sale, whether a particular owner may be difficult; and why, for example, a sale fell through with a previous buyer
- acts as a third party between the buyer and seller to facilitate negotiations
- knows who are the good contractors, septic engineers, well drillers, and soils testers to conduct feasibility studies at reasonable cost
- knows questions to ask that may not otherwise occur to you
- knows, or can find out with a few phone calls, the drawbacks of certain properties that may otherwise go unnoticed, or were not disclosed (for example, bad mosquito problem in summer, wet and boggy in winter)
- can ride herd on the paperwork and requirements as a deal moves toward the close of escrow

Last, a final note on "No mobiles:" When you first sit down with a real estate agent to look over land for sale, typically, he or she will have desktop computer access to the Multiple Listings Service (MLS) for the area. MLS features a data base that allows its members to search for properties currently for sale through realtors that match the specifications you provide.

For example, you may ask for a list of properties one acre in size or smaller, selling for $30,000 or less. Your agent will very likely instruct the MLS database to exclude from the list all properties with a "no mobiles" deed restriction. This is OK at the outset of your search because with any luck, you'll find your dream site on the list provided. But if, after

Real Estate 101

In a real estate transaction there are always at least two people involved: the Seller and the Buyer. If the Seller and the Buyer are each working through a real estate office, there can be a Broker representing the Seller, and a real estate salesperson, called an Agent or sales associate, who works for the Seller's Broker. Similarly, there can be a Broker representing the Buyer, and a real estate Agent representing the Buyer's Broker. Under this scenario, six people are now involved.

There can be only one designated Broker in each real estate office. Everyone else, even if they have broker's licenses, works as an Agent for the designated Broker. Officially, the Broker has the license and the Agents are licensees. This hierarchy helps provide a chain of legal accountability.

The designated Broker for the Seller is the person who, personally or through his or her Agent, contracts with the Seller for a commission that the seller agrees to pay at the close of sale.

The Seller's Broker, either through the Multiple Listings Service (MLS), or directly in the case of an exclusive listing, makes an offer to other Brokers and their sales Agents to share in the commission if any of them can bring a Buyer to the Seller and the ensuing purchase transaction is successfully completed.

Thus, there can be three separate agreements operating in one transaction:
1. A purchase agreement between Buyer and Seller.
2. An agreement to pay a commission between the Seller and the Broker.
3. An agreement between Brokers to share that commission.

These agreements are negotiable but all hell can break loose when people who are not a party to a particular agreement involve themselves in the negotiation. Example: a Buyer's Agent who tries to negotiate the amount of the commission the Seller will pay the Seller's Broker. War stories abound.

Last, a pop quiz trick question: What is a Realtor?
Answer: a member of the National Association of Realtors, who have registered "Realtor" as a service mark (similar to a trademark) which thereby prevents any competitors from using the word.

you've looked at everything on the list without finding something that really excites you, don't hesitate to ask your agent to pull up a list that includes properties with that deed restriction. It never hurts to look, and you might find the perfect site with an owner willing to accommodate a motivated buyer (which, of course, you are).

Purchasing raw land in a rural or semi-rural area

The three most common types of land purchases for manufactured homes are: property in a rural or semi-rural area, a lot in a manufactured home subdivision, and a lot in a manufactured home planned unit development. Let's take them in that order. The first type is the most involved because you start with unimproved raw land, however, many of the steps here also apply to the purchase of any land.

Let's assume that you have been pre-approved by your bank for a home construction loan and you have budgeted about $25,000 for the land on which to place your manufactured home. Let's also assume you will be looking at property in a semi-rural neighborhood that will require you to put in a septic system, a well, and all the utility connections. That's a lot to do, but not uncommon. People in rural settings tend to be prepared and willing to tackle the challenge. For all practical purposes you are now a land developer. Welcome to the big time.

Don't be misled by overgrown, rugged-looking parcels like this one. With a bit of imagination and TLC, many can be developed into really beautiful home sites.

Because yours is a construction loan (as opposed to a loan to purchase an existing home) your lending bank will disburse the money in chunks as various milestones are reached regarding the land, the home and the home site preparation.

Your first task: buy a three-hole paper punch, a three-ring binder big enough to hold a three-inch thick stack of papers, and a dozen separator pages with clear plastic tabs to identify subjects such as: contact numbers, property, permits, septic, bids/estimates, well, offers, house, invoices paid, County, etc. This binder serves two purposes: to keep you and your papers organized and to act as a quick-reference tool since you will be carrying it almost everywhere with you in the weeks ahead.

Let's assume, too, that you have an agent who has given you a list of properties for sale that fit your requirements. Most likely you will conduct your initial reconnaissance on your own, aided by a map showing the properties' locations. Now things start to get adventurous.

Look—and enjoy looking. Don't expect to be swept off your feet or to find your dream site on your first outing. You may spend days doing this over a period of weeks.

Don't be discouraged. Trust your first impressions and your intuition. Let each property speak to you; allow your imagination to flow. Think like a creative developer, an architect and imagine where your home could be placed and the direction it would face. Imagine the change of seasons, the views, the wind and weather, the shift of sunlight. Think about your personal preferences, how it would feel to live here.

Take your time. If a property doesn't feel right when you first set foot on it, don't fight that first impression; move on to the next offering. You can always return.

Questions to ask before making a commitment

At some point you will find a property that at first blush feels right to you and seems to match your requirements. At this point, the dreamer in you must step aside while you seek answers to important questions.

What follows is a list of general questions (together with comments) that should be answered to your satisfaction before you commit to buying the property. As for questions that need further investigation, you can still proceed to make an offer on the property but stipulate that the purchase is subject to satisfactory resolution of the questions. Not all these queries may apply to the land you're considering, and you will likely have questions of your own, but together they constitute the first test of the property's suitability:

Is there any restriction on the placement of a manufactured home on this land?

We've already touched on this. See more under Covenants, Conditions and Restrictions (CC&Rs).

Is it physically possible to transport a manufactured home to the property and to place it in the location desired?

This marks a distinct difference between you and a site-built home buyer. Make sure the approach road and entry lane are wide enough (and the grade is not too steep) for a delivery vehicle, and that there are no sharp turns, ravines, gullies or peaks in the road that could hang up the truck or the load. Trees or branches may need to be cut or removed.

If any of these obstacles are found and can't be corrected, make sure that a temporary access way can be created. Don't overlook the route from the main road to the property. If, for example, there is a bridge or trestle or overpass two miles back on the road leading to the property, make sure they provide enough height and width clearance.

The actual site/foundation must be accessible to the home placement. Wet weather and/or snow may make delivery impossible or add hundreds of dollars to the cost of home placement if planks and a bulldozer or other towing machinery are needed. If in doubt, consult a reputable dealer or a knowledgeable transport driver.

Is there well water on the site? If no well, what are the odds water will be found?

The availability of water is crucial. Chances are if a well is already there, the property owner had it put in and tested to improve the sale potential. The drilling cost (typically several thousand dollars) will likely be included in the price of the land. If no well is there, contact the well-drillers who put in wells on adjacent or nearby land and ask them what the odds are that water will be found here and at what average depth, and/or talk to the neighbors who hired them.

Drillers charge by depth drilled, averaging $23 to $26 per foot. Average depths at which water is found vary, but 100 feet is fairly common.

If well-drillers say the likelihood of finding water is high, your offer to buy can stipulate that the purchase is subject to putting in a well and obtaining the required permit. But now the question you will face is "Can I afford to spend thousands of dollars in a failed attempt to find water?"

Tip: Unless the likelihood of finding potable water is a near certainty, don't gamble. At the very least, negotiate an adjusted purchase price contingent upon the owner drilling the well at his or her expense. You will also want to know the well's flow rate. If it produces water at anything under a gallon per minute, you should consider installing a 1,000 gallon holding tank and pumps to accommodate normal household needs. This system will also add to your costs.

Has the water been tested and certified OK for drinking? Does the water have no, or acceptably low levels of non-health-related contaminants?

Well water destined for human use must be analyzed for bacteriological contamination (such as fecal coliform bacteria) and inorganic chemicals like nitrates (used in fertilizer), then certified safe (i.e., potable) by a local government agency before use of the well is permitted. But certified well water may also contain elements that, while not harmful to health, can be annoying. Examples: iron (causes rusty water, leaves orange residue), calcium (turns water hard, leaves a white residue) and hydrogen sulfide (a gas that produces a sulfurous, rotten egg smell). If any of these are present in high amounts, you may want to install a filtration system to treat your house water—also adding to the cost.

What is the fire danger? Can a turnaround area be created that is large enough to easily accommodate a fire truck? Will a water tank for fire protection be needed?

With more and more homes being built in rural areas in or adjacent to areas vulnerable to wild land fires, assess the danger in your area. Increasingly, local governments are requiring homeowners to ensure adequate access and water for fire fighting as a condition of the building permit. This can be expensive. Be sure to check if any such requirements exist.

Can a conventional gravity-fed septic system that complies with local codes be put in?

In most rural areas you can put in a traditional septic system, which includes a 3,000-square-foot drainage field for around $4,000 (again, check the costs in your area), including a design fee, provided the soil in the drain field will absorb (or percolate) the septic tank's effluent at an acceptable rate. These remarkable systems, which also handle the home's gray water (i.e., bath, shower and kitchen water) are simple, efficient, and last practically forever with proper maintenance. But the soil in the drain field must pass a percolation test, and the system has to be at least slightly down slope from the home which can limit where your home can be placed. If not, you could be looking at installing an alternative sewage treatment system such as a sand-filtered mound system operated by pumps and timers and costing thousands more in design and engineering fees, enough to kill your budget.

If the landowner has not had soil percolation tests done by a certified engineer, you should make the land purchase contingent upon a successful "perc test," preferably paid by the landowner. You will also want to determine that the septic system can be installed in relation to where you intend placing the house so that there is enough of a downslope to allow for a gravity flow into the septic tank.

How, when and at what cost will the power, phone and cable connections be made?

The answer could be as simple as, "The utility pole is right next to the northeast corner of the lot and everything can be connected within five business days for a few hundred dollars." Or the lot may be 75 yards or more to the nearest pole and require you to pay the cost of trenching and laying wire, phone lines and cable, plus a step-down transformer and other materials at considerably greater cost. In any event, you should check with each service provider (e.g., electric, telephone, cable TV) to get a cost estimate. **Note**: You may discover that 60 amps of electric power is available to the property, but this won't be enough for today's home (manufactured or site-built). You'll need to upgrade to 200 amps, which will add to your cost.

Are there any covenants, conditions and restrictions relating to this property? And, if so, are they acceptable?

Here we have the CC&Rs term that you'll hear often. These are legally binding conditions, also called deed restrictions, that accompany the recorded title or deed to the land. The Realtor representing the seller will have a copy for review. It is here that you will encounter the "no mobile homes" restriction. As discussed above, chances are if that phrase is used, it refers to the old 10-wide tin shack eye-sores, and you will have a good chance of getting it waived. On the other hand, if the language of the restriction spells out "no manufactured homes" or "only site-built homes allowed," you're out of luck.

In the not-too-distant past, until ruled unconstitutional, CC&Rs were often used to restrict the sale of homes and land to whites only, or to specify the owner must be a member

---

The CC&Rs from Hell

At first glance this rural subdivision seemed ideal: 26 one-acre lots with mountain views, plenty of water and nestled in farm country. Site-built or manufactured homes OK. It was only when one took a close look at the Declaration of Covenants and Restrictions that doubts arose. Among the covenants:

All homes to have an attached carport that must "mate" with the home....No metal awnings permitted, only those made of wood...No exterior antennas of any kind....No roof or window-mounted air conditioners or coolers....All trees and shrubs to be trimmed at all times....Nothing may be placed or stored outside the home if it can be seen by a neighbor (this includes toys, brooms, appliances, or anything that is unsightly in appearance)....Nothing, including laundry towels or wearing apparel, is to be hung outside at any time....All signs are prohibited except 'For Sale' signs and election signs 90 days before election....No trailer, boat, camper or boat trailer allowed on any driveway visible from the street....Dogs outside must be on a leash at all times...All animal waste must be picked up immediately....Ownership of no more than two dogs and two cats is permitted...No chickens, pigeons, monkeys, snakes, reptiles or other unusual animal are allowed.

In the three years the lots have been for sale, only three have sold.

---

in good standing of a congregation of the Christian faith. Happily, CC&Rs are illegal as instruments of bigotry. Still, they can serve as a kind of micro-zoning code. For example, the CC&Rs relating to the property you are evaluating may say that the owners of the adjacent property (and their guests) have permission to use the footpath that crosses the southeast corner of the property; or, No structure more than 19 feet in height may be constructed; or, No commercial business may be conducted on this property that involves customer visitation; or The owner of this property hereby holds harmless all applicable county and state agencies for any damages as a result of flooding or other hydrological events.

CC&Rs, in fact, are regularly used to preserve the tranquility and ambiance of a small neighborhood, and most are benign and well-intentioned. For this reason, pet restrictions are common, often regulating the number, type and size of animals that can be kept. You should review them with care, make sure you understand them and can live with them. Otherwise, you may find yourself trying to explain to your distraught spouse and children that you have to get rid of the family dog because he's three pounds over the weight limit described in the CC&Rs of the property you just acquired. Sometimes, too, CC&Rs can be downright quirky if not weird.

Your purchase offer—and more questions to ask

If the property successfully passes your first scrutiny, your next step is to write a formal offer with your real estate agent, including a check for several hundred dollars earnest money (essentially a deposit that is held by the broker or used to open an escrow account) and submit the offer to the property owner through his or her agent (or directly to the owner if the property is being sold By Owner). The offer will also state that the buyer will have time (typically 30 days) to obtain a report on the feasibility of purchasing the property.

Here is where you include such conditions as "subject to availability of potable water at an adequate rate of flow," "contingent upon satisfactory soils tests," and "subject to zoning studies and the procedure and length of time necessary to obtain approval for building permits." You may cancel your purchase offer during this period if any test results or other discoveries fail to meet your requirements, or the minimum standards to qualify for permits. Make sure the offer calls for a prompt full refund of your deposit in the event of cancellation.

Usually an offer gives the seller 72 hours to respond. Typically, a potential buyer offers less than the asking price, and so there will be some back and forth negotiations in the form of counter-offers until a mutually acceptable price is determined. Your agent will know, or should know, the following, but just to be sure: Do not make or accept verbal offers or counter-offers. Rather, make sure all of them are in writing. Contracts for the sale of real property that are not in writing are not recognized by the courts and are thus unenforceable.

Once you and the seller have agreed to the purchase terms, the "feasibility / contingency" period begins (30-day in this example), during which time the property is placed in escrow, usually with an agreed-upon local title insurance company that will oversee the completion (or "perfection") of the terms of the purchase agreement.

At this point your lending bank will have the property appraised to verify that the purchase price is in line with comparable properties in the neighborhood. Should the appraiser determine the property is overpriced, the bank could refuse to fund the purchase, or it could reduce the loan amount, obliging you to put more of your own money into the purchase. This way the bank doesn't exceed the percentage of the land's value it is willing to lend, called the LTV (loan-to-value) ratio.

During this escrow period you can, and should, take a proactive role in seeking answers to a second round of questions. A day or two of leg work can accomplish a great deal. Basically, what you will be looking for are any negatives that exist, or may arise in the future, that will prevent you from putting your new home on the property and otherwise enjoying the promise of living there. In most cases, your queries can be answered by visiting the county seat and talking to clerks in various departments and agencies.

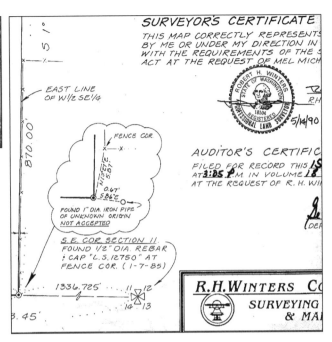

Verifying boundry markers is an important part of due diligence, but locating them can be akin to a treasure hunt if the property is overgrown. Metal detectors may be needed. Look for wood or metal stakes tied with lengths of bright plastic ribbon (above left). Remove 2-4 inches of dirt around the base to uncover the end of a 1/2 inch diameter length of pipe or rebar that has been hammered into the ground. It is often tipped with a plastic cap showing the surveyor's name and license number (above right). At right: detail of a surveyor's map.

Tip: When dealing with government officials, especially clerks and counter staff, be polite, patient, calm, good-humored and appreciative. These people are often overworked and stressed out by demanding, ill-tempered and unmannered citizens. Show them respect and cordiality and you will be amazed how smoothly things go and how easily obstacles are overcome.

Another tip: One dealer with experience helping develop scattered rural sites explains that he asks the local government agencies: What must I do to fully satisfy your requirements? "This way," he explained, "I make sure I'm not missing anything, and when I complete the checklist they provided, they're on the hook to give me the OK."

What follows are typical questions to ask, and the likely agency or official who can answer them. Again, some questions may not apply to your situation, and you will doubtless have questions of your own.

Are there any major plans, land use changes, disputes, natural threats or attempted developments in the area that could have an adverse impact? Any hazards, unpredictable weather, nuisances, or seasonal annoyances?

Start by talking with the neighbors. They will know a great deal. Examples: the area has a growing problem with fire ants; the deer population is very high and they make growing flowers and vegetables nearly impossible; the local motorcycle club has petitioned the county to put in a dirt track down the road; people are worried the water table is falling and many wells will go dry.

Next, visit the County Planning Department and ask if there are any long range plans that provide for roads or highways in the areas, zoning and land-use changes, expansion of city limits, a landfill, quarry or other potential major disruption.

Will my developing the property trigger a county demand that I pay for road improvements such as paving and drainage?

Public Works will have the answer. You want to make sure that you don't suddenly become responsible for putting in two miles of black top on a country road merely because you're the first to put a house on a lot at the end of that road. These things can happen.

Can the property's survey corner markers be easily found? What are the survey details?

The Country Assessor's office commonly maintains the survey maps for all properties, plus the records of titles, deeds, liens, judgements and related official actions. For a few dollars they will provide a full-size copy of the most recent survey map of your property. This map provides precise data on the corner markers of the property as well as related information such as easements, legal access points and exact distances.

Using the survey map, walk the property lines and locate the corner markers. You want to locate the actual surveyor's marker, usually a piece of iron rebar driven into the ground and topped with a plastic cap marked with the surveyor's license number. Don't be shy about insisting on eye-balling these markers; this is the one time when you need to be a stickler for such details.

Accessing County records online

More and more of the data concerning property and parcels (including all kinds of useful maps from various jurisdictions) are finding their way online as counties across the nation increasingly are making public records available on their Web sites. This is the wave of the future. Call your County Assessor's office (or Clerk's Office) for more information.

Is the property in a zone of regulated wetlands, streams, geologic hazards and/or the habitat of any endangered species of wildlife?

This is four questions in one, and they're all important. Maps available at the County Planning Department can usually answer all of them. Some counties also have the maps on computers and can print out those portions applicable to the property you're studying. They have, for example, maps showing flood zones and flood plains determined by the Federal Emergency Management Agency (FEMA). Other maps will show zones created by state and local governments demarcating wetlands, sensitive shoreline, wildlife habitat and locations where the presence of members of endangered species have been documented.

These special zones typically have adjacent buffer zones in which no development or improvements may be undertaken. You will want to make sure you have adequate room on the property to accommodate your home, septic system and other improvements.

Tip: If the property is in any kind of hazardous zone, check on the cost of homeowner's insurance. For example, insurance premiums on homes in Galveston, Texas, because of vulnerability to hurricanes, are one-and-a-half to two times more expensive than premiums in safer locales.

How long will it take to get the required building permit, and how much will it cost?

The Building Department will have those answers, and probably lots of handouts on every aspect of land improvements, building codes, inspections and required documentation. This department will likely be your primary (and frequent) contact point in the weeks ahead as your property is prepared for your house. **Tip**: Try to cultivate a working relationship with one staff person in that office whom you can ask for by name when you call with questions or information.

What will the taxes be?

The County Assessor's office will be able to give you a pretty good estimate after you provide them with details on your home and any additional improvements (such as a garage). Once you're moved in, someone from that office will eventually come by for a visual inspection (some do it by mail questionnaire), after which you will be able to call and learn the exact amount of your yearly property tax.

Closing escrow

If all goes well and your inquiries and inspections are satisfactorily completed, all parties will be ready to complete the settlement (i.e., close escrow), in this case on the 30th day following the acceptance of your purchase offer. Most likely you will meet at the title company with an escrow officer who will have a stack of documents for you to sign. Typically, the escrow officer will meet separately with the seller for a separate signing session. This will be a happy occasion for you, but don't let the excitement put you in a rush. Take the time to understand everything before you sign. This is the time to ask questions, not after the deal is done.

Hint: For all their thoroughness in approving home loans, banks tend to be lazy when it comes to explaining the meaning of line-item charges that appear on the settlement sheet. The task often falls to the escrow officer at the time of signing, and quite often he or she may not know the bank's precise reasoning. You will be given a copy of the escrow instructions days prior to your meeting at the title company, and that's a good time to study them and to call your lender if you have questions.

Purchasing land in a manufactured home subdivision

This type of subdivision is relatively new, and in practice, you will most likely buy a lot and simultaneously a house to go on it. But there are some important caveats. First, a little background:

Subdivisions

For generations the very image of suburban life in America has been characterized by the subdivision, or more accurately, the standard subdivision. These are properties that have been subdivided into lots on which are built single-family homes that are physically and legally tied to the land as real property and sold as such (so-called fee simple homes). Traditionally, these homes are owner-occupied. Standard subdivisions may have CC&Rs but they're often few and general in nature. The streets of these developments are dedicated to public ownership and maintained by the local municipality or county. In short, everyone is pretty much left alone.

Planned unit developments

Running a close second in traditional residential developments are Planned Unit Developments (PUDs). Like standard subdivisions, PUDs are subdivided into lots for single-family, owner-occupied, fee simple homes, but in addition, they almost always have some common interest facilities like a clubhouse or community center, green ways, a commons, private streets and recreation areas. The homeowners own these common interest facilities in so-called undivided interests with oversight and maintenance handled by the development's Homeowners Association (HOA). The HOA collects money for the facilities' upkeep and replacement as needed, and enforces the community rules and regulations (which can be quite detailed) that are a part of the development's CC&Rs. Frequently HOAs have the power to approve the size, appearance, color and general configuration of

Flyer for a lot in a manufactured home subdivision

any proposed new home. In short, you're pretty much left alone as long as you follow the rules—but you are being watched.

For anyone wishing to put a manufactured home into either of these types of developments, no matter how elegant that home may appear sitting next to its site-built brethren, the task is formidable. The old mobile home prejudice is still there. With a small, older standard subdivision, it wouldn't hurt to make a few inquiries. But with planned unit developments, generally your chances are slim to none. In sum, you can be almost assured that unless a PUD has been developed specifically for manufactured homes, getting past some of these local HOAs can truly be a nightmare.

Manufactured home subdivisions

Given this dilemma, it didn't take developers long to come up with the idea of a subdivision specifically for manufactured homes that would be tied to their land as real property. On paper the concept is a good one, but the history of such subdivisions has been decidedly checkered, but in recent years the situation is much improved.

Manufactured home subdivisions, many touted as exciting opportunities for affordable housing, began springing up around the country in the mid-80s, often on marginal land that could be purchased cheaply and where the development standards were minimal. It was not uncommon to find such subdivisions with no paved streets, or street lights, curbs, gutters or sidewalks and hardly any control of storm water runoff. Adding to these shortcomings was the absence of any CC&Rs spelling out the size of the homes, siting requirements (for example, minimum set backs with the home placed parallel to the street), installation standards, property maintenance and bans on attractive nuisances).

Compounding these negatives was a financing arrangement called an Installment Sales Contract (or Land Contract) that developers offered to buyers who couldn't qualify for a conventional home loan. With this financing instrument the title to the property remains with the seller (i.e., the developer) until the contract is fully paid. This contrasts with a conventional home loan in which the title to the property is legally vested in the buyer who can lose it only after failure to make the monthly mortgage payments and a subsequent foreclosure process.

Manufactured home subdivisions like this one are almost indistinguishable from site-built home subdivisions, especially if the developer requires all homes to have attached garages. Because these homes were sold as part of land-home deals involving conventional home loans, the homeowners can look forward to their homes appreciating in value the same as site-built homes.

Not surprisingly, these land contracts carried high interest rates similar to subprime chattel loans. In more than a few instances developers were drawn to manufactured home subdivisions because they calculated they could make more money from the high profit Land Contracts than from the business of acquiring, subdividing and selling land. Does that sound familiar?

The combination of slipshod development, minimal home restrictions and land contracts aimed at the subprime borrower was a recipe for disaster. In a few short years the appearance of many manufactured home subdivisions was deplorable: unlighted gravel streets, homes placed at odd angles on the lots with no landscaping, muddy surface flooding during rainfall, mounds of dirt and construction debris and weeds everywhere. Not surprisingly, the value of the homes in these blighted developments plummeted, robbing the homeowners of what little equity they had built.

Planned unit subdivisions for manufactured homes

The good news is that there are developers out there who understand the necessity of good sound development practices. These include special consideration of a project's over all design and adequate, enforceable CC&Rs to preserve the subdivision's character and property values. Moreover, these developments don't have to be magazine cover gorgeous to succeed. When these standards are applied to subdivisions for manufactured homes, and to planned unit subdivisions for manufactured homes, they are usually very successful.

You can expect to see more of these attractive developments popping up in regions where the labor costs for building site-built homes are high, thus allowing developers offering manufactured homes a competitive advantage. This is especially true with higher end home developments. Some developers are forging exclusive partnerships with manufactured home builders (Oregon-based Fuqua Homes is one) under which the developer builds a residential subdivision with all the infrastructure (i.e., streets, utilities, lights and landscaping) and then sells several models of manufactured homes exclusively from that manufacturer as part of home-lot purchases financed by conventional home loans.

The bottom line: manufactured home subdivisions in which the home and land are purchased as a single entity can be a good deal, especially because it qualifies for a conventional home loan, but be cautious. Recommendations:

- *Look the project over very carefully.* In general, don't be among the first to buy there, but if you're a pioneering type, there can be advantages to being among the first: the price is usually lower to attract buyers; you get your pick of the best sites and you will have a larger say in the formation of the homeowners' association. If the subdivision is partially filled, talk to a few neighbors; ask them what their experience has been.

- *Read all the CC&Rs carefully. If there are none, run.* The rules and regulations should be strong enough to give you confidence that the developer is committed to creating and preserving a quality home subdivision. Make sure the CC&Rs have been recorded with the county; if they are not, they are not legally enforceable. **Note**: While the free spirit in you may love the idea of buying land unencumbered with restrictions, the flip-side is without appropriate CC&Rs you have no control over your future neighbors.

Generally, you're best off getting a home mortgage from a bank or credit union where you will have access to many financing choices at market rates, but many reputable developers make arrangements with local banks to help home buyers secure conventional home loans at very good rates (in return for the developer's business, the banks offer lower interest rates). **Note**: Be extremely wary if a developer offers to finance your purchase with a Land Contract. As noted above, these are costly high-interest retail installment contracts. Avoid them.

The waltz begins

By the time you have completed your land purchase, depending upon its location, you will very likely be carrying on conversations with other players in addition to your banker. These can include: your dealer, who will be anticipating your lending bank's OK to order your new home; a couple of general contractors you have asked to bid on the site work for your home; a building contractor to build a garage and/or decks and steps for your home; a septic system design engineer; a well pump or plumbing contractor; and the phone, cable and utility companies.

You will find yourself waltzing with some or all of these folks at the same time as your focus shifts from nailing down a home site to finalizing your selection of your home and preparing the site for the home's installation. Your three ring binder will start to fill up and you will be spending more time on the phone. But you will have accomplished, and in the right order, three of the four steps to home ownership—and you will be well on your way to owning your dream home.

Chapter 6

Leasing a Home Site in a Manufactured Home Community

A few years ago the Foremost Insurance Company, which specializes in coverage of mobile and manufactured homes, commissioned a national survey of those who live in them. The results were intriguing. About 36% of the respondents said they live full time in a mobile home community (or more appropriately, manufactured home community), and are quite happy about it. That works out to over 7 million residents. About half of them live in communities that have between 66 and 324 spaces; the average monthly rent is $220. Among other lifestyle details, the survey also found that 49% own a dog; 41% own a cat; and the most popular magazine (with 39% subscribing) was *Readers Digest*.

Clearly a great many people, including a good percentage who can afford a site-built home, have chosen to live in these types of dwellings. In fact, the manufactured home industry was built on producing homes designed primarily to go into rental communities.

There are literally tens of thousands of these land-lease communities in the US, many of them, perhaps most, consisting of older mobile homes built prior to 1980. They range in size from 20-space mom-and-pop operations to sprawling resort communities in Florida with 1,500 to 2,000 spaces and owned by public corporations listed on the New York Stock Exchange.

The range of offerings is also large: small, quiet communities—some neat and cheery, others seedy and drab—with aging mobile homes and community facilities consisting of no more than a bulletin board and a pay phone; larger bustling mobile home communities with a front office, convenience store and laundromat; manufactured home communities with several hundred spaces offering a social center, swimming pool and an active homeowners association; huge resort locations next to golf courses or boating water ways and requiring minimum double-wide or larger manufactured homes built since 1980 and offering many amenities and social activities; and communities characterized by short streets and cul-de-sacs packed with higher end homes with rock gardens sited very close to each other, and no clubhouse or owners association.

For its part the federal government, under the Federal Fair Housing Amendment of 1988, established three classifications of communities: 1. Unrestricted, in which all ages are allowed; 2. Senior communities where at least one person must be age 55 or older in 80% of the households; and 3. Senior communities where every person must be age 62 or older.

Many communities within the first category, Unrestricted, cater to families. The most recent offering within this classification is the manufactured home community that looks

Vintage mobile homes. If you can still see trailer hitches, it's OK to call them trailer parks. There are many thousands of these enclaves around the US. Many provide decent, albeit humble, housing and a real sense of neighborhood. Despite great changes in the appearance and demographics of today's land-lease communities (see opposite page), in the eyes of some the old trailer house stigma endures.

almost identical to a subdivision with curvilinear streets and sidewalks, but consisting of rental lots (sometimes smaller than those of standard subdivisions, but not always) for new manufactured homes replete with garages and front and backyards.

What all these rental communities share in common is their occupants are in the odd position of owning homes that for all practical purposes are immovable and which are sitting on someone else's property. As peculiar as this sounds in principle, the arrangement works for many people.

But the arrangement is also the principal source of the tensions, pitfalls, controversies and outright scams that one can encounter within this sector of the housing industry.

First, here's a quick look at the pros and cons:

Pros

- The move-in cost is less because you're buying just the home, not the land. The money you save can be invested, with earnings used to offset the monthly site rent.

- You only pay personal property tax on your home, not the land (a small percentage of your monthly rent goes toward the property tax the community's owner pays). **Note**: in some short-sighted states, the personal property tax is akin to an automobile license fee: paid to the state instead of the county and declining every year on a formula scale. This approach is vociferously defended by entrenched and short-sighted dealers and community owners, but it is extremely unpopular with local politicians and a big tool for local protesters against new communities when they—rightfully—claim the manufactured homes in these situations don't pay their fair share of the local taxes.

- If this is your primary residence and you are financing its purchase, the loan interest is tax-deductible, just as with a conventional home loan.

- Your rent includes services provided by community management and staff, including lawn, landscape, sidewalk and street maintenance, and even snow removal. Sometimes the quality of these services is much higher than would be the case if the city or county were providing them.

This Seattle-area manufactured home land-lease community was developed in 1980 and today has 209 sites, all taken, all permanent, with a waiting list of buyers. Appreciating home values, a fine homeowners association and beautifully maintained properties attest to the success (and great popularity) of well planned and developed land-lease communities.

- Your community provides amenities such as a swimming pool, club house and storage facilities for boats and RVs.
- The cost is often less than a comparable apartment or condominium, the surroundings are quieter, and you have your own yard and a parking space next to your home.
- Your home is in a peaceful safe community and you can be away months at a time knowing community management and your neighbors will keep an eye on your home.
- You are a member of a true neighborhood. You share many common interests with your neighbors and enjoy socializing and activities.
- The community rules and regulations foster and preserve the community's quality and neighborhood harmony.

Cons
- Unless you are protected by a rent control ordinance or a long-term lease, you are vulnerable to periodic increases in rent and/or maintenance fees over which you have no control and which could over time greatly increase your housing costs, perhaps beyond what you can afford.
- Unless you pay cash for your home you will most likely need to finance with a chattel mortgage at higher interest rates than a conventional home loan, costing you much more and slowing down the equity build-up in your home.
- Your home is far less likely than a conventional home to appreciate in value, and, in fact, may depreciate. Many states, for tax purposes, will continue to depreciate your home over time.
- If you are unable to pay your rent or get involved in a dispute with management, the community can attach a lien on your home, preventing you from selling it or moving it until legal fees and other restitution is made. You could end up losing your home.
- Selling your home may be difficult because a buyer looking for financing will likely discover few lenders willing to write chattel loans on a used manufactured home because of the home's perceived low value. Moreover, if the community

owner plans to hit the new tenant with higher rent, the buyer will likely insist a portion of the increase come out of the price you'd be able to otherwise get for your home.

- Should you wish to move your home to another community, your chances of finding a site may be slim to none. Very few communities these days accept anything other than new homes. And in many areas the vacancy rate is zero.
- Community rules and regulations are often lengthy and detailed, spelling out rules of conduct, home appearance, types of pets and permissible activities that you may find too restricting.
- The community's homeowners association may become too controlling, meddling and intrusive and/or afflicted by petty politics and in-fighting that divides the community.
- The community can be sold to buyers who tend to be much more aggressive in their rent increase policies. Worse case scenario: the new owners intend to convert the land to other uses, requiring you to move your home.

Is land-lease a smart housing option?

Historically, the great achievement of land-lease communities has been their tremendous popularity with retired seniors who have purchased homes in communities in and around resort communities in the Sun belt—Florida and Arizona are notable examples—and who enjoy a wide range of recreational and social activities with their fellow seniors. One need only to drive through one of these thriving communities to see immediately what a great life these communities offer, and how ideally suited they are for older couples with modest, fixed incomes.

Killing the goose that lays the golden egg

What happens when the owners of mobile home parks governed by a rent control ordinance tire of seeing their tenants sell their house trailers and mobile homes for tens of thousands of dollars more than they could get without rent control? For the owners of the 124-space Vista de Santa Barbara Mobile Home Park, in Carpenteria, California, they petitioned the court to increase the monthly park rents by $900 per space, nearly quadruple the current average rate of $250.

In May, 2002, an attorney for the park's owners argued in court that the 1980 vacancy control ordinance limiting rent increases to a few percentage point annually prevented the owners from making a fair and reasonable profit from their land. The attorney asserted this is a property right a federal court in Hawaii had sustained in a recent ruling in that state.

The two days of hearings were closely watched around the state, but no more closely than by the park's 170 tenants, average age 78, most of whom live on fixed incomes and who would be forced to leave if the park owners won.

The park's owners say that unless a large rent increase is granted, they may file suit in federal court. In the meantime, the goose rests very uneasily on her nest.

If, however, you are not among this vast affinity group of retired seniors, the question remains Is a land-lease community for you? And, Is it truly a smart, affordable option? To help answer these questions, a little background is in order:

As the 20th. Century ended the great American boom and buildout of mobile home communities peaked (in California, the peak was reached much earlier, in the 1970s). Land nearly everywhere was becoming too expensive to make the construction of a traditional rental community a profitable undertaking. On the horizon were land-lease manufactured home communities which look almost identical to single family subdivisions but are more expensive to develop. In the meantime, more than 2,000,000 older mobile homes in thousands of communities were reaching the end of their useful life and were falling apart.

Many of these decaying mobiles are in communities in wonderful locations, and in recent years, as they have came on the market (often following their occupant's death or transfer to a nursing home) buyers seeking to move to prime California and Florida seaside locales, for example, will pay as much as $100,000 for an old mobile, essentially buying the site. They then have the home towed away to the wrecking yard and replace it with a new $60,000 manufactured home, a so-called community replacement model designed especially to fit the traditional smaller size community sites. In short, for $160,000 the new occupants come out way ahead: they move into a new home on prime seaside real estate, something that would cost them many times that amount had they bought a site-built home. Such a transaction is possible when local rent control and vacancy control ordinances are in effect.

Many land-lease manufactured home communities such as this one have every appearance of a conventional subdivision of site-built homes. MHI photo

The above scenario represents a high-end answer to the affordability question, one that works only for cash buyers. One would think community owners everywhere should be thrilled to see more of these transactions, for they amount to a buyer-financed modernization of America's mobile home communities. From another perspective, however, community owners are upset when they see what amounts to vacant sites on their property selling for six figures while they're completely shut out of the deal. In many instances, rent control ordinances prevent the community owner from increasing the rent to reflect the increased value of the community's land. This is a property rights issue that is not going to go away soon (see sidebar, Killing the goose that lays the golden egg).

Doing the math on a home in a land-lease community

But here is a more common situation that comes up in areas of the country outside major metropolitan centers and prime real estate locales: a getting-started-in-life couple visits an attractive well-run 20-year old community that has opened up a half dozen new sites that will rent for, say, $375 a month. They check out the community regulations and the lease agreement and everything looks OK. This is the leased land community for which they have been looking. Would it make sense to buy a new manufactured home, financed by a chattel mortgage and move onto the site?

Here's the math: The average new manufactured home sells for $60,000 (including installation). A chattel mortgage loan (i.e., consumer loan) at 12%-14% interest would require a monthly payment of around $675. Adding $375 rent brings the monthly total to $1,050. That's a lot of money when they don't even own the land under their home. By comparison, if they qualified for a conventional home loan, they could buy a used site-built home in their area for monthly payments of $800. Their home would be basic but they would own the land and save $250 a month over the community option.

This comparison argues against moving into a community. And because many potential manufactured home buyers around the country are looking at the same kinds of numbers, many communities are having a difficult time filling their new sites. Until the costs can be made more competitive, the situation is not likely to improve any time soon.

Moreover, competing for the business of these would-be-first-time home buyers (in most cases this means anyone who has not purchased a home in the past three years) are many public and private programs, many specifically designed for minorities and/or economically disadvantaged buyers with low credit ratings. One such state-sponsored program provides for a 30-year conventional home loan at 6.7% interest with only 3% down payment. Interestingly, the low loan default rate of many of these programs validates the view that people are far less likely to walk away from a home that sits on land they own.

Conventional home loan rates for land-lease communities?

Another development is a new program recently established by the Federal Home Mortgage Corporation (Freddie Mac), the government chartered organization formed to provide money for home loans by buying mortgages from lenders. Historically, because manufactured homes in land-lease communities (i.e., mobile home parks) are sited on land rented from the landowners, their owners didn't qualify for conventional home loans. In a pioneering move, Freddie Mac started a program under which manufactured home owners in land-lease communities may qualify for conventional home loan rates if they meet certain requirements.

Among the qualifications:

- The home must be permanently anchored to the foundation.
- The term of the lease must be at least five years longer than the mortgage.
- The land must be converted to real property and taxed as such.
- The home must be titled as real estate, not personal property.

What is encouraging is that owners of land-lease communities approve of this concept and are willing to make the necessary title and land conversions to meet Freddie Mac's standards. As this edition goes to press, the program hasn't really gained traction. Still, a program such as this could greatly reduce mortgage costs and help many such communities attract new residents and new homes.

With its park-like setting, ponds, walkways and a spacious club house (center), this land-lease community is a splendid example of an upscale 55-plus community allowed under federal law (at least one occupant in 80% of the homes must be at least 55 years old). (MHI photo)

Tip: Before you consider a consumer/chattel loan, find out what home-ownership programs sponsored by government and the private sector institutions are available in your area. You could be pleasantly surprised.

When a land-lease deal can make sense

In the above example, the comparison was to the average price of an entry-level home in suburban or semi-rural areas. But the equation changes when the price of homes is much higher. In many regions of the country, particularly in metropolitan areas, the higher cost of homes puts them out of reach of most working families. For these families, and for many others who have good jobs and good credit a land-lease community offers them their one chance to own their own home and to live within the familiarity and security of a small neighborhood. Moreover, living in a community within a reasonable driving distance to one's place of work provides an additional benefit of lower commute time, lower gas bills and less stress.

A dealer in Olympia, Washington, whose family has been in the community business for decades, describes how one such accommodation came together:

"We had a divorced, single-mom and her 23-year old daughter who had been living together and sharing an apartment that was costing them about a thousand dollars a month. The home prices in our area were too high for them but they really wanted to own their own home and not be shelling out all that money each month for rent. We had just opened up a few new spaces in our community, and we were able to put together a chattel loan at 11.75 percent to finance a new three bedroom/two bath home for just under fifty thousand, plus another ten thousand to cover the sales tax, a car port, storage space and a bit of landscaping. Altogether, it came to just about sixty thousand. They put four thousand down, and the monthly payment, including the lot lease, came to nine hundred dollars. That worked out really well for everyone."

While this story had a happy outcome, mother and daughter are burdened with a mortgage interest rate more than four points higher than a conventional home loan that will eventually cost them tens of thousands of dollars more. One can only hope that someday they will be able to refinance their home at lower rates.

Two cardinal rules—and a cautionary tale

While most land-lease communities are stand-alone business with no connection to home manufacturers or dealers, it is not unusual for a larger land-lease community to have close ties with a local dealership, or even to own a dealership that has a sales center in a nearby town and lot models at the entrance to the community. Other communities may have an exclusive arrangement with a manufacturer, but no lot models or sales center. Instead, they offer packages to prospective new residents who order their home through the community, which in turn is responsible for the site preparation, installation and landscaping around the new home.

All of these arrangements in the hands of reputable parties can result in fair deals, but as a prospective community resident you should adhere strictly to two cardinal rules:

Rule #1: *Do not legally commit yourself to the purchase of your manufactured home until you have secured the rental space on which it will be sited.*

Rule #2: *Do not sign any rental agreement for that space until you have thoroughly read and understood the contract and all rules and regulations, with an attorney's help if needed, and can live with them, including worst-case scenario rent increases.*

Following these rules carefully is essential to defend oneself from abuses that can be particularly heartless. Here's what happened to more than 100 homeowners in the 1990s who moved into several California communities owned by a real estate partnership:

After scrimping for years to save enough money, a couple in the Silicon Valley area purchased a manufactured home for $44,000. After looking at several communities, they had the home delivered and installed in a community that seemed particularly pleasant and with an advertised rent that was affordable. Days before their new home was ready for occupancy, the couple visited the manager's office to sign a rental agreement that they anticipated would be a mere formality. Instead, they were handed a complicated five-year lease agreement with pages of impenetrable legalese that, as near as they could tell, allowed for rent increases at management's discretion.

They felt quite uneasy but were also anxious to move into their dream home. When they asked if they could take the documents home overnight to study them, the manager replied, No, the papers could not be removed from the premises. He assured them that the five-year lease was better than one that would have to be renewed yearly, and that no community resident's rent had ever been increased to the maximum allowed by the contract.

The couple were caught in a bind: To walk away from the lease they would have to move their home to another community at a cost of $10,000, money they did not have. Despite the red flags and their great unease, the couple signed the contract.

Later, the husband told a reporter that he figured if the rent got too high, they could sell their home or negotiate a new, more favorable lease at the end of five years. He was mistaken. Unbeknownst to the couple, the fine print in their lease agreement contained a clause that automatically extended the lease for 25 years. Nor were they aware that the initial five-year lease exempted the community's owners from San Jose's rent-control ordinance, which applied only to rental contracts of 12-months or less duration.

Within five years, in spite of the community manager's verbal assurances, the couple's rent doubled from $550 a month to $1,100. Adding this to their house payments, they were looking at a crushing $1,500 a month housing cost. The burden proved too much, and the couple were forced to abandon their dream home, leaving in it the equity they had accrued, and taking with them their wrecked credit. Other residents at this community and others owned by the company were experiencing the same nightmare.

But that wasn't all: In the aftermath, the bank that had made the loan to the couple continued to pay the space rent on the home while it attempted to sell it. But after several months and no takers, the bank quietly sold the home to the community for a fraction of its original cost. The community then turned around and sold the home well below market price and still made a handsome profit. And because the community usually had half a dozen such homes for sale, other banks trying to sell repossessed homes at market rates soon gave up and dumped them to the community for pennies on the dollar.

For the same reason, homeowners trying to flee the community by selling their homes found the task almost impossible. In short, the community's owners had created for themselves a very profitable no-loss situation.

The affected homeowners banded together and raised the money to challenge these egregious business abuses in court. They won, but all had paid a steep price.

Your greatest vulnerability: uncontrolled rent increases

In some respects the pressures facing many residents of California's 5,700 communities are greater than other regions in the nation because of skyrocketing land values, the housing crunch and the intense competition between business and political interests. For the record, away from the West Coast, rent control ordinances are quite rare and are seldom an issue nationally. Nonetheless, with few exceptions, the #1 concern of the would-be community resident anywhere has to be the vulnerability to rent increases that over time can doom the homeowner.

Historically, the most reliable, safest refuge from escalating rent has been to live in a well-run family-owned land-lease community whose owners are happy with the profits they made and who worked with their tenants for the common welfare of the community. These mom-and-pop enterprises still abound, but increasingly their owners are being approached by companies that own several other communities and who offer them a great deal of money to sell out.

This same phenomenon has previously happened with much larger communities and huge companies. During the 1990s, a half-dozen companies called real estate investment trusts, or REITs, collectively bought out hundreds of the largest, most established communities, notably in Florida and the Sun belt (the A-quality and B-quality communities). One of the largest, Chicago-based Manufactured Homes Communities, Inc., owns 160 communities valued at

---

What's wrong with this picture?

It was, and still is, a lovely land-lease community in Oregon, with a number of home sites still available adjacent to the beautiful Rogue River. In the early 1990s, a just-retired couple, George and Elaine, thought they had found the perfect setting. George asked all the right questions of the park's manager and several tenants, and heard all the right answers. Several weeks later they were ensconced in their new double-wide home.

Early the first morning they were there, George was up at first light to walk the couple's dog along the river bank. The setting was lovely but something was wrong: hardly had he arrived when his eyes began stinging and burning. The pain and irritation were so bad he had to turn back.

Later that morning, after several phone calls, George learned that around midnight every night, two upstream municipal sewage treatment plants released heavily chlorinated sewage effluent into the river. By dawn each day, the treated water reached the stretch of the river where George attempted to walk his dog.

"No one told me about it because no one seemed to know," George explained. "Seems none of the tenants were in the habit of walking the river bank that early, and by nine or ten the air had cleared. I hate to imagine what it was doing to the fish."

He added that had he known about the problem, they would not have moved there. For this reason the couple eventually sold their home and moved elsewhere. "We were careful to disclose the situation, but our buyer had no problem with it. But my advice to anyone is, before you commit to a lease, visit the place several times at all hours of the day—just to be sure."

---

well over $1 billion. Wall Street investors love them. MHC's expansion continues. Currently, the company is looking to purchase both senior and all-age communities with 150-plus home sites.

Having a major corporation like MHC buy a family-owned community is not necessarily a dark portent for the residents. Many community residents hardly notice any day-to-day change, but it does mean that the corporate bottom line and shareholder value are the new standards by which rent rates will be calculated and thus residents can anticipate regular up-ticks. In some cases following buyouts by REITs and others, hefty rent increases have followed as the new owners ratchet-up the rents, ostensibly to bring them in line with the current market.

In fairness, the owners of land-lease communities need to raise rents periodically to cover cost increases and to continue providing the amenities and improvements that attract the best possible residents, and to keep those like them who are already living there.

Significantly, many of these new corporate players in the land-lease industry, in the name of property rights, are aggressively attacking rent control ordinances previously enacted by well-intentioned municipalities across the country to prevent rent gouging by owners of land-lease communities within the city limits. In many instances cities struggling with limited budgets can't afford the cost of battling these well-funded court challenges and they throw in the towel. Expect this trend to continue.

Faced with these issues, resident associations and mobile home tenant groups around the country increasingly are urging homeowners associations to buy their communities from their current owners, effectively turning the rental communities into cooperatives. From a homeowner's perspective, this transformation makes a great deal of sense.

To date the track record of such buyouts has had mixed success, but you can expect this trend to continue as well (see sidebar, A buyout success story).

Tip: When shopping for a community, you may discover the current tenants are divided between those who want to buy the place and those who don't (or can't afford to participate). Find out more. This issue can be very divisive. If you think you will be siding with the buy-the-community faction, now is the time to gauge the likelihood of success.

Your second greatest vulnerability: losing your home because of lease violations

If you are an apartment dweller who gets into a fight with the landlord who in turn resorts to eviction proceedings for some alleged violation of the lease terms, chances are the worst that can happen is you move out and find another apartment while the landlord pays for any legal costs he or she incurred. But in many states without strong laws protecting rental community homeowners, if you get into a row with your community, the community owner may not only begin eviction proceedings, but he or she can also slap a lien on your home, thus preventing its sale or removal until you reimburse the owner for (in the language of

---

Rental agreements versus lease agreements

Technically, all agreements are leases, of which there are four types:

• An estate (e.g., land or a structure such as an office, home or apartment) for a specific period of time. Typically, for several years, with a specific start date and a termination date. This is a lease in the conventional use of the term.

• As estate from period to period. Typically, a month-to-month arrangement, commonly called a rental agreement. Rental agreements are often written to cover the first year, after which the terms and conditions continue on a month-to-month basis.

• Estate at will. A variation on a rental agreement: you move in and pay monthly rent, but either you or the landlord may terminate the agreement at any time, giving 30 day notice.

• Estate at sufferance. This is when a lease expires and the tenant remains, paying monthly rent but nothing is in writing. The property owner can evict at any time.

Most states have real estate laws requiring agreements for more than a year to be in writing to be enforceable (leases), while agreements for shorter periods can be verbal (rental agreements).

---

many lease contracts) "...all attorney's fees and related costs in the event management is required to retain counsel to enforce any rule or regulation."

This is boiler plate language that is common to lease agreements, and you should not regard it in itself as a red flag, but here and there greedy community owners have used this as a license to steal homes from unsuspecting tenants or those they regard as troublemakers, or to otherwise bury them in legal bills and misery. Again, your vulnerability stems from the peculiar position of owning one's home on someone else's property.

Don't be discouraged by the above disaster scenarios. They are quite rare when one considers the millions of community homeowners who are satisfied tenants. The best way you can ensure that you, too, will be a satisfied community resident is to take your time and ask questions of the right people.

Questions to ask when shopping for a site in a land-lease community:

Shop around. Rental communities vary greatly. When you find one that has strong possibilities, take the time to get a good feel for the place. Recommendations:

- Talk to the management; ask about the community's history:
  How long in business? Is the owner local? How much turnover of homes and tenants is there? Has there been much management turnover? If so, why?
- Is the community classified as a permanent land-use in the zoning ordinances. This is one question often overlooked. Some communities were developed as temporary uses of the land, and the owners may have a right to terminate a temporary (although long-lasting) operating permit and convert to another use.
- If the community has a homeowners association, talk to the leadership. How good are the HOA's relations with the community owners? Any recent history of disputes, issues on the horizon?

When tenants buy out their park–a success story

In 1997, the land-lease community of Clausen Cove Estates, near the town of Sequim on Washington state's Olympic Peninsula, was in its fifth year of development, but things were going slowly. Only 17 tenants had taken up residence in the 9-acre community, less than half of its 41-site capacity, and planned improvements such as a clubhouse had yet to be finished.

The park's owners got along well with their tenants and when the homeowners association asked them if they would agree to give the association the right of first refusal in the event they decided to sell the park, the owners agreed. Shortly thereafter, the park's owners went a step further, offering to sell the park for $1.25 million.

The tenants got together and drew up a plan to turn the park into a co-op, with memberships costing $25,000 per homeowner. Starting with themselves, they came up with more than $400,000 cash for a down payment, and borrowed the rest from a local bank. The purchase handily closed within weeks. Everyone was delighted.

With Clausen Cove Estates operating as a co-op, rents that were $250 to $260 were replaced by monthly dues at $60. The remaining memberships were quickly sold and the co-op's bank loan was paid off within 19 months. Today, the clubhouse is finished and bustling with activity, and the co-op has more than $25,000 in the bank. Over the years monthly dues have increased all of $11— from $60 to $71.

- Talk to several community residents without the manager present. Ask if there are any negatives that you might not discover without asking (see sidebar, What's wrong with this picture?), ongoing issues with management and/or the owners. What has been the history of rent and/ or fee increases? What is the history, if any, of landlord-tenant litigation?
- Obtain from the manager specimen copies of all documents you will be required to sign, notably the lease agreement, home installation requirements and community rules and regulations. If they don't give them to you to take with you, walk out. Study these carefully. If needed, have your attorney do so as well.
- Find out if there is any local rent control ordinance. You may also want to learn more about your state's laws regarding mobile home communities. A local library may have a copy.

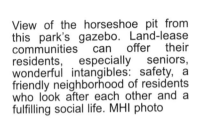

View of the horseshoe pit from this park's gazebo. Land-lease communities can offer their residents, especially seniors, wonderful intangibles: safety, a friendly neighborhood of residents who look after each other and a fulfilling social life. MHI photo

Questions to ask about the lease

Note: a lease agreement is the same as a rental agreement. If a lease is 12 months or less, it is commonly called a rental agreement (see sidebar, Rental agreements versus lease agreements).

How long is the lease?

A 12-month lease is common. Longer leases can be good for both the tenant and landlord if they are fair and provide a stable schedule for periodic, and reasonable, rent increases. But be wary: as we have seen earlier, longer term leases may be ploys to circumvent local rent stabilization ordinances that usually apply only to leases of a year or less. **Note:** Many park owners are intrigued by the possibilities of the new Freddie Mac loan guarantee program discussed earlier in this chapter, but it's too early to predict if it will catch on.

Are there any community charges for installing or removing the home?

In many states these are not allowed, especially any so-called exit fees when moving the home out of a community.

What are terms under which the rent may be increased?

The law on this issue is silent in many states, but generally requires the increases to be reasonable and with fair notice (usually 90 days). This leaves community owners a lot of leeway. There may be a local rent control ordinance. Some rates are adjusted periodically based on the CPI (the Consumer Price Index).

What is included in the monthly rent and what is not?

Usually the cost of water, sewage and garbage are included in the rent, with electricity billed separately based on a meter attached to the home. Often grass cutting is included as well. Other fees, such as snow removal or certain grounds maintenance, may also be required from time to time. **Note**: Some communities include most of these maintenance tasks in the rent, which can be a very good deal.

If the community is put up for sale, do tenants have the right of first refusal to buy it?

The inclusion of this provision in a lease is a big plus for tenants, and can be a good deal

---

When rentals turn sour

In February, 1998, Consumer Reports published a feature about the pros and cons of manufactured homes, "Dream home...or nightmare?" The magazine concluded the housing had come a long way but still cautioned "buyer beware."

In a section dealing with insecure leases, CR described the story of a gutsy young woman, Deborah Chapman, who in the late 1980s purchased a manufactured home and put it on leased land in Strasburg, Pennsylvania. She intended to live there while she saved for a down payment on a site-built home. When the time came to make the trade-up, she learned that her lease contained language that gave her landlord the right to approve the buyer. Six people made offers on her $9,500 home. The landlord rejected them all, then offered Chapman a low-ball bid of his own: $2,000.

Instead of caving in, Chapman paid $1,500 to have the home moved out of the park. A year later, after the home had sat empty, she sold it for $7,000, most of which went to cover attorney's fees to fight her landlord. Chapman had no regrets. "Had I been forced to sell," she told CR, "the landowner would have sold my home for much more than he paid for it."

Chapman went on to create the National Foundation of Manufactured Home Owners, of which she is chairwoman. Web site: www.manhousingfoundation.org. Phone (717) 284-4520.

Among its services, the foundation provides referrals to associations of home owners in your area that offer advice and resources to home buyers shopping for land-lease communities.

The *Consumer Reports* feature is available online at www.consumerreports.org. Click on the A-Z index and mouse down to "Mobile homes."

---

for the community owner as well. Should an outside buyer be thinking of converting the community to other commercial use, for example, the community's tenants would at least have a chance to raise the money to meet the buyer's price.

Will management have the right to come into my home without my consent?

With few exceptions (an emergency being one), the law of the land prohibits anyone from entering your home without your permission (even if your primary residence is a pop-up camper), but watch out for lease language that waives that right.

If the community is sold and the tenants must move their homes, will the owner provide any assistance?

A negative response should not be a deal-breaker but the question is worth asking. Many states have laws requiring the owners, in the event of the sale of the community and the conversion of the land for another use, to find new sites for the displaced tenants and to pay for the cost of the relocations.

What restrictions, if any, are there if in the future I wish to sell my home?

Read the fine print carefully here, because in states where there are few seller protections, unethical community owners have inserted lease provisions giving them approval over the buyer to prevent the tenant from accepting reasonable offers. The community then makes a low ball offer to buy the tenant's home and turns around and sells it for a substantial profit (see sidebar, When Rentals Turn Sour). For example, California law allows community managers only two reasons for disapproving a prospective buyer (or, for that matter, a prospective tenant): past failure to pay rent or past failure to follow the terms of a lease agreement. On a positive note, many managers work closely with sellers to market their homes to attract the best new homeowners.

What about any appurtenances or site improvements that I make? To whom do they belong?

If any improvements you make can be removed and taken with you, now is the time to address this issue.

Are there fees for pets or additional people?

If you have a pet, the law in many states bars a community from charging an annual fee, but make sure. In most states, too, it's illegal for a community to charge an additional per-person fee if the new arrival is a member of the immediate family.

Community rules and regulations

During your first meeting with the community's manager to discuss the possibility of your becoming a tenant homeowner, he or she will give you a copy of the community's rules and regulations (sometimes called community covenants). These are often quite extensive and detailed but most likely you will find most of the items second nature to you. You should read and understand everything before you sign anything and discuss with the manager any concerns you may have.

Typically, the rules deal with two topics: home installation and architectural covenants and community rules. What follows are excerpts from the rules and regulations typical of a manufactured home rental community:

Typical home installation and architectural covenants

Home and Size
All homes shall be newly constructed in accordance with HUD standards, have wood or composite siding and a pitched roof with composition shingles.
Setup
The home shall be recessed into the ground so that its floor level is not more than 12 inches above mean ground level. The home's site must conform to the front, rear and side setback requirements, and shall be set up according to manufacturer's specifications. Axles, wheels and hitches shall be removed at the time of installation. Resident is responsible for water, sewer, gas, electrical, telephone and cable TV connections.
Skirting
Pre-manufactured skirting, made of wood, fiberglass or composite materials, shall be installed around the entire home, including any decking.
Steps
Front and rear steps, with adequately supported hand railings, which comply with applicable building codes, shall be installed. Temporary or "dealer's steps" are not permitted.

The club house and swimming pool of a southern California manufactured home land-lease community. In many Sunbelt states, particularly Florida, many communities are built around golf courses or boating waterways. MHI photo.

Parking Pad
The parking pad shall be concrete with minimum dimensions of 12'x 20'.

Patio
A concrete patio with minimum dimensions of 100 square feet is allowed. In lieu of concrete, resident may install a wood deck with minimum dimension of 100 square feet.

Yard light
Each home site shall be improved with a yard light the design of which has been approved by the Manager. The light shall be located between the home and street, and set back five feet from the street curb.

Colors/Finishes
The standard colors offered by the home manufacturer will be acceptable. All exterior improvements, including skirting, awnings, carport covers, deck and storage buildings shall be constructed, trimmed and finished with materials and colors that compliment the finish of the home.

Storage building
At resident's election, each home site may be improved with one pre-manufactured storage building containing not less than 72, nor more than 144 square feet, with a roof height of not less than seven, nor more than, nine feet.

Typical community rules
To ensure pleasant and enjoyable surroundings, every effort will be made by Management to make certain that the community covenants are adhered to and that the lifestyle and comfort of all residents are not jeopardized. Fair and equal application of these covenants is the committed responsibility of Management.

Advertising and soliciting
Advertising, soliciting or delivering handbills by unauthorized individuals is not permitted without written authorization from Management. The residence shall not be used for the practice of any profession, trade, craft or business. Nor shall residents make any unlawful, disorderly, improper or objectionable use (as defined by Management) of the home site.

Athletic equipment and toys

Jungle gyms, trampolines, basketball goals, weight benches, play or swing sets and other such equipment are not permitted on the home site. For safety concerns, wading pools must be emptied and stored each night. For the winter season, all playhouses and pools must be disassembled and stored with all other such toys.

Clotheslines

No outdoor clotheslines will be permitted. No laundry of any kind may be hung outside of any home.

Home site

No outside storage is permitted around the home site except for grills and permanent lawn furniture. All tools, lawn mowers, toys, bikes, etc. should be kept in the garage. Each resident shall keep the home site neat and free of litter. Hoses should be kept on hose reels or hangers. Outside furniture should be kept in good repair and painted.

Landscaping

Not less than 51% of the area approved for landscaping shall be landscaped with living plants, trees and/or grass. There shall be a minimum of three living plants (trees or shrubs) two feet or more in height and/or a lawn and annuals or perennials in the front yard (between the house and the street).

Shrubs or trees or similar obstructions that will obstruct traffic vision shall not be erected. Plantings or decorative items should not be placed within five feet of the curb or the home site next to it. Vegetable gardens will not be permitted except in areas approved by Management. Each resident shall keep the lot free of weeds, tall grass and noxious plant growth.

Pets

Up to two pets are allowed per home site, subject to the following conditions: no pet is to exceed 18 pounds in weight; each pet must be approved by the Manager, in writing, prior to occupancy; all dogs and cats must be spayed or neutered by the time they are three months of age; all pets must be maintained as indoor pets and may not be left outside unattended; dogs must be leashed anytime they are off the Resident's lot; the pet owner shall immediately clean up all waste from other yards and common areas, and to maintain their own yards free of waste.

No dog house or runs are permitted; residents are responsible for informing their visitors that pets other than those owned by residents may not be brought into the community; Management reserves the right to exclude all dogs which in its opinion are of a vicious nature, breed or temperament, and to require the removal of any pet that in the opinion of Management constitutes a nuisance.

Resale of home

Written approval is required by Management (approval will not be unreasonably withheld) for the resold home to remain on the home site. If the home is not in conformance with the community standards it must be brought into conformance prior to the new buyer occupying the home.

Prior to finalizing the sale of any home, the prospective purchaser must apply for residency of the home site and pay all applicable fees or deposits. Qualification for acceptance of the buyer will be based upon his or her acceptance of the Community covenants, credit report and income qualifications.

Residency

Two persons per bedroom are permitted to reside within a home. Any person residing within a home for more than one month will be considered a permanent resident and must be registered with Management.

Right of entry

Management or its designated company reserves the right of entry upon the land on which a home is situated for maintenance of the utilities and protection of the community.

Subletting

No home may become a rental home. Subletting shall not be permitted. The owner must occupy the home as well as be party on the lease.

Vehicles

Vehicles kept on the home site or in the community parking areas shall have current license plates, be operable and not leaking fluids. Loud exhaust and flat tires shall be repaired immediately. Trucks in excess of 3/4-ton shall not be parked on a home site or in community parking areas. No mopeds, mini-bikes , motor scooters, go-carts, dirt bikes, all-terrain vehicles or snowmobiles may be operated within the community.

Vehicle washing, repairing and storage

Vehicles may be washed on home site driveways. Minor repairing of vehicles, such as changing tires, spark plugs or fan belts, requiring the vehicle to be inoperative for a period of two hours or less, is allowed. Vehicles may not be put on ramps or blocks. Boats, motor homes, unmounted truck campers, all-terrain vehicles or trailers of any kind may not be kept on the home site unless garaged.

Covenant violations

A resident who has violated a covenant may be contacted by means of a visit, a telephone call, a notice or a letter. If the infraction is not corrected or if the violation is continually repeated, legal proceedings may begin.

Management thanks you for selecting our community as your new residence and anticipates a long, enjoyable and rewarding experience.

In all, a trade-off that can work

While the detailed character of community rules and regulations may be very off-putting to someone unfamiliar with land-lease communities or planned unit subdivisions, comprehensive covenants generally work very well, preserving tranquility and neighborhood ambiance in a community characterized by small home sites packed closely together. Clearly, the community manager has a lot of discretionary authority, and good managers use that power wisely and fairly. In sum, despite the tenant-landlord tensions latent within the system, land-lease communities provide a trade-off that can work very well indeed for a great many manufactured home owners.

Chapter 7

The Anatomy of a Dealership

At last count there were roughly 4,000 manufactured home dealerships nationwide, down from over 8,000 at the height of the boom in the late 1990s. Inasmuch as a good percentage of these are community owners and builder-developers, the actual number of retail sales centers (street dealers in industry slang) is probably closer to 3,500. The shrinkage was been brutal in some states (in Georgia alone 200 dealerships went belly up in an 18-month period). These dealerships run the gamut from mom and pop operations with a half dozen lot models and a mobile home for an office, on up to slick superstores with landscaped grounds, lots of flags, spacious sales offices, two dozen home models and well-coifed motivated sales staffs.

Given the industry's roots, the business model for distributing and marketing manufactured homes is very similar to that of the automotive industry. Say what you will about dealerships, and you'll find a lot of opinions, practically the only way you can buy a new manufactured home is through a dealer, not direct from the factory. Even developers who increasingly are choosing manufactured homes over site-built dwellings for subdivisions and in-fill developments, must purchase through dealerships or become licensed dealers themselves.

Retailers are organized pretty much the same, regardless of size, although the level of professionalism varies tremendously. Here's a brief overview of the typical dealership and how it operates.

There are two kinds of dealerships: independent and factory-owned.

Independent dealerships

Most dealerships are independent businesses whose owner (or owners) operates on a leased sales lot large enough to accommodate from six to ten home models and a modest sales office. The dealer represents two, sometimes three, brands of manufactured homes, each model line designed to appeal to a market segment, e.g., low-end, mid-range, high-end. Some dealerships focus on just one market segment, for example, low-end homes providing affordable housing, or high-end homes favored by affluent retirees.

To obtain the display model homes, the dealer takes out a loan from a bank or financial services company (the latter may be a subsidiary of a manufacturer) that provides so-called flooring loans (a term borrowed from the auto industry where new models are displayed on a car dealership's showroom floor). The loan is used to pay the factory in full for the homes, usually within 15 days of delivery to the dealership, as well as the costs of transportation from the factory to the dealership and setting up the home on the lot. But the flooring lender attaches a condition: the manufacturer must sign a repurchase agreement, guaranteeing it will buy back from the bank any floored inventory, at the existing loan balances, if the dealer

This pitch to "payment buyers" still works at the market's lower end. Is it any wonder that most mainstream consumers would never consider a manufactured home as a viable housing option? Photo: Consumers Union

becomes insolvent. If the dealer has repaid the flooring loan to the lender, the manufacturer is off the hook. This way the bank is protected.

For several months, or until a lot model is sold, the dealer pays interest only on its flooring. When the home is sold, the buyer (or the buyer's lender) pays the dealer who in turn pays off the flooring loan on the home. What's left after the cost of the home's delivery and setup, and sales commissions, is the dealership's profit. However, if six, eight or 12 months (terms vary) pass without the lot model selling, the flooring lender will require the dealer to begin paying down the principal as well as the interest, which ties up cash. To avoid this happening, and to sell the home quickly, the dealer often lowers the home's price and adds a sales incentive bonus of several hundred dollars (called a spiff) to the sales commission. Purchasing a spiffed lot model can sometimes be a good deal for a smart home buyer.

Typically, one or two of the lot models will feature a number of dealer-ordered options (called "flash" in the trade) such as solid oak cabinets, a ceiling fan, skylights, larger master bath and/or a fireplace. To increase appearance appeal some dealers also add furniture, wall art, and other decor to one or two models. These are not sold with the home. Some dealerships have all, or none, of their models decorated.

A typical dealership will have a sales staff of two or three, while the largest sales centers may have six or seven. Salespeople ("home consultants" in industry parlance) are generally paid minimum wage (about $1,000 a month) plus commissions, usually based on 20% of gross profit of each home they sell. If all goes well and the economy in the region is healthy, a successful salesperson can earn $40,000 to $60,000 a year.

Working closely with the dealership, but not on the payroll, are subcontractors who specialize in setting up and installing the homes, including interior painting, putting in carpeting and installing gutters and downspouts. Some of these, installers in particular, are specialists trained in joining multi-section homes, leveling the home on its foundation and completing the installation of the home's heating and central air conditioning. Many, but not all states require installers to be licensed. Typically these subcontractors will have agreements with several dealerships to work on setups and take-downs. Legally, dealers are not allowed to sell a home without being responsible for its completeness once placed on site.

Many first time manufactured home buyers have no real idea what is involved in the setup and installation phase, yet this is an area where improper installation and shoddy workmanship can cause major long term headaches. Chapter 11 provides inspection guidelines for this phase.

If the home is going into a new subdivision or raw land that is being developed, a local general contractor will be involved, either hired by the buyer or by the dealer as part of an optional package. Some dealers are themselves licensed contractors, while some states, notably California, require all manufactured home dealers who are not so licensed to hire a licensed contractor to install the homes. The general contractor is responsible for the site preparation (including constructing a concrete foundation if required), water and utility hookups, the septic system, the driveway and landscaping. In the absence of a nearby water main, these contractors may also oversee the drilling of a well.

Often the dealership's salesperson takes an active role in seeing that the necessary building permits are submitted to various county agencies and to keeping the home buyer abreast of developments. This can be a very busy time for all concerned, especially if a septic system and a well are being put in.

Lastly, many dealerships often have jack-of-all-trades people on staff (or under contract) to handle follow-up warranty service on homes previously sold. Typically the dealership is reimbursed these costs by the manufacturers but not infrequently problems arise that are not under warranty protection but which the dealership resolves at its own expense to keep its customer happy.

Factory-owned dealerships

As the name indicates, this type of retailer is owned by the manufacturer. These dealerships operate very much like their independent counterparts. Theoretically, factory ownership arrangement makes sense inasmuch as, by owning all the components of the enterprise—from design and manufacture of the homes, to distribution and sales—the manufacturer gains an additional revenue source (the retail home buyer) while offering the advantages of a single chain of accountability, warranty service and customer care. In addition, since the dealer presumably does not have to pay the costs of flooring, that savings can be passed on to the customer.

The reality has been far different. With few exceptions, the idea has flopped. Manufacturers have proven ill-equipped and unschooled for the demands of retailing, customer care and the responsibilities of managing far-flung sales organizations. For example, most factory-owned dealerships, lacking the authority to OK warranty work, often require weeks to get authorization from company headquarters. In contrast, an independent dealer can take care of problems right away, even non-warranty service, in the name of keeping the buyer satisfied. As for the savings on flooring costs, even though a flooring bank is technically no longer in the equation, the capital that is sitting in each home on that sales lot has to come from somewhere. Either the corporation borrows the money or ties up its own funds. What has actually happened is 90% of the factory-owned dealerships ended up flooring their homes through traditional lenders, not the parent company. Elsewhere, many factory-owned dealerships are obliged to sell their homes at higher prices than the independents because they are now part of huge corporations that have correspondingly huge overhead.

In addition, manufacturers who own their own dealerships tend to favor keeping their very expensive production factories humming rather than heeding the recommendations of their dealerships about particular housing needs of the potential buyers. As a consequence

This Home Max retail sales center near Raleigh, North Carolina illustrates what can be done to display home models in a manner very similar to the approach of many major site-built home developers. Welcoming, well-landscaped grounds, attractive display models and low key professionalism can go a long way to attracting mainstream home shoppers who are turned off by the tacky street dealer image.

the manufacturers tend to load their dealerships with lot models unpopular with local buyers. This disconnect, coupled with burdensome demoralizing corporate oversight, has led to a higher than average turnover of sales staff.

In short, at this point, the industry consensus is that a locally owned independent dealership run by reputable professionals generally holds the advantage over its factory owned counterpart and can thus provide the home buyer a better deal and better follow-up warranty service. But there are exceptions. Some manufacturers—Clayton and Palm Harbor Homes—have effectively addressed the problems and made the concept of integrated ownership work well.

A dealership's profit centers

The principal source of revenue is the profit margin on each home sold. This can vary depending on how big the demand is, but it's not as great as many think, currently 20% to 30%, with the average in the 20%-to-25% range. Here are other ways profit is generated, some of them questionable:

Packages. (also known as "Packs" or "PACs"), generally offered as all-inclusive bundles for one price. Typically, three are offered:

Setup PAC. Also called the Sales PAC. This is the cost of transporting the home to the home site, setting it up on the foundation, finishing the interior (taping, painting, carpeting, cleaning), and performing minor work to bring the home into conformance with local codes. Exterior work includes installation of gutters and downspouts and skirting. This PAC is almost always included as part of the home's base price, and in concept is not subject to a dealer markup, but some dealers have been known to skimp on what they pay subcontractors, and pocket the rest.

Park PAC. Includes the above Setup PAC, plus the costs of site preparation in a land-lease community, construction of foundation (if needed), landscaping, driveway, utilities hookup, and an optional garage or car port. This PAC can involve an outside general contractor who in turn hires sub-contractors ("subs" in the trade). Sometimes hidden in the package cost is an informal kickback to the dealer in return for steering the business to a particular contractor.

Land-Home PAC. A comprehensive land development package that includes the sale of land for the home, site preparation, home setup and installation, well, septic system, permits, landscaping and often a garage or carport. A general contractor (who can be the dealer, if licensed) is required. Typically, the dealer doesn't own the land being sold but instead has a prior agreement with the landowner for a share of the profit from the land sale, which is perfectly legitimate. These PACs, excluding the price of the land, can easily run $25,000 to $35,000 and up.

To a dishonest dealer, this "We'll–take-care-of-everything-for-you" package can be a license to steal. If no one is looking too closely, there are ways to overcharge the client. When these PACs are part of a construction loan, the lender typically keeps a tight rein on the process, giving close scrutiny to every line item, often insisting on bids, to ensure the costs are fair.

A few dealers who can afford to do so, will actually buy land and take title to it, then prepare it as a ready-to-go home site for a land-home PAC offering. This is a perfectly legitimate enterprise, almost identical to the role of a land developer who builds a "spec" home (i.e. on speculation) on purchased land and puts it on the market.

Financing. One reason dealers prefer financing homes through their own lending sources is that, when the manufactured housing market is hot, many of those lenders offer a rebate of 2%-2-1/2% of the total loan, sometimes more. On a $60,000 loan, this amounts to $1,500.

This arrangement is OK as long as the rebate doesn't end up hidden somewhere in the loan. Less than reputable dealers will sneak into a purchase contract charges for loan origination, documentation fees, points, credit checks and other "routine" items that are nothing more than line item rip-offs that go directly into the dealer's pocket when the loan closes. **Note**: The good news for home buyers is this rebate, while common during the boom years of the 1990s, has virtually disappeared.

Insurance. Typically, insurance purchased through dealers is much more expensive than policies purchased through general insurance brokers. Laws vary from state to state, but dealers can often earn meaningful commissions on hazard insurance, extended warranty coverage and creditor life insurance.   (**Note**: You should never buy creditor life insurance. Buy term life insurance instead, if at all.) To be fair, reputable dealers offer competitively priced policies not so much for the commissions (which are nominal) but as a convenience to the home buyer.

Rebates. This is an important profit center. Almost every manufacturer offers a dealer incentive rebate program under which the manufacturer periodically pays the dealership a percentage of the cumulative total wholesale purchases the dealer has paid the factory for homes ordered during a 12 month period (see sidebar). This can be a substantial chunk of change.

About factory rebates

Rebates are a universal legitimate practice in the world of commerce. Not only are they powerful incentives to retailers, but they also help ensure that participating dealers pay their bills on time (a typical rebate program excludes from the dealer's cumulative total those invoices that are not paid promptly). Prior to the start of every 12-month rebate cycle, each manufacturer forecasts the total amount it will need to pay in rebates, then includes that cost in the price it charges dealers as a percentage of each home sold. Sometimes this cost component is called a hold back. In the manufactured home industry rebates can run anywhere from 5% to 10% and higher. The greater the volume, the higher the percentage.

For example, under one program, a dealership that reaches $950,000 in wholesale orders gets a 7% rebate check worth $66,500. A larger dealership that breaks the $1.4 million total earns a 9.5% rebate totaling $133,000. Really big dealerships often have the power to negotiate their rebate percentages with the manufacturers.

Rebates can actually benefit the consumer because many dealers, in order to get their cumulative numbers up, will sometimes beat each other to death lowering prices to move the homes. In short, a dealer can sell a home at cost and yet still make a profit from the year-end factory rebate. Often, a dealership's entire annual net profit derives from factory rebates.

Unfortunately, the losers here are the dealership's sales staff; they receive no commission on a home sold at cost (one more reason why the industry traditionally has a high turnover of salespeople). A few enlightened dealerships, as an incentive, share with their sales staff a proportion of the rebate money received above a certain annual sales goal.

Wild and crazy profit centers

For the typical reputable manufactured home dealership, the sources of profits are straightforward: income derives from the markup on the homes, the annual factory rebates, the sale of property in a land-home package, and rebates from lenders and insurance companies. But over the years, enterprising dealers have cooked up amazing strategies, not all of them legitimate, to mine extra dollars from pliable home buyers and, in some instances, willing lenders. A few examples:

One dealer created a side business in household furnishings. He shopped closeouts and liquidations, buying low quality inventory for pennies on the dollar, then offered a furnishings package to home buyers at steep markups. Over time, his "Home Amenities PACs" grew to include dishes, silverware, TVs, appliances, and even motel wall art—until the lenders caught on.

Other dealers have started their own outside landscaping or construction companies (sometimes both) to perform the work involved in dealer-offered landscaping packages or garage, barn or carport construction projects. These enterprises can be legitimate—reputable

---

A typical factory rebate program

Here's how one major manufacturer structures its dealer rebate program:

During the 12-month period beginning January 26, _____, the company will pay dealers a retroactive bonus based on a percentage of the combined total wholesale purchases of qualifying homes from the manufacturer. The purchase volume is the sum of the home's base price and the factory's product options only. Bonus checks are mailed quarterly.

Annual Combined Purchase Volume Plateau	Retroactive Bonus
0 to $400,000	0.0%
$400,001 to $600,000	1.0%
$600,001 to $800,000	2.0%
$800,001 to $1,000,000	3.0%
$1,000,001 to $1,500,001	4.0%

...and so on in increments of $500,000 until reaching a bonus of 8.0% for any total over $10,000,000.

In addition, if the dealer's growth from the previous year's total purchase volume is 15% or higher, a year-end bonus of an additional 1% will be awarded. Big volume dealers (over $10,000,000) need only post a 10% gain.

A key incentive is that the qualifying purchase volume carries over from quarter to quarter. Thus, for example, when a dealer reaches a plateau of $600,000, the bonus is 2%, payable at the end of that quarter. But in the following quarter, the dealer need only purchase an additional $200,000 in homes to reach $800,000 in cumulative totals, to earn a 2% bonus for that quarter.
These incentives encourage dealerships to load up their lots with models to earn rebates, particularly near the end of the 12 month period (in this case the dead of winter) even if the homes aren't selling. This way the manufacturer keeps the factories running during the slow season.

---

dealers who are also general contractors are a welcome trend—but in these cases, because the jobs were not put out for bid, were overpriced, and the dealer profited nicely.

During the go-go years of the 1990s, when major subprime lenders let it be known they would not require bulletproof documentation that a down payment was actually made by the borrower, the result was a torrent of "false downs." Some dealers would offer to "buy" a loan applicant's hat (or skiff or motorcycle) for $3,000, which the owner would then use for the down payment. As Chapter 3 noted, in Oregon, one preferred item of trade was the dealer's Jet Ski, made famous in a series of articles exposing dealer fraud by the *Portland Oregonian* newspaper. The Jet Ski, of course, never left its owner's garage. The $3,000 was tacked onto the back end of the loan, increasing the amount from which the dealer's rebate was calculated. The borrower was happy with a Zero Down purchase while the lender looked the other way as long as it could sell the loan to Wall Street or others in the financial community.

This practice came to a screeching halt when the avalanche of repossessed homes began in 2000. Not to put too fine a point on it, the above borrowers who were happy with a "Zero

Sympathy for the Dealer

In all fairness, selling manufactured homes is one of the toughest jobs in retails sales. Tedium, frustration, angry shoppers, clueless shoppers, paranoid shoppers, window shoppers who play head games, long hours of effort for nothing, sales that fall through at the last minute, self-doubt, unpredictable pay days, pressure from creditors, guilt by association and Murphy's law—all these come with the territory. Those who endure, let alone thrive, have patience, a sense of humor, drive and a kind of passion for their work that, considering the pressure pit environment in which they must work, is remarkable.

Spend any time getting to know personally a dealer or salesperson and it won't be long before you hear a few Buyer from Hell stories. Here are a few excerpts from interviews.

The Incredible Hulk goes shopping "One afternoon I showed this couple one of our low-end models and the guy, who was as big as a pro linebacker, suddenly turned into the Incredible Hulk. He started storming from room to room complaining how cheap and flimsy everything was. 'Look at this,' he yells, and, Bam! he punches a hole through the dry wall. He goes into the bath and rips the front off the vanity sink and holds it up, yelling "There's supposed to be a drawer here. This is crap!" I had to ask them to leave."

The grinders "You don't always spot them until it's too late. They get four or five dealers working overtime to cut the best deal, each thinking they earned his trust and that he's going to buy from them, then he proceeds to grind everyone down mercilessly with back and forth last-minute changes of heart, until finally one of us caves in and sells the house virtually at cost just to end the BS. Maybe the buyer walks out feeling OK but in his wake is a lot of ill-will. It can be exhausting."

Splitsville "We spent weeks with this one couple who had already bought a piece of property. They were cash customers; they spent a lot of time looking at options; they ordered a nice high-end house; and made a down payment. The factory built it—then the very day the home comes off the line, the couple split up in a huge clash of attorneys. Bank accounts are frozen. And we're stuck in the middle, looking at many months of delays and legal fees before we ever get paid, and in the meantime we have ten business days to pay the factory."

Blamers "This was one of those construction loans that was plagued from the beginning with mishaps and problems. I was blamed for just about everything, but we worked our tails off to correct things, and at our own considerable expense. Then the well we had drilled came in at only a gallon a minute. When I suggested that a thousand gallon holding tank and an additional pump would be needed, I was blamed for the low flow rate and blamed for never suggesting that a tank might be needed. And this was on land they had owned for some time. Sometimes nothing will make it right."

The clueless "They were a nice middle-age couple who'd lived in cities all their lives and whose Realtor found them property, and money was no problem. The home was ordered, and they said they would take care of the site prep. But they had no idea what was involved, even though we'd gone over everything. They had no idea what a septic system was, let alone how it worked. Wells and pressure systems were mysteries to them. Again and again we had to sit them down and patiently explain how the property is developed and what a general contractor is, and how the electricity is brought in, and how the permit process works—and then they'd forget everything. They seemed to think they were buying an instant home that somehow you just plugged in."

The gamers "I like people, I really do. If my flight is delayed I can sit in an airport and people-watch for hours. But what has jaded me about human behavior over the years is all the times I've had home shoppers sit in front of my desk and sound terribly sincere, and I know they're flat out lying. It's like it's a game to them, like, 'Every dealer is out to screw you, so don't ever tell them the truth.' I don't mind negotiation. The back and forth is part of the striking a fair agreement, but the cynicism and distrust and veiled hostility of these types of shoppers are so difficult to deal with."

The endless be backs "You expect people shopping for a home to make several visits before they get serious. They're called 'be backs' in the business. But the be backs who can wear you down are the ones who come in twice a month for months on end, asking endless questions and taking up lots of your time, and always giving you the impression that they're about to commit to a home purchase. And then after ten months or a year, they simply disappear. It's like you were their bi-weekly entertainment , a place they came to get their dream-fix about owning a home someday, all a fantasy. It's one of the great frustrations of this business."

The complainers "As soon as they moved into their new triple-wide they started complaining about everything. Of course you expect to make a few service calls during the first few months of a new home as the owners discover things that need fixing. We take pride in our warranty service. But this couple called at least twice a week for months on end. They wouldn't change a light bulb or the temperature on the wall thermostat without calling to complain. I swear you couldn't please 'em if you hung 'em with a new rope."

Down purchase" were in effect colluding with the dealers to cheat the system. Home buyers who knew they were being dishonest deserve some of the blame for creating the mess that the industry found itself in at the end of the 90s.

The trapped entrance, locked homes, up rotation and other mysteries

When you first set out to visit manufactured home dealerships, you may be surprised to discover you can't simply walk onto a lot and wander unaccompanied through the home models. This of itself should not be a matter of concern. How a dealership handles walk-ins depends very much on the region of the country, the dealership's sales philosophy and the demographics of its customer base—and these vary considerably. At one end of the spectrum are dealerships, usually smaller ones that don't have a lot of foot traffic at any given moment, whose salesperson will greet you casually without asking your name and welcome you to explore on your own and invite you to stop by the office if you have any questions. Typically, the lot models at these dealerships will have an information sheet taped to the refrigerator showing the home's base price, plus a line item listing the options and their costs. At the other end are large dealerships surrounded by cyclone fences and a single entrance (called a trapped entrance) that forces you to enter by way of the sales office where you are assigned a home consultant who won't allow you to tour the lot models until you have been subjected to an hour-long sales presentation, have volunteered personal information so your credit score can be obtained, and been cleared by the sales manager, following which your host accompanies your every step. About the only control system missing is the use of cattle prods.

A great many, perhaps most, dealerships are somewhere in the middle of this range. They keep their lot models locked but are happy to give you the keys as soon as you sign the guest book in the office (and they don't check IDs.)

Whether or not you are accompanied by a salesperson as you go through the lot models often depends on the level of sales pressure the dealership employs, but there can also be a second factor: how much they trust you not to trash or steal from the lot models. The latter concern is no trivial matter. Most dealers really don't like people going through their models unaccompanied because, sad to report, they end up losing a zillion knickknacks: range knobs, the hot and cold buttons on Delta faucets, range hood grease filters, shower heads, faucet strainers, even pieces of furniture. It drives them nuts. Add to this chewing gum on the carpets, cigarette burns on counter tops (and rugs), ashes and phlegm in the sink, and an occasional surprise caca deposit in the toilet (the water is off), and it's no wonder some dealers won't allow visitors to inspect their lot models unaccompanied. They simply don't trust them.

There is a third reason why dealerships want at least a bit of personal interaction with you before you look at the lot models. Typically, the person who greets you when you enter a dealership is the sales person whose turn it is to be up and ready to meet walk-ins. Should you end up working with this person to buy a home from this dealership, he or she will earn the sales commission. Salespeople take turns in rotation throughout the day being "up," i.e., the designated greeter for the next walk-in. Up rotation is not only fair and orderly, but very important to the sales staff, since "ups" are the principal way in which salespeople connect with eventual buyers.

Hint: Even if you only visit a dealership for a quick first look, and assuming the salesperson who greets you makes a favorable impression, make a note (or take a business card) and ask for them by name the next time you visit. Not only will they appreciate it—after all, you're protecting their potential sales commission—they will work harder for you. If you don't, whoever is up to greet you will usually be free to take over as the salesperson of record in the event you purchase a home there.

"Write ups" and the blight of high pressure sales

For too long manufactured home dealers have tended to regard their customer base as not only the least creditworthy, least informed and least educated but also the most easily manipulated and most susceptible to high-pressure sales techniques. Historically their assessment may have some statistical basis in fact, and their low-brow, fast-pitch, close-the-deal-now sales strategies may still work in many regions of the country. But this sign-here-now tactic can spell big trouble for you, and you should not tolerate it.

The principal tip off that you're being gamed by this kind of approach is the pressure during your very first visit that the salesperson will exert on you to "write up" a contract and get your signature before you leave the lot. The contract (or purchase agreement or loan

The Home-Mart dealership in Tulsa, Oklahoma. Single-wide homes (upper right) account for a large percentage of home sales in this region (as well as the Southwest). With more than 30 lot models, this is a large well-established sales center. In contrast to many retailers, Home Mart posts sticker prices in its lot models, which are not locked, a marketing strategy that has worked well.
(MHI Photo)

application) can have a lot of "to be determined" written in the blanks where hard numbers will come later, but the idea is to get you locked in to some kind of deal, any deal, with that dealer, even if it's one you eventually walk away from (and even that may not be easy). Chapter 10 goes into this practice in detail—please be sure to read it.

The goal of that salesman is to get as many write ups as possible, to get you hooked to that dealership waiting for them to run a credit check on you and then shop your loan application to various lenders. These tactics are designed to dissuade you from talking to any other dealers, let alone sign any other purchase contract. This practice is borrowed straight out of the retail car business where floor salespeople often receive a $25 "spiff" for every write-up they produce.

Salespeople are often graded by how many write-ups they get each month, even if a lot of the contracts failed to get funded, because their ability to get walk-ins to sign any contract or application is regarded as a mark of superior salesmanship. From this perspective, it is, but guess who ends up at an early disadvantage?

Bear in mind that on average the typical buyer of a manufactured home makes between nine and 12 visits to a dealership before they commit to a purchase.

Where are the price stickers?

Elsewhere, it is a sad commentary that the great majority of dealerships still refuse to put sticker prices on their lot models (in California a Manufacturers Suggested Retail Price sticker (MSRP) is required; the figure is generally 40%-45% over the dealer's factory invoice). It's hard not to believe it's because dealers want to keep the option of quoting the price depending on how much they think they can get out of the customer. Often, that's the reason, pure and simple. But there are two other explanations:

1. Not posting the sticker price allows a dealer or salesperson to disclose the price in person and to prevent or minimize sticker-shock by suggesting ways that a deal might be structured to meet the home buyer's financial situation—thus saving a potential lost sale.

This explanation is credible, but it can't justify no sticker prices. The practice is also short-sighted. Site-built home developers, who really know their market, without exception post sticker prices in all their models.

2. If the home shopper indicates an intention to trade in his or her existing manufactured home, the dealer needs to determine its market value, which in turn will effect the price quoted on the home—a tactic directly lifted from the car industry. It works like this: Say a prospective home buyer owns a single-wide that will likely appraise at $8,000. To sweeten an offer, the dealer offers a $14,000 trade-in allowance toward a new home. That will leave the dealer with $6,000 in so-called "negative equity" in the trade-in. No problem. That $6,000 is merely tacked onto the quoted base price of the home. The home shopper is thrilled to learn the old house is worth so much, and has no idea that he or she is paying $6,000 more for the new home.

Of course, if confronted, the dealer might explain, "OK, we could take the trade-in at its fair market value of $8,000, and quote the home price at $6,000 less, and the buyer would still end up needing to borrow $6,000 more. No one gets robbed. What's the difference?" Sounds like a perfect "Ethics 101" quiz question.

Unfortunately, there are dealers out there who really don't know the difference—and they'd flunk the quiz. Attitudes like this, together with high-pressure sales tactics, remain a blight on the industry.

But as the product has improved dramatically, a new generation of educated, affluent buyers are beginning to show up at dealers' lots. For these customers, which include boomers, or boomers shopping for aging parents, or simply solvent middle-age singles, these high pressure sales approaches are offensive, insensitive, laughable and counterproductive.

In fact, astute dealers have already discovered that treating even the least creditworthy shoppers with respect and patience pays big dividends. For example, in Tulsa, Oklahoma, the Home-Mart dealership has adopted "open doors" and "posted prices." True, they have a trapped entrance and they ask visitors to fill out a card, and they prefer to have a salesperson accompany visitors, but on busy days with high traffic, visitors are free to roam about on their own, with no salesman dogging them.

Owner Doug Gorman, who has a degree in marketing, explains he posts the sticker prices because, " I figure that may be the best and only opportunity I'll get to tell them what we're willing to sell the homes for."

Despite fierce competition from more than a dozen retailers in the same neighborhood, and a high credit risk customer base, Home-Mart has become one of the most successful dealerships in the country.

Knowing the territory

Understanding how manufactured home dealerships are set up and run, knowing their sales tactics and the ways they make money, are essential to being an informed home shopper. Not surprisingly, some dealers interviewed for this guide refused to discuss any of these subjects, let alone even admit that things like factory rebates exist. It's as though their guarding of these "secrets" is the only advantage they possess over the customer. By contrast, every reputable dealer approached was happy to talk, confident that the more informed the buyers are, the easier their job would be in selling their products and services. The chapter that follows will help you find and select that good, reputable dealer.

Chapter 8

Finding a Reputable Dealer

At the outset, let it be said once again that the majority of manufactured home dealers are honest and attempt to give the home buyer a square deal. Unfortunately, as noted previously in these pages, virtually everyone interviewed for this guide agrees that this industry attracts more than its share of less-than-reputable retailers and lenders.

Unless or until the industry cleans up its act and rids itself of these elements, the prudent consumer is left with no choice but to assume every dealership is suspect until it has demonstrated it can be trusted. Put another way, if you see flags in front of a dealership, color them red until proven otherwise.

In this environment your two best defenses are, first, knowing where the abuses occur and how to prevent them, and second, finding a reputable dealer. Of the two, hooking up with a reputable dealer worthy of your trust is essential. Hence this cardinal rule:

Finding a reputable dealer is as important as the decision on which house you buy.
To which should be added:
Buy from a reputable dealer close to home.

Purchasing from a dealership closer to where your home will be sited (within an hour's drive at the outside is a good rule of thumb) ensures that you will have access to prompt warranty service, something you should require of your dealer.

By the time you're ready to check out a dealer's reputation, you will most likely also be looking at homes at various dealerships and narrowing down your preferences. And since you will need to ask important questions on both counts, this is the right time to bring into the picture your personal advocate (described in Chapter 4) if you are the least bit shy about making pointed inquiries.

What follows are questions, recommendations, tactics, litmus tests and things to look for when checking out a dealership. There is no hard and fast sequence. Several of these are inquires you absolutely should make; others are optional. Together they provide more than you will need. You will most likely be able to make a confident assessment after following only a few of these recommendations.

As you make your inquiries, here are some guidelines to keep in mind:
- Don't come on like "Gangbusters." Take it easy, be polite. Enjoy shopping. Remember, the first salesperson you encounter may be the one you end up choosing. A show of mutual respect can work wonders. When it comes to asking hard questions, don't be confrontational. Preface your query by saying something like "Buying a home is a big decision for me and I'm looking for a comfort level

here. It would help me if I could ask you a few questions that fall in the category of due diligence."

- Trust your intuition, your feelings, especially your first impressions. They're rarely wrong.
- Don't go with a dealer who offers the lowest price but with whom you don't feel completely comfortable; stay with a reputable dealer who provides a high comfort level; you may pay a bit more but you will be a happy, satisfied buyer.
- Be reputable yourself. Don't lie. Not only is it unethical and unnecessary, but doing so undermines your own credibility. Good salespeople have a well-developed ear for false notes. The dealer you're looking for will be checking you out as well— mutual trust is very important.

Getting the local lowdown

It's quite amazing how much you can quickly learn about the dealers in your area by tapping into the local network of banks, credit unions, mortgage brokers, Realtors, and other professionals who know and do business with the dealerships. Chances are you have met one or two already. Start with a loan officer at a bank or credit union who handles manufactured home loans. Ask for an informal interview. People like being asked for advice.

Be prepared for them to avoid saying anything negative about any specific dealership, but ask the questions anyway. Most banks have internal "Do-not-do-business-with..." lists for their own staff. Conversely, many lenders will happily provide a list of recommended dealers. Take note of names missing from their lists—these could be the local "bad apples".

Realtors, too, will usually be wary of revealing dealerships with less than sterling reputations, but don't hesitate to ask questions, especially of the real estate agent with whom you may be working. Most every agent has a list of contractors and other specialists they recommend to their clients, and those they don't. In the interests of protecting your interests, he or she will usually find a way to hint to you which dealers have a poor track record.

Along the way, check out the ads you see in the local newspapers and other area media. Dealerships that proclaim "$1 over dealer invoice," "Zero Down," "Factory Clearance Sale," and similar come-ons are also revealing their identity as bottom feeders whose target audience is the uninformed, the unwary and the vulnerable. If you visit such dealers, anticipate being treated as such.

With any luck at all you'll come away from these interviews with a good idea of who's best and who to avoid.

Ask around. Talk to your friends, your associates at work and neighbors. Don't be shy to approach those traditional fountainheads of local knowledge within most any community: hairdressers and mixologists. Gossip is information. You may find yourself chatting with one or two recent home buyers to learn of their experiences and opinions.

Checking out a dealership

At some point you will begin to zero in on a particular dealership. Before you go too much farther, you should make a few phone calls, and/or online inquiries:

- Contact the Better Business Bureau and request a report on the dealership. You can also do this online by going to www.bbb.org and filling out an on-screen form. All you need is the dealership's name, city and state. The response will tell you how many complaints have been registered with the bureau during the previous three years, how may of those have been resolved, how many closed as disputed, how many remain unresolved and how many remain unanswered. The Bureau takes an especially dim view of businesses with unresolved and unanswered complaints. If its report concludes: "This company has an unsatisfactory record with the Bureau..." take your business elsewhere.

- Phone your state office of consumer affairs and ask them if they have had any complaints about the dealership or the manufacturer. In the case of a dealership owned by a chain or a manufacturer, you may find there have been no complaints against the dealership but other sales centers owned by the chain have been the subject of complaints (this is not a good sign).

- If the dealer is a licensed contractor, contact your state licensing board to confirm this and to ask if there have been any complaints, suspensions, revocations, judgements and/or claims against the dealer's bond. Often this information is available online.

- Check the online archives of the local paper for any news about the dealership. Many newspapers will allow you to search their archives online at no charge. You pay a modest $2 to $3 fee to download an article.

- Using an Internet search engine such as google.com, search for any Web pages mentioning the dealer's name. This is something of a shot in the dark but you never know what may turn up.

- Here is an optional inquiry, and may require a trip to the clerk's office of the superior court of your county courthouse: Call and ask the clerk on duty if there are any active court cases involving the dealership. If the dealership's name is on any active file, they can usually tell you, and will provide the case number. You can then visit the courthouse and read the file.

Questions you or your personal advocate should ask the dealer

How long has this dealership been in business? How long representing this line of homes?

You're looking for long-term stability, someone who will be around to help long after they've sold you your home.

How long have you been with this dealership? Your sales staff?

Again, you're looking for stability. If there appears to be a high turnover of sales staff, that could be a warning flag.

Can you provide the names and phone numbers of three or four satisfied customers who have purchased homes from this dealership in the past twelve months and who would be willing to talk to me?

If you get anything less than a firm "Yes" to this question, don't go any further with this dealer. Leave. Some industry observers downplay the importance of references, claiming that all dealers, even the sleazeballs, have a list of happy customers willing to talk. This view is mistaken. The key here is "within the past twelve months." You want to talk to customers who have been in their homes awhile, six months or more, and who are thus quite removed from the dealer's influence. See below for questions to ask references.

About your warranty service, do you have a local crew? Do they work under your supervision? Are they paid by you? Do you perform factory warranty work? Can you promptly authorize such service and repairs?

There are two warranties involved here: the dealership's warranty covering the setup and installation of your home, and the manufacturer's warranty covering the structure of the home itself, including electrical and plumbing systems, floor construction and the roof.

Every home will need some warranty work during the first year after move-in. A reputable dealer will have a capable local crew working under the dealer's supervision, promptly responding to service calls, under the dealer's warranty coverage. The dealer's crew may also perform factory warranty work, billing the manufacturer.

A less acceptable (many would say unacceptable) alternative, usually found with factory-owned dealerships, is combined dealer and factory warranty service performed by factory representatives. These are crews dispatched from central hubs out of the area who periodically visit your area when enough service calls accumulate to warrant a trip. You can wait weeks before someone shows up, during which your dealer, who has been paid and is off the hook, may sympathize but claim, " Sorry, it's out of my hands."

Unfortunately, factory service personnel, in general, have a mixed record of getting complete jobs done without having to come back at some future date to, "We didn't bring the right material." Sending crews out hundreds of miles on numerous calls ensures there will be a high hit-and-miss rate. Still, there are always exceptions, and one can find excellent warranty service using any of the above programs. Ultimately, the quality of service depends on the reputation of the manufacturer and the dealer.

Questions to ask "satisfied customers" the dealership provides as references:

In general, how would you rate your experience with the dealer?
What problems, if any, did you encounter, and were they resolved to your satisfaction?
How would you rate the warranty service from the dealer and the manufacturer?
Would you buy another manufactured home from this dealer?

Warning signs, encouraging signs

Very often the manipulative sales tactics, misrepresentations and abuses that have been described in previous chapters are preceded by behavior that an observant visitor can interpret as warning signs. Similarly, a sales staff with a reputable dealership will behave in ways that represent encouraging signs. But there are no hard and fast rules. This is where your judgement and intuition come into play—and nowhere more so than during your first visit to a dealership.

For example, as mentioned in the previous chapter, some dealerships follow what they believe is a tried-and-true sales system whereby, before you are permitted to look at lot

What to look for when visiting a dealership

Here is a list of warning signs and encouraging signs. Many have been previously mentioned. Others are described in later chapters. Some behaviors are major red flags, others suggest caution. Your own good judgement will be your best guide.

WARNING SIGNS	ENCOURAGING SIGNS
Within the first few minutes of your first visit aggressively questions you about your personal finances.	Does not ask about your financial situation (provided you explain the price range of the homes you're evaluating).
Asks a lot of questions to draw you out about your personal circumstances.	Refrains from asking a lot of questions about your personal circumstances.
Behaves in a controlling manner as though following a technique, a scripted pitch.	Relaxed and low-key in demeanor, professional but not programmed.
Won't let you inspect home models without a sales person present (and talking).	Happy to have you to look over the models on your own if you prefer, but may ask that you first sign the guest book.
Specifications, options, and base prices of the lot models are not posted anywhere.	An information sheet is posted in each home, showing the specifications, dealer options, base price, and base price plus options.
Won't quote a base price of a home "until we learn a bit more about you" or similar excuse.	Happy to give you the base price of any home without even knowing your last name.
Won't quote a lot model's base price, only the total price as is with dealer options.	Will provide a complete breakdown of pricing, with and without dealer options.
Pushes to get your social security number to run a credit check on you.	Does not push for your social security number, waits until you discuss your financial situation.
Seems in a hurry to get you to sign a purchase agreement, loan application, or other contract.	Is in no rush for a "write up." Waits until you're feeling comfortable with the product and the dealership.
At a certain early point, refuses to become any further involved in discussions without your signing a purchase agreement.	Same as above. Willing to continue discussions during repeated visits.
Refuses to provide promptly the names and phone numbers of references who purchased within the past 12 months. Or promises to provide you the references but never does.	Gives you an up-to-date list of at least three or four references and phone numbers of buyers who have agreed to talk.

WARNING SIGNS	ENCOURAGING SIGNS
Won't raise the possibility that you may qualify for a conventional home loan, pushes for financing through the dealership only.	Willing to recommend the names of area lenders, and advise you of any special programs to aid first time buyers.
Pushes you to purchase homeowner's insurance through the dealership.	Will invite you to purchase a policy through the dealership but won't push hard.
Urges you to buy expensive unnecessary additional insurance such as credit life insurance.	Will tell you that these coverages are also available through the dealership but won't push them. Will advise you which policies are not required as conditions of the loan.
Won't agree to give you a verbal estimate of the deal terms on a home purchase financed through dealer's lender, based on a credit score which you provide (without disclosing your social security number).	If you are regarded as a credible shopper trying to narrow down the choices (and not playing dealers against each other), will agree to give you a verbal estimate of deal terms based on your credit score, usually within 24 hours.
Has no warranty service people on staff.	Has one or more service people on staff.
Won't allow you to talk to the home installer (or stalls your request), and won't provide you a copy of the installation manual for review.	Happy to put you in touch with the installer or other members of the setup team, and provide you a copy of the installation manual for review.
Doesn't return phone calls, or call at a time promised; keeps changing his or her story; often claims the need to plead your case to the sales manager.	Returns phone calls and/or calls on time, provides timely updates, keeps promises, doesn't change the story, and doesn't need to plead your case to anyone.
Refuses to allow you to take home for study any contract or other document prior to signing.	Invites you to take home any contract for study before signing and recommends your attorney or other adviser call if any questions.

models, their sales people insist you sit down with them and experience their flip-book presentation, followed by a polite interrogation about your personal financial situation, all in the interest of "helping you find solutions to your housing needs."

Other dealerships may be more informal, but their salespeople will still ask you first to sit down with them for a folksy get-to-know-each-other discussion. Many dealerships prefer this approach because A., they believe a bit of personal interaction and presentation about their company will engender early trust and give them a leg up on the competition down the street, and B., they can weed out the financially hopeless who would never qualify for a loan, thereby preventing the sales staff from wasting time showing lot models.

These arguments are not without merit, but you as an informed shopper should not have to disclose any personal financial information about yourself during a first visit to any dealership nor should you have to sit through a presentation if you would rather not.

What you do need to do, however, is provide the sales person with the price range of the homes you're considering, so that he or she can point you to the right lot models.

For example, you should be able to say (politely, of course): "Look, I'm not here to buy today. I'm evaluating several homes in the fifty-five to seventy thousand dollar range and I just want to look at your lot models in that range and take notes. If you've got something that interests me, I'll be happy to come back another time and we can talk. If it's OK with you, I'll just sign your guest book and take your business card, and you let me look over the homes."

If your sales person is even half way on the ball, he or she will gladly comply, and you can take that response as an encouraging sign. On the other hand, if the sales person denies your request, either take your request to the sales manager, or leave.

One couple interviewed for this guide told of visiting a fancy factory-owned sales center and making a similar request of a young sales person who was about to launch into a 20-minute presentation. She apologized and said she really couldn't do that, then after a furtive glance about her to make sure no one was nearby, she lowered her voice and pleaded, "Please. If I let you go on to the lot without doing all this first, they'll fire me."

The couple took pity on the woman and invited her to continue, but afterwards excused themselves as quickly as possible and left, never to return.

Note: If each time you visit a dealership over a period of weeks you find yourself dealing with a different sales person, this could be a sign of a dealership in chaos with a high turnover of sales staff. This is not a good sign. There are others (see sidebar).

In the best of all possible worlds, news of your search for a reputable dealer will reach a trusted friend who knows someone they trust completely and who just happened to recently purchase a manufactured home from a wonderful, good, honest dealer. You will be put in touch with this person who will personally introduce you to the dealer—and you'll be on your way. Short of that happy coincidence, you will be searching on your own, at least in the beginning. But if you follow the guidelines in this chapter, you will be pleasantly surprised how many people will be willing to help you, and how quickly you will succeed.

Chapter 9

Selecting the Right Home

In the mid-1990s, *Consumer Reports*, the trusted periodical that provides ratings of just about every product that Americans buy, turned its attention to manufactured homes with the idea of rating the manufactures and their various makes and models. *CR*'s researchers soon discovered, however, that the task was impossible. Unlike the auto industry where, for example, a Chevrolet S-10 truck sold in Maine is the same as an S-10 California, the same model of, say, a Fleetwood double-wide sold in California could be quite different than the same model sold in New England. One reason is that the dealers routinely order lot models with options and floor plans suited for the weather and the preferences of their local customer base, both of which can vary widely from region to region. Another reason is that the quality of factory construction depends on the caliber of the plant manager and its work force, factors which can vary from plant to plant.

Consumer Reports settled for an overall, and still useful, assessment of manufactured homes, published in 1998. Among the article's assertions was the view that shopping for a manufactured home combines the headaches of buying a car with the complexities of buying a home. So true.

Rating the manufacturers and their brands

Although *CR* abandoned as unwieldy a consumer rating of specific makes and models of manufactured homes, what still seemed feasible, and potentially very useful, was a more generalized rating of the product lines built by the manufacturers, especially considering that most producers build homes for a fairly narrow segment of the market. Accordingly, not long after the publication of the first edition of this book, I began researching the backgrounds and products of all U.S. HUD-code builders—79 in all. The results of that undertaking was *The Grissim Ratings Guide to Manufactured Homes*, the first-ever survey and ratings assessment of every manufactured home builder and their brands. That guide, published in 2006, is designed to be used as an essential companion resource with this book (end of commercial).

The core measuring stick used in the *Ratings Guide* to determine a manufacture's construction rating is the same one provided in this chapter to help you evaluate the homes you are looking at—The manufactured home construction features and specifications comparison table. We'll get to that in a minute, but first, here's a quick overview of pertinent background facts:

• In the manufactured housing arena, the HUD code is the only constant. Every home must meet HUD's minimum safety standards in areas such as electrical wiring, plumbing and   structural integrity, but beyond that there is enormous variation in the product, especially the quality. The product spectrum ranges from bare-bones 14'x 56' single wides with phony walnut wood cabinet veneers and window "drapes" stapled the walls, all the way up to luxurious two-story, three- and four-section homes loaded with amenities and featuring first rate construction throughout.

•   Despite scores of brands and hundreds of models, ten manufacturers annually produce 80% of all the homes. Their quality varies considerably.

•   These ten companies together operate scores of production plants around the country, and, as mentioned above, the quality of homes can vary from plant to plant, even in the same region.

•   Dealers offer only a small selection of lot models (average five to ten) and usually try to display the low end and high end of product line with a couple of in-between examples. Unless a particular lot model meets your every requirement, you will most likely find yourself using one of the lot models as a starting point from which you will order a home similar to it with a floor plan and options that you specify.

•   Despite the claims and surface differences, in general the homes you will inspect in each price range are quite similar in many respects, including general appearance. Aside from design details and floor plan variations, the real difference will be in the quality of construction and prices. Still, appearances can be deceiving. Some builders use pool quality construction where it can't be seen; conversely, others build in high quality construction where it's not evident. New Era and Wick Building Systems, for example—are known for their "heavy sections," i.e., much more solidly built, and several tons heavier than comparable sections, attributes that are not visually apparent. These manufacturers are also more likely to offer two-story models.

•   In general, better built homes are found in the northern tier of the U.S. where harsh winter weather mandates stronger, higher quality construction. Below average construction quality abound in the southeast and the south central U.S. where Sun Belt weather is more forgiving of cheaper materials and lower quality construction, and where demographics suggest the need for affordable shelter more frequently trumps the desire for a home that has a site-built appearance and which will hold its value, let alone appreciate.

A quick look at the price range—and some tips

Chapter 10 provides methods for determining a fair sale price of a home, but as you begin your search, you should have an idea of the price ranges you will be encountering. The ranges below are for new homes (including lot models), not including the sales tax. Normally, a dealer's quote includes delivery and installation on piers or blocks, frequently the air conditioning, and sometimes skirting and steps or a small deck.

Again, keep in mind that these prices do not include land, permanent foundations, garages, fencing, concrete sidewalks, landscaping and utilities hookup—all things that are included in the turn-key price of a new site-built home—or a manufactured home—in a planned subdivision.

The dividing line between ranges is not carved in stone—a $64,000 price tag may be a mid-range number in one region but regarded as high-end in another.

Low-Range
$19,000 to $44,000
Average: $31,000

Your $19,000 will buy you a stripped down 12'x 50' single-wide with a lot of plastic fixtures, barely acceptable construction and the aforementioned stapled drapes. You could probably kick you way out of it, but it will be a basic HUD-code dwelling that with TLC and good maintenance will be a decent serviceable home. This model will most likely not appreciate in value, and you would have a hard time finding one for sale (or to order) outside the less prosperous regions of the country, but it's an affordable home and that's nothing to sneeze at.

Actually, there are a few small manufacturers at the wild and truly low end of the market who are producing single-wide housing for around $10,000 to $12,000. **Tip**: If you have that amount in cash, you can find some excellent bargains in used and repossessed single- and double-wide homes that originally sold for two and three times that amount.

The $31,000 average price will buy either a reasonably good quality 14'x 70' single-wide or a small (1,080 square feet) double-wide. Higher quality single-wides are available in the $36,000-$42,000 range but increasingly home buyers are opting to buy small double-wides offered in the same price range. Pushing the envelope in the single-wide category are 18'x 80' behemoths with more than 1,400 square feet—popular in Texas, where there's lots of room for them.

Mid-Range
$45,000 to $75,000
Average: $60,000

By far the most homes are sold in this range. An entry-level double-wide, 28' x 44', with features comparable to a site-built starter home commonly offered in a new subdivision (i.e. 1200 square feet, painted and textured walls, double-pane windows, composite shingle roof, residential-size doors and an appliance package) runs between $50,000 and $70,000. The upper end of this range would be represented by an 1800 square foot double-wide with three bedrooms, two baths with a few options such as a sliding glass door, a larger master bathroom, skylights and an upgraded carpet.

High-Range
$75,000 and up
Average: $85,000

High-end triple-wides can top out at $186,000 or more, but most homes in this category are in the $80,000 to $95,000 range, mostly double-wides, characterized by top-grade components, quality construction and interior finish work, lots of options (including skylights, extra windows, and tile trim on kitchen counters) and upgrades on carpeting and appliances.

Tips before you begin shopping

According to the Manufactured Housing Institute, based on all manufactured homes sold in 2005, the average sale price was $63,000 (including typical installation cost) for a 1,500-square-foot home, at a cost of $42 per square foot.

Before you put on your shopping shoes, here are a few tips:

1. Buy the highest quality home you can afford. There are a lot of tacky boxes out there wearing the manufacturer's red labels certifying they're in HUD compliance, which they are. Yes, you'll pay more to move up to higher quality, but not that much more

2. Keep in mind that the prices you will see don't include sales tax. As discussed in Chapter 4, if you budget, for example, $60,000 for a home purchase and your state's sales tax rate is 5%, the maximum price tag you can actually afford is $57,000. See the section Calculating your buying power in chapter 4. **Note**: You also pay sales tax, in effect, when you buy a new site-built home; the builder, who paid the sales tax on the materials, passes that tax on to you by including it in the sale price.

*3. If you have the time, attend a trade show where you can inspect many home models and pick up a lot of useful informatio*n. Most any local dealer will know when and where the next show is. In some regions, home models are also exhibited at state fairs. Many states also have a manufacturer's association (see appendix) that keeps a calendar of upcoming events and will be happy to provide details.

Checking out the lot models

Let's assume you've done your research, qualified for a land-home deal, nailed down a home site and calculated you can afford a home in the mid-range with several options. You're also prepared to shop defensively and may have with you your personal advocate. Make a day of it (or a weekend) and visit several dealerships. In fact, promise yourself you will. Don't get bogged down. Enjoy yourself. After all, you're looking at candidates for your future happy home. Get a feel for what's out there, collect brochures, especially the single page descriptions of the specifications ("spec sheets") of the lot models you examine. Collect business cards, too, so that you will have a sales contact with each dealership. **Note**: If any dealership balks at letting you look at their lot models without your first sitting through a presentation and/or a "pre-qualifying interview" or similar tactic to extract your social security number for a credit rating, say "No, thanks," and leave.

Three things to do as you look over each lot model:

1.   How does it smell as you first walk in? In contrast to the mildly intoxicating "new car smell" that we all know and love, some cheaper manufactured homes can smell of chemicals, including formaldehyde, widely used in all kinds of adhesives and bonding agents: carpeting, laminated counters, interior veneers and joinery. The phenomenon is called outgassing; it happens in site-built homes as well, but because manufactured homes are built in a few days (instead of a few months), the odor is more prominent.

You can often detect at least trace amounts of this distinctive odor in all homes; it will disappear over several months as the home "cures," but here's an unscientific rule of thumb (or nose): The cheaper the home construction, the greater the smell (low grade carpeting is a common odor source). Don't be misled by the explanation that the home is so magnificently air-tight that some residual odors remain in the absence of ventilation. This is only partly true. The nose knows. Another indicator: If musty or mildew-y smells are present, go on high alert. Also, if air fresheners are in the home, be cautious and inquisitive.

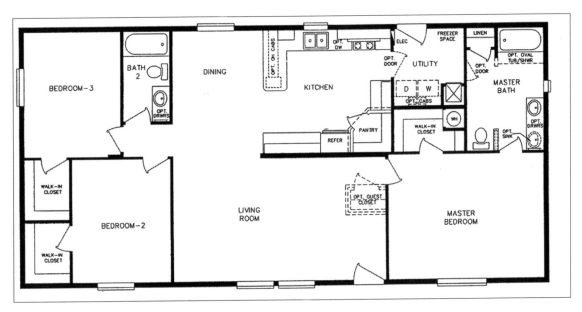

Floor Plans—the good, the bad and the point of departure

You will quickly get a feel for floor plans after looking at a few lot models. Here are two floor plans for a 3 bedroom, 2 bath, 1500 sq. ft. home. The plan above is all perpendicular walls and a boxy layout that cuts off sight-lines, making for a cramped feeling. The model below features several diagonal interior walls, angled kitchen counters, and open sight lines that give a much more spacious, inviting feeling. Consider any floor plan merely a point of departure for your own design ideas. You can move or add sliding glass doors, skylights, and windows, even flip the entire floor plan so the master bedroom is on the left, instead of the right. Some builders, Palm Harbor, for one, will try to make whatever floor plan you come up with, even if it's not on their model list. True, there is only so much one can do with a rectangular box, but it's quite amazing how much designers have been able to achieve. The irony is the HUD code does not prevent builders from designing less boxy homes identical to site-built dwellings. A few are starting to move in that direction but the entrenched attitudes of the street dealers need to change before real change will come. See Afterword.

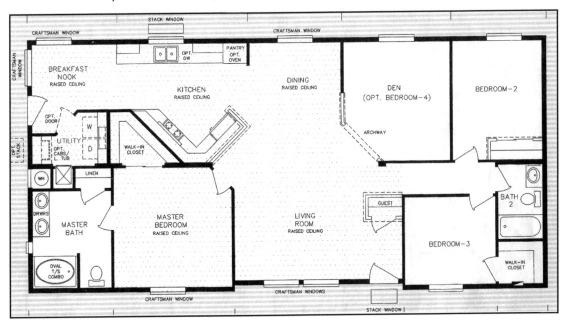

2.   Look for the manufacturer's information label (formerly known as the Data Plate) that is required to be posted in every home. Ask to see it if you can't find it. It is usually found on the inside of one of the utility room cabinets, on the inside of the home's circuit breaker panel or inside a bedroom closet. The label will tell you the factory of origin, the date the home was made, relevant information about appliances, heating, water heater capacity, etc. and the HUD wind-zone and snow-load zone for which the home was designed. The information should also give you a good idea how long the model has been sitting on the lot.

Note: The law allows lot model homes that have never been sold to be advertised and sold as "new" even though they may be several years old at the time of sale. Lot models that have not been properly blocked and sealed, or stored properly on a lot, can have significant problems when reinstalled on a home buyer's site.

3.   Look for a spec sheet listing the home's base price, list of options on this model, and the total price with options. Usually this will be found taped to the refrigerator or a kitchen counter. If you don't find one, ask for the numbers. If the salesperson stalls or becomes evasive, consider it a red flag, and move on to another dealership. A few states require the posting of a Manufacturer's Suggested Retail Price, which can give you a lot of details.

There's a lot you can tell right away about any home you walk into, and there is no need to conduct a close inspection until you have narrowed the field of candidates.

Taking a close look: the construction features & comparison table

Once you've completed your first foray into the world of MH lots models and developed a feel for things, you're ready to take a close critical look at the models that interest you.

First, take a few minutes to study the exploded diagram on the next page and the three-page construction features and specifications comparison table that follows. The table describes not only the principal construction features and specifications involved in the production a home (I've chosen 56 in all), but presents them within a one-to-ten scale representing their comparative quality. Granted, it appears a bit overwhelming at first, but with the help of the accompanying notes and the glossary of common terms, you'll quickly become comfortable, even downright conversant.

The table serves two main purposes:

1. You can take the list of features and specs of a home you are considering and see where they line up in the table, thus enabling you to arrive at your own construction rating for that particular model, independent of what a sales center may claim.

2. You can see how construction features are measured, enabling you to ask knowledgeable questions. For example, if a sales person says a home has an "upgrade carpet and pad," you can ask "How many ounces?" for the carpet, and "How many pounds?" for the pad, and learn precisely how much of an "upgrade" you're dealing with.

 This table is also reproduced in the companion resource to this book, *The Grissim Ratings Guide to Manufactured Homes.* There, it serves a third purpose: Using a manufacturer's construction rating—say, for example, 7—you can examine the features and specs in the table that fall beneath that number to get a good idea of what likely goes into that builder's homes.

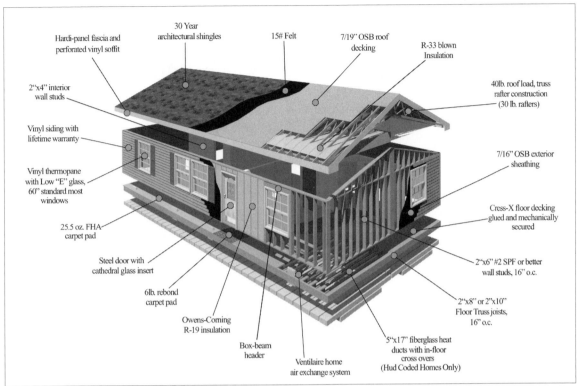

This cutaway is of Patriot Homes' Heritage American model, a well-built higher end home that retails in the low 70s. Shown are the principal construction components of a factory built home. This model features a number of desirable upgrades such as 30 year architectural shingles, Low E thermopane windows and 2"x6" exterior wall studs 16" on center. Illustration courtesy of Patriot Homes

A few notes on the construction table:

In my opinion, some specifications and features are indicative of below average or poor construction. These include:

- electrical outlet boxes attached to walls with wings or clips instead of nailed to studs
- carpet attached to floor w/ staples instead of tackless strips
- single pane windows
- 2"x 4" exterior wall studs
- 2"x 3" interior wall studs 24" On Center
- 5/16" wallboard

In some cases, determining the dividing lines between quality rankings in the table— average versus above average, for example, is more art than science, and you may have your own opinion, but the goal here is to provide you with a useful tool to help you quickly get up to speed on any MH builder in a matter of minutes and to enable meaningful comparisons of different manufacturers and their products.

The notes that begin on page 135 are pegged sequentially to the 56 construction criteria and contain additional commentary and recommendations. Many deal with issues that an informed home shopper should consider before making a purchase decision.

Manufactured home construction features & specifications comparison table

See accompanying notes to this table for details, comments — Item	Mainstream site-built home and some high end manufactured homes		Manufactured home mid-range to high-end			Manufactured home low mid-range	Manufactured home entry level & low end		
	10 EXCELLENT	9 SUPERIOR	8 VERY GOOD	7 GOOD	6 ABOVE AVERAGE	5 AVERAGE	4 BELOW AVERAGE	3 POOR	1–2 VERY POOR
Aesthetics: Exterior	Attractive, indistinguishable from site-built		Attractive, comparable to site-built if w/ steeper roof slope, attached garage, etc.			Unmistakably identifiable as a manufactured home/"mobile home"			
Aesthetics: Interior	Excellent floor plan, pleasing sight-lines, high ceilings, superior fit & finish		Good floor plan with design accents (plant shelves, alcoves), good fit & finish			Utilitarian floor plan, small rooms, low ceilings, poor fit & finish			
Customization	Great flexibility, many options/upgrades. Can build to customer's plan, design engineers on staff		Quite flexible: flip/mirror plans, move walls, windows, increase roof pitch			Some, but limited	None		
Roof pitch (or slope)	4/12 to 12/12		4/12 to 7/12 (3/12 for triples)			3/12		2/12 only	
Roof sheathing	1/2" plywood or OSB					3/8" plywood or OSB			
Shingles/ roof under-layer	30-year architectural shingles 15 lb. felt			25-year shingles, 15 lb. felt		20-yr. shingles, 15 lb. felt	20-yr. shingles, 15 lb. felt (roofs less than 3/12 require 30 lb. or 2 layers of 15 lb. felt		
Eaves and extension		All sides, 12" to 16"		Front and ends, 8"-12"		Front /back, 8"	Front and back, 3"	None	
Roof insulation R-value		R-38 or more			R-33		R-21		R-7
Sidewall insulation R-value		R-19 or more			R-13		R-11		R-7
Exterior wall studs		2"x 6" 16" O.C.				2"x 4" 16" O.C.		2"x 4" 16" O.C.	
Exterior sheathing		7/16" Plywood			7/16" OSB			3/8" Plywood	
Exterior siding	Fiber-cement siding, painted e.g.,, HardiPanel, HardiPlank			Quality vinyl siding (foam backed)		Economy grade vinyl siding or 4'x8' sheets of 1/2" dia. hardboard, manufactured wood or particleboard			
Exterior sidewall height	9-10 feet			8 feet		7-1/2 feet		7 feet	
Exterior house wrap	Yes (e.g. with Tyvek or equivalent)						No		
Interior wall studs	2"x 4" 16" O.C.			2"x 3" 16" O.C.		2"x 3" 16" O.C.		2"x 3" 24" O.C.	
Drywall or wallboard to-stud fastening	Screwed and glued			Nailed and glued		Stapled and glued			
Drywall or wallboard thickness/finish	1/2", bull nose corners tape & textured or tape & painted			1/2", square corners, taped & textured/primed/painted		3/8" vinyl covered wallboard with battens at seams, corners		5/16" vinyl on wallboard	
Molding, interior finish	All molding, baseboards, jambs, sills, casings set, nailed, caulked, painted		Pre-finished/ pre-painted wood used	Pre-finished wood, set and primed, customer to paint		Vinyl covered wood molding	Vinyl on particleboard	Paper on particleboard	

Left-side section groupings: Roof system · Exterior walls, siding · Interior walls

	Mainstream site-built home and some high end manufactured homes		Manufactured home mid- to high-end			Manufactured home low mid-range	Manufactured home entry level & low end		
See accompanying notes to this table for details, comments — Item	10 EXCELLENT	9 SUPERIOR	8 VERY GOOD	7 GOOD	6 ABOVE AVERAGE	5 AVERAGE	4 BELOW AVERAGE	3 POOR	1–2 VERY POOR
Floor decking	1-1/8"' plywood	3/4" Plywood or OSB	5/8" plywood	3/4" Cresdek or Novadek		5/8" Cresdek or Novadek	3/4" generic particleboard	5/8" generic particleboard	
Floor insulation R-rating		R-33		R-21			R-11		R-7
Decking fastened by	Glued, screwed			Glued and nailed			Glued and stapled		
Floor joists		2"x 8" 16" O.C. (2"x 6" OK for single-sections)				2"x 6" 16" O.C.		2"x 6" greater than 16" O.C.	
Carpet	32-50 oz.		26-31 oz.		22-25 oz.	19-21 oz.	16-18 oz.	15 oz.	15 oz. or less
Fastened to floor		Installed over cushion w/ tackless strip using power stretcher or knee kicker				tackless strip and staples	Stapled only	Stapled, glued	
Carpet pad		6 lbs/cu.ft, 1/2" dia. bonded polyurethane ("rebond")					5 lb. rebond, 7/16" dia		3/8" foam
Vinyl covering		High quality tiles or rolled vinyl w/urethane wear layer		Heavy, quality rolled lineoleum with no seams, urethane wear layer		Middle grade lino	Economy grade vinyl lino		
Front door		36"x 80" 6-panel steel front door (insulated core) w/ dead bolt lock and peep hole				36x80 steel			
Rear door (to outside)		36"x80" steel, dead bolt, dual glaze window (doors to attached garages are 32" wide)		36"x80," dead bolt		steel, 32"x74," x 76" or x 78"	Aluminum, 32" x74, 32"x 76" or 32" x 78"	Aluminum, 34" or 35" x 74," 76" or 78"	
Matching key locks			Yes				No		
Interior doors	30"x 80" solid wood, 6-panel	30"x 80" wood frame door, hollow core		30"x 80" paneled, hollow core		28"x 80" plain luan, foam core	26"x74" plain luan, hollow core		
Interior door hinges		3, full mortised: both door and casing				2, mortised to door or casing		2, surface mounted	
Windows	White vinyl vacuum sealed dual glazed w/ low-E,		White vinyl, dual glazed Low-E			White vinyl, dual glazed		Single pane, aluminum frame, w/ self-storing storm windows	
Water piping	Copper				Pex or CPVC				
Pipe fittings	Copper/brass			Brass				Plastic	
Water shut-off valves		At all fixtures					Main water shut-off only		
Outside faucets	2				1				None
Energy Star certified			Yes						No

Floors, floor covering

Doors and windows

See accompanying notes to this table for details, comments — Item	Mainstream site-built home and some high end manufactured homes		Manufactured home mid-range to high-end			Manufactured home low mid-range	Manufactured home entry level & low end		
	10 EXCELLENT	9 SUPERIOR	8 VERY GOOD	7 GOOD	6 ABOVE AVERAGE	5 AVERAGE	4 BELOW AVERAGE	3 POOR	1–2 VERY POOR
HVAC — HVAC register locations	Cool climate: perimeter (in toe kicks in kitchen/bath(s)/ Hot climates: ceiling						Middle of floor		
HVAC ducting	Sheet metal, caulked w/ mastic, wrapped w/ fiberglass insulation					Fiberglass, wrapped	Fiberglass, taped only		
Air return system	Through dedicated return air floor ducts		Through wall vents, ceiling vents on both sides of wall connected to attic ducting, openings beneath interior doors				Openings under doors only		
Electrical outlet boxes			Nailed to studs				Attached to wall w/ wings, clips, screws		
GFI outlets	Additional GFI outlets				20 amp outlets in kitchen and bathrooms - required by HUD code				
Kitchen — Phone/cable/Internet	Yes, Cat. 5 ready (home networking, security alarm)		2-3 phone jacks, cable ready boxes, customer or contractor to wire			No			
Kitchen faucet	High quality brand name metal single lever			Single lever (metal)	Dual knob (metal) with sprayer	Dual knob (metal)	Dual knob (metal works, plastic shell)		
Kitchen sink	High quality cast iron, 8" deep	Corian 8" integrated with counter top	Full size, stainless or white enamel on metal (porcelain), 7" deep			Stainless 6" deep	Smaller, non-standard size, acrylic, 6" deep		
Counter tops/edging	25" wide, granite, w/ 4" hand-laid tile backsplash	25" wide, Corian, 4" ceramic tile backsplash	25" wide, laminate, edged w/ wood/tile, 4" ceramic backsplash	25" wide, Formica, beveled edge, ceramic or rounded edge, 2" tile backsplash		25" wide, Formica or post-form, self edged	24" wide, Formica, self-edged w/Formica backsplash (requires smaller, non-standard sink)		
Cabinets	Full-size: base ht.. 36" (31" overhead ht.), stained wood, raised stiles, quality knobs or finger pulls, Melamine interiors, hidden hinges.		Full-size, stained hardwood face, raised stiles, plywood walls, hidden hinges			Full-size, MDF, vinyl-wrapped stiles, open hinges	Smaller size, MDF, no lining, exposed hinges, economy knobs, no toe-kicks, no bottom shelf in base cabinets		
Cabinet shelves	1/2" Melamine or equiv., fully adjustable				1/2" MDF adjustable		1/2" particleboard, not adjustable		
Drawers	Hardwood face, plywood, glued/screwed, 18" deep, 2-1/2" & 4"-plus ht.		Hardwood face, plywood, stapled/glued, 16" deep, 2-1/2" & 4"-plus ht.				Vinyl-wrapped face, 12" deep, stapled/glued, face serves as front of box		
Drawer guides/rollers	Metal/metal, full suspension		Metal/plastic, full extension		Metal/plastic w/ drawer stop		Plastic/plastic w/ drawer stop		
Bath — Bath sinks/countertops	Vitreous china/ Corian		Vitreous china/ laminate w/ ceramic edging or both made of cultured marble			Acrylic, Formica self-edged			
Vanity sink(s) overflow			Yes				No		
Master bath tub/shower	60" 1-piece fiberglass			48" 1-piece fiberglass			48" 2-pc. plastic		54" 1-piece tub/shower
Toilets	Vitreous china, elongated			Vitreous china, round			Acrylic, round		
Water heater	50 gal.			40 gal.			30 gal.		20 gal. elec.
Refrigerator	20-25 cu. ft. FF, side-by-side w/ water/ice		18-22 cu. ft. FF, side-by-side w/ water/ice			16-17 cu. ft.	14 cu. ft. over-under, auto-defrost		
Plumbed for ice maker/water			Yes				No		

Notes on the construction features & specifications comparison table

Aesthetics: Exterior & Interior Curb appeal is an important consideration for many home buyers, including those who would prefer their new home not have the appearance of a conventional manufactured home. MH interiors can be very attractive, fully comparable to site-built.

Roof pitch. Measured by the number of vertical inches a roof pitch rises for every 12 inches of horizontal distance. Example: a 3/12 roof rises three inches for every lateral foot. A 4/12 pitch is regarded as a minimum pitch for a residential appearance to a site-built home. A 5/12 roof will usually be hinged. Higher pitched roofs will all be hinged. Note: A number of insurance companies, nervous about writing homeowner's policies on poorly constructed "mobile homes" that are vulnerable to severe weather, refuse to insure manufactured homes unless they have at least a 4/12 roof pitch. That's discriminatory, of course, but their thinking is the vast majority of homes with 3/12 roof pitches or less are of average or less construction quality. Statistically, probably true.

Roof shingles. Commonly, 25-year fiberglass or composition shingles with a Class A fire protection rating. If severe weather and high winds are a concern, you may wish to upgrade to 30-year quality for around $2,000.

Eaves. Ideally, at least a 12-inch overhang on the front and all sides (16 inches is better, although if the home will be sited in a MH community where homes are cheek by jowl, it may exceed width limitations). Alternatively: a six inch overhang to which can be added a five inch rain gutter. This is one of the unattractive quirks of most manufactured homes: typically the home's rear (or backyard side) roof has no eves. Because most highway transportation laws include the roof overhang in the allowable width, manufacturers eliminate the rear roof overhang to avoid having otherwise to reduce the floor area of the interior living space. **Note**: many manufacturers now offer rear eves as an option, but ship them "loose" (uninstalled) for the setup crew to complete on-site.

Front and rear roof lines, same house. The absence of rear eves really detracts from a home's appearance. Consider spending several hundred dollars more to have them put on when the home is built at the factory (or shipped loose for later installation).

Roof insulation The higher the R number, the greater the insulation. R-values will vary depending on the region of the U.S. The legal minimum for HUD code is R-14/7/7 (for roof/ceiling, walls and floor. As a general rule, higher R values mean less energy is needed to heat and cool a home. Most manufacturers insulate the roof by blowing in cellulose; others use fiberglass battens identical to those in the sidewalls. Both work fine.

Exterior sheathing This may not be needed if the ext. siding is HardiPanel or some other 4'x8' wood or cement-fiber product.

Siding. Exterior siding such as horizontal wood, hardboard or vinyl siding – or stucco-type surfaces—over an underlayerment, or sheathing, for example, 3/8-inch OSB (short for oriented strand board, a strong composite material). Alternatively, fiber-cement exterior side board. **Note**: Vinyl installed over OSB sheathing is an excellent exterior siding. Extremely popular in the Midwest, Northeast and Mid-Atlantic areas, even on high-end stick-built homes. Culturally, vinyl has yet to win the hearts of buyers in the West or Southwest. But the odds are it will.

Sidewall insulation R-value R-19 is insulation designed for a 2x6 sidewall. R-13 is a high-density insulation designed for 2x4 exterior sidewalls.

Exterior wall studs 2"x 6" 16" O.C. is the standard, for two reasons: It allows for more insulation (yielding lower energy costs) and adds needed strength to the home during transit (minimizing cracks in dry walls, for example). In my view, 2"x4" exterior wall studs is a strong indicator of below average construction quality.

Exterior sidewall height A site-built home will almost always have a minimum 8' side wall height, and usually a flat ceiling. Nine feet is becoming ubiquitous with site-built homes in many regions.

Interior wall studs. Some manufacturers argue that 2" x 3" on 16" centers is fine for non-load-bearing interior walls. Probably true, but if on 24" centers, that merits a poor construction rating.

Interior walls. Recommended: all walls covered with sheet rock at least 1/2-inch thick, taped, textured, and painted. Rounded sheet rock corners. Avoid the cheap alternative: 3/8-inch thick sheet rock with a vinyl covering that provides a prefinished surface (although families with small children may appreciate the washability of this wall type).

Dry wall or wallboard thickness/finish Also called gypsum (mostly in the east). If it's covered with vinyl or wall paper, it's called wallboard. Paper is no longer common. Hence vinyl on wallboard, or VOG. A home may also be delivered with its dry wall "blue nailed," i.e., unfinished and ready for the home buyer to finish, paint and/or texture.

Molding, interior finish There is far more emphasis on crown moldings, casing, and baseboard moldings in the Eastern US than the West, reflecting regional tastes. For example, in the West, crown molding (where the sidewall meets the ceiling) is rarely found.

Floor decking. Subfloor decking of plywood, at least 5/8-inch thick or better is fine, but 3/4" is better. Several brands of specially treated particle board are very good: Cresdeck, NovaDeck and Willcraft (3/4-inch thick). Decking comes in very large sizes which minimizes the amount of floor seams. Good quality particle board treated with waterproof glues is OK. Avoid particle board treated with water-soluble glues; when wet it crumbles, peels and contracts. All particle board floors need extra care to prevent water damage.

Floor joists Under "below average," "greater than 16" O.C." is a bit over 19 inches.

Carpets If possible avoid anything less than 16 oz. Much better: 31 oz. or better, lasts much longer. Low end carpeting carries disparaging nicknames such as Dog hair, fuzzy-side up and the ultra-cheap, Essence of carpet, not much more than a beach towel.

Carpet pad It's very important to have a good carpet pad. Get one with at least a 6 lb. rating (about 1/2" thick). Avoid 3/8" foam padding. It wears quickly, turning into granules, a huge irritation for housekeepers.

Carpet, how fastened to floor Most plants in the Eastern US do a full installation of carpets; in

The living room of this low-ceiling home is vastly improved by the triple skylight and the larger craftsman style windows. These options are not that expensive in the context of the total home cost. Tip: Ceiling fans are also worth getting, but you can often save by having the factory install only the wiring (connected to a wall switch). After you move in, buy your own fan and install it yourself. MHI photo

the West carpeting is installed in single-wides, but shipped loose in sectionals, for a subcontractor to install. A carpet stapled to the floor is a big tip off of less than average construction.

Vinyl covering Whether as hand-laid tiles or "rolled goods," vinyl (or "lino") can be an amazingly high quality product. The difference is the wear layer. The thicker that layer, the higher the quality. Consider available linoleum upgrades. Linoleum is often used for the entry foyer. Suggestion: upgrade to tile in that area. Unlike carpet, which is easy to pull up and replace, replacing vinyl is both difficult and expensive.

Doors. Look for white, insulated, vinyl-clad steel, 36" x 80" entry door. If the home has a glass sliding door on the rear side, it should be 72" x 80" with dual glass panes and a screen. Interior doors should be 80 inches high. Make sure the door stops will prevent a door knob from punching through a wall. Watch out for bedroom doors that are only 28 inches wide, instead of the house standard 30 inches. They can make moving furniture very difficult. Get mortised hinges that allow you to remove the door by pulling the hinge pin. Interior doors: the industry standard for site-built homes is a 30x80 wood frame door, hollow core.

Windows The phrases dual glazed and thermal pane (also thermo-pane) are synonymous. Recommended: dual glaze vinyl-clad windows throughout. Avoid single pane, aluminum frame "interior storm windows." The aluminum frame "sweats, " can crack at joints, and the single pane glass offers poor insulation.

Skylights. These can be wonderful optional (at approx. $350-$400 each) that add value and ambiance to a home (see photo above) but be aware that in hot sunny climates like the Southwest, they also let in heat-producing sunlight that increases air-conditioning costs.

Plumbing/piping. Copper is considered best and is standard with site-built homes, but PEX and CPVC (both are types of flexible pipe) are also excellent, proven, and virtually equivalent in quality and performance. Be sure to have shut-off valves at each fixture (e. g., under the kitchen sink, guest sink, toilets, etc.). Get at least a 40-gallon water heater. Depending on your needs, you may want to consider upgrading to a 50-gallon water heater. Toilets: white China, 1.6 gallons per flush. All fittings and valves of metal, not plastic.

The kitchen area of this double wide shows an excellent use of space: the range is built into the center island, the breakfast nook is inviting, while in the right corner a built-in desk with a computer can double as a child's homework table. A skylight (not visible) adds to a spacious airy feel to the room. (MHI photo)

Outside faucets Make sure you have at least one if you plan on having porch plants.

Energy Star certified This is a big deal and highly recommended. Cost: $1,000-$1,500 for upgraded windows, insulation, etc. Homes with this certification meet the Environmental Protection Agency's standards for homes using at least 30% less energy to heat and cool than the older standard. This efficiency is achieved through better insulation, low-E thermopane windows, tighter construction and more efficient heating/cooling systems and ducting. In addition to significantly reducing your energy bills, Energy Star certification adds resale value to your home. Bonus: some utility districts offer up to a $1,000 rebate for certifying your home.

Heating, ventilation and air conditioning (called HVAC). All manufactured homes have a central heating and ventilation system (usually gas or electric) and the furnaces contain a cavity to accommodate a refrigerant coil that is connected to an on-site installed condenser unit to provide air conditioning. If air conditioning is a must for your region, be aware that it is considered an add-on option that can cost $1,600 and up, and will be installed by a subcontractor. Make sure the manufacturer has included the "air conditioning ready" option. Alternative cooling systems such as evaporative coolers (also known as swamp coolers) are popular in the regions of very dry, hot weather. In other regions, the Northwest, for example, heat pumps are gaining in popularity. Consult your dealer.

Note: Ventilation of the entire home is extremely important, and the HUD code ensures there are systems that help get rid of stale, moist inside air. You will find range hoods that exhaust to the exterior, power fans in the baths, an air-injection system in the furnace, and open-able windows in all bathrooms.

HVAC register locations Registers in the middle of the floor are a hallmark of manufactured homes built to average (or less) construction quality. **Floor registers**. These should be located at the room perimeters or under toe kicks (vertically mounted) where people normally stand, e.g., to wash dishes. Air return vents should be over interior doors but manufacturers will often cut the interior doors a couple of inches short at the bottom to allow air flow. **Note**: In regions where cooling is the prime concern, some manufacturers offer ceiling ducts, better for dispersing cool air into a room.

HVAC ducting There is a third type of ducting: a round, flexible insulated duct made of a wire coil (for strength) and wrapped in plastic, widely used for crossover ducting between home sections. In smaller diameters, it's also used in attic areas for up-flow systems. All three types perform well (i.e. no leaks) if conscientiously assembled.

Air return system Dedicated return ducts are by far the best. Ceiling vents on either side of a room wall are less intrusive visually (Karsten does this).

Electrical outlet boxes If attached to walls, not nailed to the studs, this is a strong indicator of less than average/poor construction quality. It doesn't take too many yanks on the vacuum cleaner cord to eventually pull a wall-mounted outlet box out of the wall.

GFI outlets HUD code requires them over all drain boards, sinks, anywhere an electrical appliance could contact water, as a safety measure. Some high end builders will add them elsewhere, e.g., utility room.

Phone/cable/Internet High end homes may be pre-wired to allow a wide range of consumer electronics, including Internet, home entertainment and security alarm systems. Mid-range homes may have wall boxes with cable/wire tubes down to the crawl space, ready for wiring.

Kitchen. Many builders boast of a single-lever kitchen faucet, but these vary widely in quality. Be sure to check specifics, insist on metal workings, preferable a brand name such as Moen. Sink: which is best, stainless or white enameled metal sinks, is a matter of taste, but Palm Harbor's stainless sinks have a sound-deadening coating on the bottom, a welcome touch. Acrylic sinks are below average.

Stove: 30 inch free-standing gas or electric range and range hood that exhausts to the exterior. Optional: matching microwave above range hood. Refrigerator space to be plumbed for ice maker.

Kitchen counter tops A 24"-width counter top is indicative of low quality construction, often requiring a smaller non-standard sink that can't be replaced by any sold at home improvement stores.

Cabinets, hinges, fixtures. Nice but not gotta-have quality item: concealed cabinet and door hinges. Make sure all door knobs, drawer pulls and similar fittings are metal, not plastic painted to look like metal. Recommended: cabinet interiors should be fully finished (no visible fasteners or cleats). All overhead cabinets with adjustable shelves. As for cabinets, until recently, the rule was get at least base-grade hardwood (no printed or prefinished exteriors) but some cabinet-door and drawer-front makers have come up with really good prefinished products. Ask about availability; you could save $800 to $1,000.

Master bath tub/shower The 54" 1-piece tub/shower is notoriously inadequate as a tub. The drain is in the middle and the tub is so shallow and confining that one must sit with knees bent nearly to one's chin.

Plumbing. PEX or CPVC (both are types of flexible pipe) for the fresh water system, with a main shut-off valve and shut-off valves at each fixture (e. g., under the kitchen sink, guest sink, toilets, etc.). Standard ABS drain system (i.e., made of black plastic pipe, widely used), 40-gallon water heater. Depending on your needs, consider upgrading to a 50-gallon water heater. Toilets: white China. All fittings and valves of metal, not plastic.

Glossary of common terms in manufactured home construction

Architectural shingles An upgrade from the standard, flat 3-tab shingles, having a thicker looking, more three-dimensional appearance that adds to a home's curb appeal (and hides the fold line of a hinged roof that can sometimes be seen otherwise).

Auto-defrost A de-frost cycle on less-expensive refrigerators that needs to be manually selected to activate.

Batten strips Vinyl tape placed over the seams of vinyl on gypsum wallboard sheets, imprinted with the same decor pattern as the wallboard to disguise the seam.

Bull nose A rounded corner or edge, associated with a wall or counter top.

Cathedral ceilings Also called vaulted ceilings. Ceilings that slant up to the center ridge line, at roughly the same angle as the outside roof pitch, usually meeting at the ridge line in the center of the home.

Cape Cod A home with a steep roof (usually 8/12 or greater) and two or three dormer windows. With HUD code versions, typically the attic space is finished as a second story by the home buyer after move-in.

CPVC Chlorinated Polyvinyl Chloride, plastic piping approved for potable (drinkable) water, usually white in color. Can be connected with either threaded components or glued fitting

Cresdek The trade name of a brand of engineered particleboard, widely used as floor decking. See also, Novadek.

Corian The trade name of a high quality faux marble product. See cultured marble.

Cultured marble Also **cultured granite**, **cultured onyx**. A cast polymer product mixed with colorants to create "veining" and/or the appearance of genuine marble, granite or onyx, made with a high-gloss "gel coat" coating. The process yields an attractive, durable, rock-hard product, highly regarded.

Dormer, or dormer window A vertical window on a projecting structure built out from a sloped roof. See also Cape Cod.

Dry wall sheets of gypsum, usually 4'x8' in varying thicknesses coated with paper or vinyl and attached to wall studs and/or ceilings. Also called wall board when covered with patterned vinyl or paper.

Double-wide A two-section home

FF Frost-free. Self-defrosting refrigerators, typical of better quality models.

Floor Industry jargon for a section. A double-wide consists of two floors. Factory output is measured by the number of floors produced per day or week.

Floor joists structural members placed perpendicular at regular intervals between floor beams to form the floor structure

Full-finish Dry wall that is taped, prepped, primed and given at least one coat of paint.

GFI – Ground fault interrupt. Special wall plug outlets, usually in wet areas such as kitchens and bathrooms, that are built to instantly shut off in the event of a short circuit, to prevent electrical shock. Required by the HUD-code.

Gypsum see Dry wall

Hardiplank, Hardipanel Trade names for James Hardie siding, made from fiber cement, in many patterns and finishes, well regarded.

HVAC Heating, ventilation, air conditioning.

In-line registers Floor registers that are located in the middle of the floor (instead of along the perimeter or ceiling), typical of average or less construction quality

Interior storm windows Also called **self-storing storm windows**. These economy panes fit on the inside edge of a window casing, held in place by clips. Found on low construction quality home.

Lavy Bathroom sink, also called a vanity sink

Low E glass Refers to low emittance. Window and skylight glass treated with a microscopically thin, invisible metal oxide significantly cut down on heat (or cooling) loss.

MDF Medium density fiberboard. An economy quality fiberboard used for cabinet doors and shelving.

Melamine The trade name of a high quality, high density fiberboard, usually painted white on both sides, widely used for cabinetry shelving.

Mortise A shallow indentation made in a door or window casing (and on the edge of a door or window) into which a hinge plate can be placed and secured so that it is flush with the surface. Hinges are said to be mortised.

Novadek The trade name of a brand of engineered particleboard, widely used as floor decking. See also, Cresdek.

O.C. On center. Used to describe the intervals between studs. 16" O.C. means the centers of the wall studs are placed at 16" intervals in the wall.

OSB Oriented strand board. a very strong composite material comprised of thin strands of wood bonded with a strong adhesive, highly regarded.

Perimeter heat Floor registers mounted on the perimeter of a room, either in the floor or the wall (in contrast to registers in the center line of the room)

PEX Cross-linked Polyethylene, a flexible tubing with crimped-band fittings, tat connects to metal pipes and other plumbing. Widely used, well-regarded.

Pod See Tag.

Proud seams Edges of dry wall panels that buckle outward slightly as a result of a slight torquing or bending of the wall, often during transport or from poor installation

Prow porch A covered porch on the gabled front end of a home extending across the entire width of the home, with the roof and porch extending out in a shallow angle similar to the prow (or bow) of a ship. Popular with mountain retreats.

PVC Polyvinyl Chloride, a plastic pipe (usually black) used for wastewater drain and septic systems. Can be connected with either threaded components or glued fittings.

Rebond A rug cushion comprised of bits of polyurethane glued together, i.e. re-bonded. Usually green and white in appearance. Widely used.

Roof pitch A measure of roof slope, the number of vertical inches the roof rises every 12 inches of horizontal length.

Sectionals Homes comprised of two or more sections, e.g., double-wide, triple-wide.

Self-edged A square, 90 degree edge on a counter top.

Single-section A single section home, same as single-wide, also SW

Single-wide A single section home, also SW

Stiles Raised strips of wood used decoratively, usually on kitchen cabinets.

Studs Vertical lengths of wood spaced at intervals in a wall.

T&G Tongue and groove

T/T Taped and textured throughout

t/o Throughout

Tag Also called a pod. A small section, usually room- or porch-size, that is attached, or tagged, to a home to serve as a family room, den or other living area.

Toe-kick A recessed area abut two-inches deep at the base of counter and sink areas (typically kitchen and bath) that allows one to stand comfortably closer to the counter.

Turn-key A type of home sale transaction in which the seller, in this case the sales center, performs all the tasks associated with preparing the home for move-in—i.e., site preparation, permits, well, septic, utilities hook-up, home delivery, installation and trim out, garage and deck construction, landscaping—and then turns the door key over to the home buyer.

Vaulted ceiling See Cathedral ceiling.

Vanity sink A bathroom sink, also called a lavy.

Vinyl siding Exterior siding made of vinyl designed to look like wood lap siding or wood paneling, sometimes like cedar shingling. Popular in the Midwest/East, gaining a foothold in the West.

Vinyl-wrapped molding Molding (usually made of particleboard) wrapped with a vinyl cover printed with a wood grain pattern, typical of lower quality finish work.

Vitreous china Also called porcelain (which it isn't). The strong polished ceramic material widely used to cast toilets and sinks.

VOG Vinyl on gypsum, i.e., dry wall covered with a vinyl sheet, usually with a color and/or pattern. Also called wall board.

Wall board Dry wall/gypsum, usually 3/8" dia.) covered with a vinyl sheet. See VOG.

Narrowing the field: getting to apples-to-apples

Don't be concerned if the information packed into the preceding ten pages seems a bit boggling. There's certainly a lot in there, but as your home search continues you'll likely refer to that section regularly and soon will regard it as a handy reference tool.

One question that home shoppers face in the early going is "How can I determine which home is the best deal when I'm looking at different models and brands, and at several dealerships, and each has different options?" Indeed, the dilemma is like comparing apples to oranges.

Your task may be further complicated because, emotionally, you simply like one house more than the others. Trust that feeling, especially if you're in the hands of a reputable dealer. However, if you don't have a favorite at this point, your objective is to have before you at least two finalists, in the same price range, with similar specifications, options, and general features. Here's how:

1. Almost all manufacturers have a one-page handout for each home model series that lists most of the construction features included in the homes (they sometimes omit mention of features that are missing or below competitive standards). Place these sheets next to each other and compare the lists with each other and with this book's construction features comparison table. Not only will you easily spot any differences, including what may be missing, you'll be able to calculate a pretty accurate construction rating on a one-to-ten scale for each home model. What you're also doing is sifting through what appears to be apples

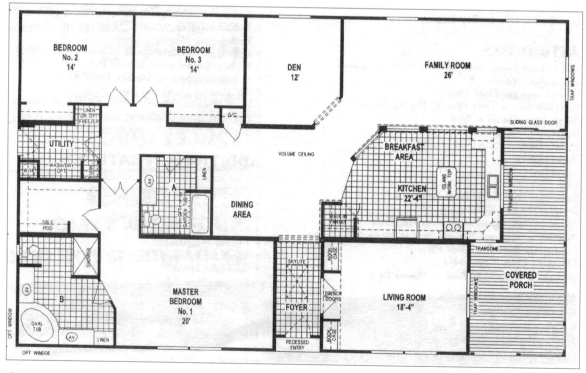

Floor plan of one of the Lexington series by Skyline. This 3 bedroom, 2 bath triple wide palace takes up 2,472 sq. ft. and features cathedral ceilings throughout, a large covered porch, and a recessed entry. Base price: $105,500, installed. To vacuum, plan on moving through two time zones.

and oranges to identify key features of interest in each model so that you can now compare as apples-to-apples.

2. Next, meet with the salesperson representing each home model and "spec" out the home—that is, calculate the actual final price each dealer would charge you for that home with the options and features you want. For example, you could specify a floor plan, then add a sliding glass door off the dining room, a skylight and a fireplace in the living room. You might upgrade the kitchen appliance package, select a larger master bath and upgrade the carpet.

Spec-ing out each home can easily take an hour or more, but the sales person should be happy to do so, and give you a complete breakdown in writing with the line item cost of each option. Be up front about what you're doing, and don't hesitate to assure him or her that if your consideration comes down to price, you will give the dealership a chance to improve the terms.

Note: As a general rule, don't reveal to a dealer any prices quoted to you by another dealer. But if you feel it's important to disclose some numbers, be straight with all the players. If at one point you say to Dealer A that Dealer B down the street is offering to sell an almost identical home at a lower price, be prepared to show to Dealer A Dealer B's written offer. Be assured that all the dealers in a given market keep close tabs on each other and usually can tell with surprising accuracy how low each is willing (or able) to go.

If you conclude that going to a second dealer to spec out a house is just too daunting a task—and it is indeed hard work—consider this: In early 2005 Consumers Union issued a report dealing with manufactured home sales in Texas and the Southeast and concluded that home buyers who visited three or less sales centers before buying paid on average 10% more for their homes than those who shopped at four or more. CU also discovered a significant differences in prices for the same models, some by as much as 20% for some low-end homes. Granted, such a price disparity is unlikely with higher end homes but clearly, shopping several dealers in the early going is a smart strategy.

All those spinning plates

By the time you get to the point where you are spec-ing out houses, you may begin to feel like you are keeping a great many dinner plates spinning on the dining room table of life. You'll be right. Your three-ring binder will be filling rapidly, and you may be talking to potential contractors, conferring with a septic system designer, narrowing your search for a reputable dealer, perhaps talking to your lender, losing a bit of sleep, and probably feeling pretty darned excited. You should be. Buying a home is a major life experience for most of us, and can be quite stressful. Hang in there. You're closer to the finish line than you might think.

MHI photo

MHI photo

Above, the retail sales center loop of the stand-out New Colony Village in Maryland. Right, a more modest (and typical) dealership. Below: sales people at a home exhibit at the Oklahoma State Fair. The venues may differ but the key to a successful home purchase is the same: take your time, shop around, be informed, and don't hesitate to negotiate.

Photo courtesy of Home-Mart

Chapter 10

Getting to a Fair Price and a Square Deal

To get straight to the point, this is the most important chapter of this guide. You are now out where the rubber meets the pavement: on the lots dealing face to face with sales reps and sales managers. Many will be really grooved in with polished sales techniques. Their abilities must be respected. To level the playing field, this chapter arms you with information that a great many dealers don't want you to know. Regardless of whether you are paying cash or have a construction loan or need dealer financing, what you learn here could save you thousands of dollars. It could also greatly reduce the level of anxiety of one of life's most stressful experiences—buying a home.

When Americans shop, they are accustomed to seeing price tags on merchandise and paying that price without any thought to bargaining. In a way this is unfortunate, for in many cultures the world over, bargaining, with its gentle banter and give-and-take, is one of the joys of shopping. The ability to do so is something of an acquired skill—and it's rarely more useful, or more needed, than when purchasing a big ticket item such as a car or a home. So, if you feel unsure about your negotiating skills, rest assured that you have plenty of company. The goal of this chapter is to provide you with what you need to know to determine a fair price for your future home (and, if needed, acceptable terms of dealer financing) and to negotiate with confidence a square deal that you will be happy with long after you sign on the dotted line.

Keep your options open—don't sign anything

The more informed you are about the way manufactured homes are sold and financed, the stronger your position as you approach the negotiating process. But you can easily surrender much of your advantage early in the game if you get cozy with a dealership, even a reputable one, before you have comparison shopped, done the numbers and understand what options are available, not only in home prices, but, if you're looking into dealer financing, loan terms. Hence this cardinal rule:

Don't sign anything in the early going, and don't reveal your social security number.

Your signature and social security number are your power, two highly prized items dealers want from you. Safeguard both, keeping all your options open until you have all the facts and are ready to commit to a purchase and/or seriously pursue a loan application.

If you will be shopping for dealer financing, you also possess (or should by now) a third powerful resource: your own credit score. The prudent use of all three is the essence of shopping in control.

If you have recruited a personal advocate, this is the time when he or she should be by your side, ready to step up to the plate on your behalf. Reason: the strategies suggested here, notably involving your use of your own credit score, may be met with resistance by retailers long used to dealing with compliant, uninformed shoppers. You will likely encounter some initial tension. Just remember:

You, the customer, are crucial to the dealerships. They need you, not vice versa. Don't be a victim, or a codependent care taker, or throw yourself at their mercy. Make them earn your trust. They're the ones who must past your test. The good ones will.

A common cutthroat tactic

There are three distinct documents commonly associated with the purchase process: an authorization to obtain a credit report, a loan application and the purchase agreement. Of the three, only the purchase agreement will be involved in all cases. For example, if you're a cash customer, or have a pre-approved loan from your bank, the first two documents are not needed.

It's important to know what each of these documents is—and isn't.

- An authorization to obtain your credit report can be a single sentence on a visitor card on which you write your social security number and sign your name. This gives the dealer authorization to "pull a bureau score" on you. You may be asked to pay a fee for this, usually around $25, but typically the dealer absorbs the cost if a deal eventually goes through.
- A loan application is more formal, requiring much detailed financial information, as well as your social security number and signature, but you are under no obligation to accept any terms that a lender may offer you.
- A purchase agreement is precisely that, a legally binding contract to buy a home.

The classic example of getting too cozy early in the game is signing a purchase agreement (and putting up a deposit, or earnest money) during the first visit to a dealership, the so-called "write-up," when the very most that may be needed is a loan application. Don't do this under any circumstances. There is no need to, for at this point you are simply gathering information, and you may be doing so for several visits to come.

To be sure, your salesperson may tell you that your signature doesn't commit you to making a purchase, and that it's a mere formality needed to start the loan application process, "to see what kind of deal we can get for you." This is complete nonsense. If this were true, then why not simply fill out a loan application?

The phrase "to be determined" will likely be written in many spaces in the contract where numbers go. Further, he or she may ask for a modest deposit of a few hundred dollars in earnest money, assuring you that you can walk away at any time and your deposit will be refunded. That may sound OK, but the document you are being asked to sign at your peril commits you to a great deal more: You're taking yourself out of the marketplace and giving up a huge negotiating advantage.

By signing that purchase agreement you, as the buyer, are entering into a legal contract with that dealership, a.k.a., the seller, who now has a lot of discretion over whether or not to hold you to the contract's terms. Example: frequently buried in these contracts, in the fine print under the section titled Financing, is a land mine that contains something like the following:

"If Buyer cannot obtain required financing within a reasonable time, Seller may seek financing for Buyer, and if obtained, this condition shall be deemed satisfied."

This means that if you can't get your own financing (and likely that's why many sign the contract in the first place), and the dealer comes up with an approved loan loaded with hefty fees, pre-financed "points" and an interest rate that borders on extortionate, you're legally stuck with the deal. Technically, if you walk out, the dealer can take you to court.

Actually, very few dealers ever exercise that option (time and expense are prohibitive), but if the dealer is anything less than reputable don't expect an easy time of getting your deposit back. Some write-ups allow the dealer to keep from your deposit any out-of-pocket costs incurred by the Seller in applying for financing or other such expenses. These can eat up a lot of your deposit. **Note**: If you find yourself in this predicament, inform the dealer you are prepared to report your difficulty to the State Attorney General and the Better Business Bureau—and follow through if necessary, sending a copy to the dealer.

So, why do many dealers push their salespeople to get write-ups on the first visit? They do so because it's a cutthroat tactic that works, tying shoppers to the dealership. Write-ups effectively lock in the customers (freezing them out of the marketplace) before they go anywhere else, preventing (or at least seriously discouraging) them from signing other contracts with any other dealership, thus greatly increasing the likelihood that, in the event the customer qualifies for financing, the dealership will land the deal.

The principal rule of most sales strategies is, "Don't let the shopper leave without making every effort to get a write-up." For the record, only about one out of every four write-ups (i.e. loan applications) results in a loan offer.

Dealer financing—don't be a Charlie the Tuna victim

Should you have a low credit score and believe dealer financing is the only way you will be able to swing the purchase of a manufactured home; you may be right, but shop for the best financing the same way you shop for the best home price, without signing anything. You do this by arming yourself with your own credit score (which Chapter 4 describes how to obtain). **Note**: Be prepared to tell the dealer which of the big three credit bureaus you contacted to obtain your score.

This fact cannot be over-emphasized:
Providing your own credit score for the purpose of helping determine what kind of loan terms you may be able to obtain is a powerful tool and powerful protection.

This said, expect every dealership you visit to tell you that no lender in their right mind will work up a formal quote on a loan package without having your full name and social security number so that they can properly assess your creditworthiness. They will be right, but tell them this: You're not looking for a quote from a lender; you're looking for some informal numbers from the dealer. You're prepared to provide your credit score and approximate figures for the home price and the down payment. You don't even need anything in writing.

Again, be prepared for salespeople to reply that providing you with estimated loan terms based on a credit score you provide is unheard of, or impossible without your signing some kind of document. This is nonsense. They may argue it's against company policy. Advise them that banks and credit unions, for example, routinely furnish likely loan terms without requiring a signed application, that *Consumers Union* as recently as February 2002 strongly urges manufactured home shoppers do precisely what you're doing.

Truth is, with that simple number you effectively demolish any argument a dealer may have for obtaining your signature and social security number until you are ready to seriously pursue a home purchase.

Don't let any dealer kid you that they can't come up with ballpark numbers. They live and breathe this stuff. Most can easily tick off the likely interest rate changes for every ten point difference in credit scores over a 200-point spread—for the last three years.

It's a safe bet that if you tell them how much you're thinking of paying for a home, and the likely down payment, they can pencil out the numbers within a few minutes. And if they're not deliberately low-balling their estimate to lure you into their fold, the estimated terms will be very close to what a lender would offer after receiving a formal loan application.

Tell them you don't expect to get a quote with terms in concrete and that you understand any eventual loan approval will be contingent on your providing your social security number and other required information so that the lender can verify everything, including your credit score. Tell them you're in no hurry, that you'll call them sometime tomorrow.

If your request is refused, offer to provide a contact phone number in case the dealer has a change of heart—then leave.

Note: Don't be discouraged if this happens. Unfortunately, there are a lot of old mobile home guys out there who simply won't get it, and are not about to change the way they do business. They'll squint at you suspiciously with a look that says "What kind of stunt are you trying to pull?" Don't let this get to you. There are a lot of fine dealers everywhere who will quickly understand who they're dealing with and will be happy to provide you deal terms, and on company letterhead to boot.

The reality is many dealers are afraid you will take any deal terms they give you and go down the street to another dealer who will beat their offer. If they actually voice this complaint to you, feel free to nod politely and reply "Gee, compare prices before you buy—what a concept."

Sadly, the pitfalls of the first visit write-up can be particularly costly to the very people who most often sign them: uninformed consumers with low credit scores who tend to be far less concerned about the price of a home than they are about their chances of getting financing. As a consequence, they're happy to do whatever the dealer offers—"Gee, honey, isn't this wonderful? They're going to help us." In so doing, these Charlie the Tuna victims surrender almost all their power to bargain over the price of the home, let alone negotiate better terms on the loan package the dealer is able to get for them.

The dealers pat them on the back and gush, "Isn't this wonderful! We were able to get you financing for your home," knowing that the buyers will be so grateful they won't even think about quibbling over the home's full retail price tag.

These same grateful new home buyers may also be unaware that the dealer they relied on to get them financing may not only have obtained from a lender the maximum amount of money they were qualified to borrow, but somehow also made sure to find them a house with a price tag that just so happened to equal that maximum amount. How resourceful.

It is tempting to suggest that if more consumers with low, but still qualifying credit scores understood these sales ploys and refused to put up with them, dealers would begin to drop these deceitful pressure tactics—or lose sales. Unfortunately, as long as uninformed consumers continue to walk in with: "WRITE ME UP, I'M ALL YOURS" written on across their foreheads, change will come slowly, if at all.

How one reputable dealer operates

One Midwest dealer whose clientele is largely entry level buyers with poor credit and who need dealer financing explains his approach: "Don't get me wrong, I'll always want to write up customers the first time, but we don't pressure them. We have a visitor card we ask people to sign that has a space for them to fill out if they want us to run a credit check for them. Purely voluntary. We then offer to go over the report with them. Very few have ever checked their credit themselves and sometimes we spot mistakes that can be corrected.

"If at some point the customer is serious about buying one of our homes, we give them a printed explanation that spells out exactly what we will be doing. We agree to help clean up the credit record, which sometimes improves their scores. They can then apply for a loan to one of our lenders, or go right to a purchase agreement for a particular home they want, and give us a deposit. The difference is spelled out. If their loan is approved, we absorb the cost of the credit checks. If they're turned down, we refund their deposit minus the credit check costs, which are usually well under a hundred dollars. It's fair and it works for everyone."

As you shop in control, follow these additional guidelines:

- Be up front with the salespeople (but don't disclose any more than you must). Not only is this polite, but they'll also quickly understand that you are an informed consumer and will (or should) adjust their behavior accordingly.
- Don't shop just for the lowest price. The dealer's reputation and service should figure heavily in your purchase decision.

A word about the Kelley Blue Book and the NADA Appraisal Guide

Given the manufactured housing's historical roots in the automotive industry, you would think that there would be a publication akin to the *Kelley Blue Book*, the auto industry's standard reference for the wholesale and retail prices of cars, trucks, motorcycles, motorhomes and trailers. There is, and you can find a copy in the reference section of many public libraries. One might think that knowing the price of last year's model home would help in determining a fair asking price on this year's new model. The problem is the *Kelley*

Blue Book on manufactured homes focuses on appraising pre-owned homes in land-lease communities (i.e., parks) based on the model, age, size, equipment, the park's location and the park's amenities, and thus, is of little help. If a copy of the book is easily available at your local library, it might be worth a quick trip to browse the listings, but not much more.

The same is true of the *National Automotive Dealers Association's Annual Appraisal Guide to Manufactured Homes*, the NADA guide for short. This hefty volume, like the *Blue Book*, is really geared to mobile home appraisers and lenders concerned with older homes (usually much older), by geographical region. The guide does provide some useful data on the average per mile cost of transporting a home, price ranges on air conditioning and other options, as well as ballpark figures on setup costs in various regions, but is otherwise of little use to the new home shopper.

Strategies for determining a home's fair market value

There is no absolutely sure method for determining whether a price quoted to you is fair, but there are a couple of strategies that can help you answer the question with a pretty high level of confidence.

Method 1

The first is to compare the base retail prices offered by several dealers within your area, described in the last chapter. Yes, the process is work-intensive, but by comparing quoted prices you should be able to determine quickly if the prices are in-line with the fair market values. You will also have a useful grasp of the price spreads, which is very important for negotiating.

Strangely, it appears that only a minority of manufactured home buyers seriously comparison shop—or, for that matter, seriously bargain—before purchasing their home. One explanation is that conscientious comparison shopping is plodding work, often involving long drives to dealerships, inspecting models, face-to-face meetings to spec-out a home, deflecting the ever present sales pressure and studying the numbers. Many buyers who find an initial comfort level at one dealership (after visiting one or two others) may lose enthusiasm for the effort that comparison shopping requires. As a result, without the information that comparison shopping would give them, they have little or no strength with which to negotiate a discount on the home's price. They don't even know what kind of price reduction (or discount) to ask for—and they literally pay a price for it, sometimes thousands of dollars.

If you think you, too, won't have the enthusiasm for the above comparison effort, don't despair. As you'll see in a minute, an important strategy is never to agree to pay the full price quoted you. Hence this cardinal rule:

Always ask for a discount. The amount of the price reduction you eventually get may not be substantial, but it's always there. You simply have to ask.

Method 2

The second method for determining fair market value involves a bit of mathematics using a few costs that a dealer or sales person will usually be comfortable sharing with you. But first, here are brief definitions of some of the terms involved.

Dealer invoice. The wholesale price the manufacturer charges the dealer for the finished home FOB factory, that is, Freight on Board (also Free on Board) at the factory, ready to be transported.

Transportation. The cost of transporting and delivering the home to the home buyer's site, usually placing it near a prepared foundation (but often directly on it, if accessible). If the home is a lot model, the cost would be the total of two trips: factory to dealership and dealership to the home site.

Set-up. Also called **Installation.** The cost of placing and securing the home on the foundation (often called blocking), removing wheels, hitches and running gear, connecting all utilities, painting and texturing interior portions, installing (or completing the installation of) carpets, and cleaning—in short, preparing the home in all respects for owner occupancy. May also include installing steps, exterior trim and skirting around the foundation perimeter.

Mark-up. Also called margin or **profit margin.** The profit the dealer adds to the wholesale price of the home (the dealer invoice), often expressed, and calculated, as a percentage of the home's wholesale price.

Base price. Also called the **retail base price** of the home. The price, most often excluding sales tax, quoted to you. Comprised of the dealer invoice price plus the cost of transportation and setup. Sometimes the setup cost is not included. Be sure to ask.

Base price plus options. Same as above but includes all the options, those on a lot model or those you select when spec-ing out a home.

MSRP. Manufacturer's Suggested Retail Price. Similar to the MSRP in the auto industry. This is a printed sheet listing the home's base price, plus options, that some states, notably California, require dealerships to post in every manufactured home on display. As with the car industry, MSRPs don't reveal the markups, but they are certainly better than no posted prices at all.

Gross profit. The amount left after subtracting from the retail price of the home the dealer's invoice, and the actual costs of transportation and setup.

Sales commission. The amount paid to the person who sold the home, usually 20% of the gross profit, but sometimes as much as 25%.

Net profit. The gross profit minus the sales commission.

In general, dealerships shoot for a 30% mark-up when setting the retail base price. This allows them wiggle room for negotiating prices. But this percentage varies. During the hot market in the mid-1990s, markups of 35% and 40% and higher (sometimes much higher) were not uncommon. When times are tight and competition is ferocious, margins of five and ten percent, or less, are the norm.

Here's the rule of thumb: reasonable profit on a home sale is 25%. Keep this number in mind.

Dealers have no hard and fast rules for arriving at their markup, and understandably no dealer is going to tell you that number. However, if you know the transportation and setup costs, you can determine the retail base price of the home after the markup. Then, using different markup values—for example 20%, 25% 30%—you can calculate the dealer invoice of the home.

Let's take a look at an example:

Say, you're looking at a 1,600 sq. ft. two-section home that has a retail base price of $71,000. You're also considering options that total $6,500, bringing the total to $77,500. The price excludes sales tax but does include the cost of transportation to the site and set-up. In response to your questions, the sales associate says that the transportation costs will run about $2,500 and they've budgeted about $4,500 for the set-up/installation of the home. Note: Don't expect dealers to do much more than provide you with approximate numbers. For one, actual costs can vary depending on the transport distances and any installation problems encountered on site. For another, understandably they're not anxious to help you to figure out their markup. But you should ask these questions of every dealer you visit.

Subtract the transportation and set-up costs from the total retail base price:

$77,500	retail base price, including $6,500 in options
- 7,000	(transportation $2,500 + set-up $4,500)
$64,000	retail base price excluding transportation and set-up

This number also represents the dealer's invoice cost (including options) plus the mark-up. To determine what that dealer invoice cost is, and using a fair mark-up of 25%, divide that $64,000 by 1.25, a number equal to 100% + 25%.

$64,000 ÷ 1.25 = $51,200

This yields the dealer's invoice cost (including options) of $51,200. Granted, this figure may not be precisely accurate, and it assumes the retail base price is not inflated. It also assumes the dealer is marking up the cost of options by 25% (some dealers don't). Nonetheless, having a good idea of the dealer's invoice before transportation and set-up give you a good point of departure for negotiating a fair price.

Using a 30% mark-up, dividing $64,000 by 130 yields a dealer invoice of $49,230 or a gross profit of $14,770. That's a hefty profit—too much, in fact, when you add the factory rebate the dealer will later receive.

Thus, to reduce **Method 2** to simplest terms:

• A fair asking price for a home is dealer invoice plus a 25% mark-up.

• Calculate that price by subtracting from the quoted retail base price the costs of transportation and set-up and dividing the amount remaining by 1.25.

How one dealer calculated a sale

Here is how one sales manager for an average-size dealership in the Pacific Northwest breaks down the numbers on a popular three-bedroom, two-bath double-wide with a price tag, excluding sales tax, of $53,800:

"Our dealer invoice was just under 38,000 dollars—37,967 to be exact. Our markup at the time was 23 percent, which worked out to $8,733. The transportation costs from the factory to the home site averaged $2,500 and we budgeted the setup cost at $4,600. Those two came to $7,100. That total plus the markup brought the price to $53,800. That was the home's retail base price. Of course, people would order options but our policy is we don't add any margin to them—they pay what the factory charges us.

"Our gross margin of $8,700 and change may sound like a lot, but actually it didn't leave us much room to bargain. Out of that comes the 20 percent sales commission, or $1,747, leaving $6,986 for our net profit. Call it $7,000. Now, the dealership absolutely has to make at least five thousand dollars of that amount to cover operating expenses. That leaves me with two thousand dollars of bargaining room.

"If the customer asks for a thousand dollar discount, that's easy to accommodate. If he asks for two thousand, I have to first look at where the home will be sited to make sure we won't be looking at possible additional costs because of difficulties in delivering the home and getting it onto the foundation. All things being equal, I will usually OK a two thousand dollar discount. But if the customer insists on any more than that, I let the deal walk."

Depending upon the home's price tag, a dealer's gross margin generally varies between $8,000 and $20,000, the latter would apply to a top-of-the-line triple section home in the $100,000 to $125,000 range. Obviously, a $20,000 markup leaves a lot more room for negotiating because the transportation and set-up costs are not substantially greater than those for a double-wide (about 40 to 50% more).

To be sure, factory rebates periodically paid to dealerships based on gross sales are a very important part of the revenue stream. In a cutthroat market, particularly on the lower end, many dealerships will sell homes on a break-even basis just to move the homes, then make their profit from the end-of-the-year factory rebates which are based on gross sales.

Negotiating a square deal on a home price

Let's assume you will be paying cash or have obtained a loan commitment from a lender other than a dealership. Once you have determined to your satisfaction that the asking price (i.e., the base price) of the home you desire is fair, your objective is to pay the least amount possible. You do this by negotiation—and you have to make the first move, and you must be patient. Many home buyers, for whatever reason, make no move at all to ask for a price reduction, and it costs them.

You should approach this moment the same way you would for any home, whether or not through a Realtor: *You make an offer.*

I recommend my clients seek a face-to-face meeting with the sales associate or sales manger. Never make an offer over the phone. If you have a personal advocate, have him or her with you. Verify the total package and the total price that the dealership is offering, including all options and every line item expense. Then, offer to purchase the home for 10% less than the base price of the home (which includes delivery and setup).

In making your offer you can explain that as you've assembled all the numbers, the costs have been higher than you anticipated and your budget is very strained (which is quite often the truth with the clients I have helped). But you don't need to offer any justification.

On a home that's competitively priced in a tight market, that discount will likely be more than the dealership can give up—it amounts to dealer invoice plus a 15% mark-up—but it may not be. You don't know, and the only way to find out is to put an offer on the table. It's a starting point. In a sense, you've got to get to "No" before you get to "Yes".

Don't appear in a hurry. Keep it easygoing and polite. Give the dealership a day or two to think it over. Or, if they flat out refuse on the spot without making a counter offer, or respond with a discount that is far less than you asked, reply you'll think about it, and leave. Remember, they want your business. True, there will be a touch of theatre in all this as Buyer and Seller play their roles, but it's an honorable and serious game, with perhaps thousands of dollars in the balance.

Very likely you will be negotiating with a reputable dealer who has the home you really want and whom you sincerely like. In fact, another dealer may have already quoted you a home price that is a bit less, but you prefer this dealer and are prepared to pay more because of a better reputation and service. This is the way to go. You may even be prepared to accept a response that no discount is possible because the home has been priced as low as the dealership can go. This is very unlikely—dealers always leave a little wiggle room in the price in case they need to sweeten a deal—but you won't know until you ask.

Getting to a square deal on a home price and dealer financing

Here you are negotiating, not one, but two things: the price of the home and the terms of the loan the dealer is offering. Your task is a bit more complicated, not so much because there is more to negotiate, but because many dealers will at first refuse to give you any prices on homes or loan terms without first writing you up.

As noted above, many dealers love those first visit write-ups because they get their hooks into Charlie the Tuna who becomes strongly obligated to take whatever deal is offered, both on home price and deal terms. These retailers have been doing it for so long this way, and have become so accustomed to gaining an early advantage over pliant, unquestioning customers, that many simply cannot conceive of doing business any other way.

Fortunately, there are dealers who do understand, and accept, your approach to home and loan shopping, and are perfectly willing to work with you because they believe they have the best reputation for product and service.

Typically, when dealers discuss the needs of a prospective home buyer who will require dealer financing, they think in terms of the four corners of a deal: the monthly payment, the amount of the down payment, the home desired and the financing terms (interest, length, points, etc.). This approach is perfectly sound, as long as you don't have to sign anything to have that conversation.

A good strategy to follow when you find a dealership with the kind of home you're looking for, and feels comfortable, is to sit down with the salesperson or sales manager and paint a picture for them—your picture. Explain that you're in the market to purchase a home and that you have determined the best option for paying for it is through dealer financing. Tell them you are visiting several dealerships to see what's available both in home prices and loan packages but that you will not be signing any agreements until you've been able to compare informal quotes. Add that you would be happy to provide your credit score and what you can afford for a down payment and monthly payments to assist the dealer in obtaining a quote.

Explain that you are not solely price-driven, that you're looking for a dealer you feel good about, one who has a good reputation and who will do a great job, including warranty service, and that you'd be willing to pay more to have those things.

A reputable dealer who understands and respects your position will be happy to work with you. He or she might even offer to review with you the credit report you have already obtained to identify ways by which your credit score can be improved (such as paying off an auto loan to reduce the debt ratio). Again, reputable dealers are not in a hurry to get your business. They're confident they will earn your trust, and will do so by helping you pull together the useful numbers without insisting you sign anything.

Negotiating the terms of a loan package

The very fact that you can negotiate the terms of a loan offer is the clearest sign that you are shopping in control. Unlike the final price of a home, the terms of a loan, including many line items and small print, are complicated, but dealing with them is not rocket science either. Chapters 3 and 4 cover the critical elements of a chattel loan (or chattel mortgage), but don't hesitate to get help from your personal advocate, attorney or advisor.

There are many ways to adjust a loan so that it works for both parties. The length of payments, amount of payments, the down payment, number of pre-paid points, interest rates—all these and more can be varied. If at all possible, you will want the funds disbursed by the lender in a phased manner that ensures a portion of the money is held back until the job has been done (see below).

Be sure to review and understand all charges, fees and costs that must be disclosed somewhere in the term sheet. Remember, too, that successful negotiating is never confrontational. Rather, it's a polite conversation, full of goodwill and earnest reasoning. Keep in mind that your dealer will want you to be happy with the package and will work with you to meet your needs, and to earn your signature.

Deal terms: important details

Assuming you have found a reputable dealer, you should not have difficulty addressing the following topics and deal terms. But always keep in mind the maxim, the devil is in the details. The details should be a part of your discussions and negotiation and, as needed, put in writing:

Cardinal rule: Never sign any purchase agreement contract unless it contains in writing everything agreed to, together with line-item costs clearly listed, including all options ordered, all agreements made by the dealership (especially oral commitments), and anything important to you that you believe should be stated in writing—and made a part of that contract.

Just one of many examples that comes to mind when this rule is not followed: A dealership promised a retired school teacher they would build a two car garage as part of the purchase deal on her home, but didn't put it in writing. The day after she signed the contract they demanded $8,000 to pay for lumber to build the garage. She was stuck.

Dealer and buyer responsibilities. A reputable dealer will have an information sheet clearly spelling out the tasks for which the dealer and the home buyer are responsible once the purchase contract has been signed. If not, there should be. Ask for one, and go over the items with your dealer or salesperson. You don't want to be surprised by a costly buyer responsibility as you come down to the wire. Be aware that the countdown to move-in is time-sensitive and there will be important tasks you need to do before the dealership can move on work for which it is responsible.

Disbursing funds. When asked, dealers will often say it makes no difference to them whether they're paid by a bank, finance company or cash customer. This is not entirely true. The rebates that many finance companies once offered may be history, but dealers certainly prefer whomever has the most liberal payoff policy. That could be you if don't know how and when to disburse your money, and don't know how to protect yourself.

Whether you're paying cash or using a bank loan, payments are made at certain milestones, either by you or the lender. These disbursements, especially their timing, can become contentious issues if they are not discussed and agreed upon prior to signing a contract. However, if you are paying for your home through dealer financing, you may have little or no leverage to negotiate the conditions for these disbursements—another reason why dealer financing should be your absolute last choice. Keep in mind that before signatures, a purchase contract can be amended, and often is. You should feel free to suggest changes and offer addenda as needed. Here are recommendations:

Task sheet. If the dealer does not provide a sheet that clearly explains the tasks that all parties agree to do (and when), ask them to provide one, or make one up yourself. It can be part of the contract that is signed at closing.

Deposit. If you're paying cash, the dealer will ask for a deposit at the time the contract is signed and the home ordered. Usually he or she will ask for 5% or 10%, sometimes more. At this point you should have the property or home site legally nailed down with no complications and all funding needs in place, and no loose ends elsewhere that could jeopardize the completion of the project. If so, a 10% deposit at the time of signing should be fine. There is certainly no need for a larger deposit.

Down payment. If a lender is involved, you won't be making a deposit, but a down payment—at least 10% in most cases—in accordance with the schedule that your loan officer will provide. If escrow is involved, you will probably make your payment at the close of escrow. If yours is a land-home deal and you own the land on which the home will be sited, and its appraised value will be used for the down payment (not uncommon), the lender or lender's agent will file a lien against the property.

Payoff of the remaining purchase price. This issue can become a real sore point between dealers and buyers if not addressed before contracts are signed. In the case of construction loans for land-home purchases, banks have differing policies on paying off the total cost of the home contained in the purchase agreement (this number almost always includes the cost of transportation/delivery and setup). If the note for your loan is to be secured by a mortgage or deed of trust on the land, your bank will very likely require that the house be affixed to the foundation, and inspected, before it pays. The bank may even insist that the payment be part of an escrow transaction during which the appropriate document is filed with the county recorder that legally ties the home to the land as real property.

Some banks pay the dealership the entire amount right after the home is delivered to the site, whether placed on the foundation or off to one side. This is great for the dealer but can put you at a great disadvantage. If any significant problems arise during the setup phase, the dealership has less incentive to quickly correct them because it has already been paid.

Banks with this full payout policy know this but will argue that they only deal with reputable dealers and not to worry. What they likely won't disclose is that the policy is a serious sweetener that encourages dealers to bring them their loan business—and it works.

Ask your lender about their payoff policy. If they do a full payout at delivery, push for a holdback of a few thousand dollars until after the final walk-through inspection. It's only fair; it's also your most powerful leverage. Your request is appropriate and demonstrates you are a careful informed buyer—and, after all, you have the most at risk.

Note: don't be surprised if your lender does not make an inspection, which they, or their agent, should. In some regions lenders are lazy, requiring only a phone call from a dealer to say that all is well ("...and send me the check immediately.") If so, be proactive, insist at the very least that you be consulted before any payment is released.

Here is reasonable arrangement, one used by many banks that regularly make manufactured home construction loans: When the home is delivered to the site, placed on the foundation and bolted together, the bank inspects the home and issues a check to the dealer to pay for the dealer invoice (i.e. the wholesale price of the home, plus transportation costs). This payment allows the dealer to pay the manufacturer within the 10 to 15 business days normally required. (Still, not all dealers prefer this—see below.) When the setup of the home is finished, completing all of the dealer's responsibilities, a bank representative meets (or at least they should) with the homeowner and the dealer's representative and together they conduct a walk-through inspection.

After the inspection, if everything is satisfactory, the bank pays the dealer in full the remaining amount due per the purchase contract, and the homeowner takes physical possession. If items are discovered during the inspection that are the dealer's responsibility to fix, the bank withholds payment until the dealer fixes them. Only when the dealer is subsequently paid in full is the homeowner permitted to move in. This process, which is fair to both parties and protects the customer, is agreed to in writing at the time of the signing of the purchase agreement.

Note: Typically, your bank will have you sign a release each time a specified project milestone is completed and before disbursing a payment. Advise your loan officer that you intend to be an active participant in this process. If at all possible, don't sign a blanket release form that allows the bank to disburse funds "as conditions are satisfied" without first obtaining your signature.

The 10-80-10 payout

If you are a cash customer, you control the checkbook. Because you are not a bank, your dealer may ask you to pay the full amount of the purchase contract at the time your home is FOB the factory. Don't do this under any circumstances. You may not be a bank, but you're not Charlie the Tuna either. Bad things can happen between the factory and the home's final destination. Say, you've paid 10% down; you want to see that home on the site and kick the tires and make sure it's the one you ordered, with the options you ordered, before you make any further payments.

Ideally, your payment schedule and conditions are identical to the bank policy above; however, when the time comes for payment following the home's delivery to the site, your dealer may be reluctant to disclose to you the dealer invoice on your home, for it would allow you to see what the markup was (a reasonable concern). Here's a solution: pay the dealer 80% of the total purchase contract at that time, with the remaining 10% to be paid upon completion of the walk-through inspection and the fixing of any problems. You would agree not to move in until the dealer fixed all problems and you issued the final payment.

This ten percent holdback is similar to that widely followed in the site-built home industry: ten percent of the contract is held back until 30 days after completion—to correct any mistakes or omissions contained on what is commonly called a "punch list."

Thus, for example, with the double-wide in this chapter that retails for $53,800, let's say you tacked on options worth $3,500, bringing the total to $57,300, then successfully negotiated a $2,000 discount, to $55,300. Assume the tax in your state is 5%, or $2,765, yielding a total purchase price of $58,065. You would hold back 10% of that amount, or $5,806.50 until after the walk-through inspection and, if needed, the completion of any fixes for which the dealer is responsible. Again, everything is negotiable, but in this example, at an absolute minimum hold back $2,000-$3,000.

Note: In the category "Another way manufactured homes differ from site built homes," some dealers are extremely hesitant about delivering a home onto a cash buyer's property without first receiving the 80% payment. Reason: Should the buyer for whatever reason delay or refuse payment, the dealer is legally prohibited (without a court order) from entering the property to retrieve the home. These dealers bring the home to the edge of the property, then take payment by cashier's check before proceeding onto the buyer's land.

Disputes. This is a judgement call: Consider a paragraph in the purchase contract that commits all parties to go to binding arbitration in the event of a dispute that cannot be resolved. On the other hand, this may not be to your advantage. The arbitration programs in some states have poor reputations for fair dealing, with the homeowner frequently on the losing end. A lawsuit may be the most effective recourse for you. Consult your legal advisor on this topic.

Clearly, disbursement milestones, and their conditions, can be fairly involved. This is why some home buyers, especially those paying cash, will open an escrow account, either with a title company or an attorney acceptable to both parties. Give this serious thought. For the cost of a few hundred dollars, split between buyer and seller, a disinterested third party disburses funds according to the mutually agreed-upon written instructions of both parties. **Note**: this process is mandatory in California where the laws require all manufactured home sales go through escrow.

Before you sign the purchase contract

This may seem a little off-topic, but you should be aware of it before you sign a purchase contract: A reputable dealer will alert you to the importance of obtaining all the required permits for your home before ordering it. In fact, many dealers won't order a home until all the permits are acquired. Rounding up these documents is your responsibility. They include county permits for building, sewer, water and electrical. Ideally, have all the needed permits in hand, and provide copies to your dealer, before you sign your purchase contract. This way you avoid getting caught in a particular frustrating, and sometimes costly, dilemma: the dreaded permit delay.

Tip: Some dealers have their installers obtain these permits and include the costs in the purchase contract. Be sure to ask about this, and if this is the dealer's policy, ask for a detailed breakdown of the cost, and don't hesitate to negotiate terms.

Last, here is a recommendation that may require disciplined behavior: There will come a moment when the purchase contract has been completely filled out, with all the i's dotted and the t's crossed, and is ready for your signature. Your dealer will slide the document across the table to you, inviting you to sign. Don't. Tell him or her you'd like to take it, or a photocopy of the entire contract, with you for one final review—overnight, or for a couple of hours. A reputable dealer will have no difficulty agreeing to your request.

Take the contract and read it through one last time at home, or review it with your personal advocate or lawyer, your spouse or significant other. At the very least, go to a coffee shop or sit in the car and look it over one last time, without pressure. Reason: you're making what may be the biggest purchase of your life and this will be your absolute last opportunity to spot any problems or language you don't understand. Given all the work you have invested to reach this moment, you owe it to yourself to do so.

When it's over and you and the dealer shake hands, you will both feel good that each of you worked hard to get to a square deal that made you both happy.

The new rules of the game

This chapter illustrates how you, as an informed consumer armed with your own credit score, can now shop on a level, and fair, playing field. In so doing you are changing the rules of the game. You are insisting on it, or you will take your business elsewhere. The number of consumers like you will likely grow because few incentives in the free marketplace are more powerful than the prospect of saving thousands of dollars. Here's a thought: the principal factor that will force the retail arena of the manufactured home industry to finally clean up its act will be you, the swindle-proof consumer.

Chapter 11

Site Preparation, Delivery and Set-up

If you have followed in sequence the tasks recommended by this guide in purchasing your manufactured home—and finding a site for it—you have come a long way. Give yourself a pat on the back. Few projects require as much homework, research, caution and attention to detail as purchasing a new home, all the more so if you are placing a manufactured home on property that you are developing. Now, things get exciting. You are now weeks away from moving into your home, and you are finally going to see some real action: the preparation of your home's site and all that goes with it, including your new home.

This is where finding and doing business with a reputable dealer really pays off. Installers and contractors will be involved, people your dealer knows and trusts to do a professional job in a timely manner. This said, here's a caveat to keep in mind:

A weak link in the chain

Because the HUD-code requires special certification to set-up (or install—these words are used interchangeably) a manufactured home, in most states you will find set-up contractors (a.k.a., installers) who perform this task only, leaving the work of site preparation, laying the foundation, bringing in utilities, landscaping and all other tasks not directly related to the home to a general contractor. Elsewhere, you will encounter general contractors (GCs) who have both a GC licence and a HUD ticket to perform home set-ups.

These distinctions are important because many, if not most, major problems that new homeowners encounter are not due to factory construction errors but rather poor or sloppy work by the set-up contractor. Anecdotally, this finding is more prevalent on the lower end of the market. Because the dealer is almost always responsible for hiring the set-up contractor, some less than reputable dealers, to cut corners, have an incentive to hire the cheapest set-up crews they can find. Unfortunately, too, the requirements to obtain a HUD-code installer's licence are not as stringent as they should be (but this is starting to change). The result is that an incompetent or sloppy set-up contractor becomes the weak link in the chain. And when things go wrong, you can end up with everyone pointing fingers at each other and no one stepping up to fix the problem.

Growing dealer involvement in the process

In this chapter, we'll be describing the most common scenario: work performed by a general contractor and a set-up contractor, each with distinct responsibilities.

If you're moving into an established manufactured home community (i.e. a park), there may not be a great deal to do beyond the delivery and set-up of the home, including hooking up to existing sewer and utility connections and pouring a concrete path or parking pad (called flat work). Your dealer will likely do all this as part of a park package (often called a Park PAC) that you purchased.

On the other hand, if you're moving to a new manufactured home subdivision, or onto undeveloped land, the task is more complex, sometimes much more. If you purchased a land-home package for either of these projects, your dealer is under contract to complete the task for the agreed-upon cost, leaving nothing more for you as the new owner to do than step up and turn the key in the front door (known as a turn-key arrangement). If there are any cost-overruns or mistakes, the dealership, not you, is responsible.

Because these turn-key projects involve quite a few contractors whose work must be coordinated and overseen, with very few exceptions (see below), using a general contractor is by far the best way to go. In California, where many laws in the manufactured home arena were first enacted to correct past abuses, dealers are required to hire a licensed general contractor to do site preparation or be licensed general contractors themselves. This requirement promotes an orderly process under which the project is overseen by a licensed and bonded individual or company and provides you, the customer, with legal protection in the event a dispute arises. Interestingly, California has a special GC license, called a C-47, that allows a qualified general contractor to do everything connected with setting up a HUD-code home, plus hire all the licensed trades needed to do the site prep, even built garages and do all the landscaping, in short, everything needed. A very promising concept.

Increasingly, as land-home purchases with conventional home loans constitute a growing percentage of manufactured homes sold, savvy dealerships are becoming more involved in all aspects of site preparation. Some are obtaining general contractors licenses. This is a good trend, for not only does this involvement protect less-than-knowledgeable buyers from being overwhelmed (or taken advantage of), it provides an important additional profit center for the dealership.

In cases where you are purchasing a home only, whether for cash or with a construction loan, you as the buyer assume some responsibility for site preparation, but legally HUD law holds the dealer responsible for ensuring the home's conformance to HUD code, and this means the home must be completed on site and ready for occupancy. Here a reputable dealer will provide you with a list of recommended general contractors and subcontractors from which to choose. If you are in this category of home buyer, discuss the list with your dealer. Some contractors have better client relationship skills than others, and your dealer may suggest one or two names that would be a particularly good fit for you.

Site preparation—what, and who, is involved

Just how complex can site preparation be? Let's consider an increasingly common occurrence: putting a modest double-wide home on a poured foundation on an acre of semi-rural land, together with a well and a septic system. Here is a list, not in precise chronological order, of the providers involved (and the likely number of employees for each in parentheses):

Well driller (1-2)—Drill water well, do required purification tests

Septic engineer (1)— Perform percolation tests on land to confirm suitability for septic system use, design septic system

Bulldozer operator (1)—Excavate and level foundation site

Work crew (2)—Prepare forms for concrete foundation pour, lay and tie rebar

Concrete pump truck (1)—To pump concrete into the foundation form (often, but not always used).

Concrete delivery trucks (2)—Deliver ready cement to pump truck

Work crew (4)—Spread concrete, finish foundation surface

Backhoe operator (1)—Dig trenches for water, utilities, phone, TV, propane

Work crew/backhoe (2)—Install 10 cu. yd. dry well, fill with rock aggregate, connect to rainwater downspouts from home, backfill.

Set-up installer (2)—Block and level house, seal and paint exterior of home at roof joints and end seams. Connect to water, septic system and electricity Finish interior trim at seams of the ceiling, marriage line and end walls, repair stress cracks. Test appliances.

Set-up/tape & texture (1)—Prepare interior marriage line joints for painting, taping, then texturing, followed by painting.

Carpet installer (1)—Install (or complete installation of) carpet pads and carpeting.

Rain gutters/downspouts contractor (1)—Install gutters and downspouts.

Skirting contractor (2)—Construct skirting around house perimeter, with access opening (to underside).

Well pump contractor (2)—Install well pump, water pipes, pressure tank and electrical switches.

Work crew (3)—Excavate for septic holding tank and leech field, install same, connect to house septic outflow, backfill.

Local power utility district (2)—Prepare power connection from pole or transformer at property's edge.

Electrical contractor (2)—Lay wire from power pole at edge of property, install J box (junction box) on exterior, connect wires to inside power panel. Install meter.

Air conditioning contractor (1)—Install outside AC unit (or heat pump or swamp cooler) and connect to home's inside central ventilation unit.

Telephone service (1)—Connect and bury phone line from terminal next to property to exterior of home; second visit: hook up phone junction box to home, install inside jacks, test phone.

TV cable (1)—If cable service ordered (as opposed to satellite dish): connect buried cable wire from terminal at property corner to cable splitter at home exterior; install inside TV jacks

Propane service (1)—Place propane tank 30 feet from home, lay underground gas line from tank to home, plumb gas connection to house.

Backfill/compaction (2)—Fill in all trenches, backfill around foundation perimeter, compact.

Driveway (2)—If crushed rock/gravel: haul in, spread and compact several truckloads of rock/gravel for driveway; if concrete or asphalt: construct with machinery as required; work crew may be three or more.

State and local inspectors (2-3)—Visit job site as needed to sign off on all work requiring inspections (per HUD requirements and the local building code).

House cleaning (3)—Vacuum and dust, clean walls, windows (both sides), fixtures, remove all trash, leave home ready for occupancy.

Some of the listed providers are counted more than once (e.g., the work crew), but the total doesn't include those involved with the construction of decks and stairs or a detached garage or fencing. In short, you can expect more than three dozen professionals will have tromped across your work site before you are handed the keys to your new home.

Hiring a general contractor

Very likely the well has already been drilled and the ground successfully perc-tested for a septic system, but the remaining tasks will need to be completed within a matter of weeks, starting with building a proper foundation. To this end, engaging a general contractor (GC) is the first item on your agenda. As mentioned previously, more and more dealers are becoming licensed contractors to provide turn-key home purchases, but for now, let's assume you'll be hiring your own general contractor. Typically, these are small companies that own earth moving equipment. Other general contractors may focus on building and construction, assigning the earth-moving tasks to subcontractors. All should be licensed and bonded.

After you have reviewed with your dealer the recommended names, solicit bids from at least two. If you have a construction loan, chances are your lender will require only one bid, but getting two gives you a better basis for comparison. Ask each to meet you at the property so they can get an idea where you plan to site your home, the size of the driveway and any approaches, distances to the well head and septic system and any grading that may be required.

Note: During this initial visit do not ask, or permit the contractor (or his representative, usually a foreman), to measure and stake out the foundation. That should be done only by the contractor you select. But of course it's OK for them to take whatever measurements they need for purposes of preparing their bids.

If, for whatever reason, only one contractor is available during your project time frame, be sure to review the submitted bid with your dealer and/or others familiar with such estimates to make sure the prices are in line.

Unless your site presents significant challenges, the bids you receive should be straightforward and competitively priced. If you are a cash client (i.e., not using a construction loan), the contractor you select may require you to sign a contract, but sometimes a signed copy of the bid will suffice. In either case, the agreement should be signed by both parties and contain the following two terms in writing:

1. A payment schedule, detailing when partial payments will be made for specified tasks completed. If you have a construction loan, this element will be spelled out by your lender.

2. A provision that states that ten percent of the project costs will be held back following completion until the following conditions are met:

- Contractor to correct any mistakes, omissions or other shortcomings noted during an inspection with the client.

- Contractor to provide a statement of warranty or guarantee of all work performed.
- Contractor to provide a paid-in-full statement and a lien waiver.

A lien waver is a statement signed by the general contractor stating that the contractor has been paid for all work performed under the contract and hereby waives all rights to file any lien against the client's property. Filing a property lien, also known as a mechanic's lien, is a legal process whereby a contractor who has not been fully paid for work completed may file a document, called a lien, with the country recorder that states the amount still owing.

This lien, which may be legally contested by the property owner, is attached to the property's title as a recorded addendum, and in effect prevents the property from being sold or transferred (or even used as collateral for a loan) until the matter is resolved. On some big projects, many general contractors routinely file a lien at the commencement of the job, then lift the lien within 30 days following project's completion and receipt of all payment due.

Title insurance companies refer to such properties as having a clouded title. A lien gives contractors and other providers, who would otherwise have to resort to prohibitively expensive lawsuits, an inexpensive way to compel (at least eventually) a resolution of the issue. If the claim is upheld, the owner usually pays the contractor's legal costs as well.

As you may imagine, property liens can be much more than a nuisance; they can be disruptive and costly. For this reason, banks routinely require contractors to certify full payment and provide a lien waiver before issuing checks. You should, too.

As for the ten percent holdback, this is standard procedure throughout the construction industry, providing the contractor with incentive to complete the job to the client's satisfaction. Typically, after completion of a site-built home, the homeowner takes note of items that need correcting or completion. This "punch list" is given to the builder to complete before a final inspection. This is an orderly procedure that you, too, should follow.

Should you be your own general contractor?

The short answer is "No". Some home buyers may be tempted to conclude they can save a bundle on the cost of site preparation if they dispense with a general contractor, do a lot of the work themselves and put the rest out to bid. Here is why this is a bad idea for all but a very few:

- The contractors you hire (e.g., electricians, excavators, well water pump installers, carpenters) know you are a one-time client whom they will likely never see again. Human nature suggests you'll be regarded as a nice plump pigeon. With no general contractor to crack the whip and to threaten to withdraw the promise of future work, they may put you last on their to-do list, especially during a busy building season. Result: intermittent progress at the job site, or delays of several days at a time, for any number of excuses.
- Work delays can snowball into big problems. If some subcontractors can't begin work until others finish, everyone must adjust. The project may come to a halt for weeks at a time—costly weeks.
- You may be surprised to learn that the low bid you accepted didn't include certain

items because you didn't specify them; they need to be done, and now you're being charged top dollar, perhaps overcharged, and you're stuck. Similarly, even minor requests to modify plans result in change orders that quickly add up to significant costs. All this takes a hefty bite out of the money you're saving by not hiring a GC.

- You encounter site problems that require additional equipment and/or work force resources that a general contractor would routinely provide at no additional expense to you. Instead, you're on the hook to pay for them—yet another hefty bite out of your pocketbook.
- You discover that if you have to purchase any tools, equipment or materials or rent machinery, you pay full retail.
- In contrast to subcontractors who frequently work for the same general contractor, and who know each other and work smoothly together, some of the "subs" you hire may be unpopular with the local work force and/or may have spotty track records that you don't know about. Result: poor coordination and friction between subs, uneven quality of work.
- With multiple subs working directly for you, you're more vulnerable to mechanic's liens than if you worked with a general contractor, and potentially more prone to lawsuits resulting from injuries on the job site (your homeowner's insurance may not kick in until the home is completed).
- Without a secretary, office manager and project foreman at your disposal, you alone must do the work of all three: constant phone calls, scheduling, coordinating visits by inspectors, cajoling your subs, keeping track of expenses and often working into the night to stay on top of the myriad details involved. As de facto project foreman, your field supervision skills are frequently put to the test. Your daily emotional landscape includes frustration, anxiety and constant worry.

When being your own general contractor makes sense

For a small percentage of home buyers, acting as one's own general contractor can be a prudent cost-saving move. For example, if you yourself are in the construction trades and know how to do a lot of the required tasks, if you know and regularly work with many of the people you plan to hire as subs, if the preparation of your site is a fairly straightforward proposition, if you can bargain for a discount on equipment and materials from your local supplier (or better yet, can borrow needed equipment), if you have a comfortable time frame within which to get the job done, and if you have friends and/or family in the trades who are willing to moonlight for you at a reasonable hourly rate—if you can answer "yes" to most or all of these—then being your own GC makes sense.

Surprisingly, a fair percentage of new home buyers, by virtue of being in the building and construction trades, handily meet the above requirements. Many banks that provide construction loans for land-home purchases of manufactured homes routinely allow their borrowers to "general" their own site prep.

Explained one bank loan officer, "Of course, we require them to get bids on the work that they don't do themselves, and we pay at the completion of certain milestones just as we do with a licensed general contractor. But this way they do save a few thousand dollars which lowers the amount they have to borrow, or provides them with a little extra to add a few improvements."

If you're contemplating this option, be prepared for the dealer who is selling you your home to require you to sign an agreement stipulating that if all work is not properly completed by a specified date the dealer may come in and finish the job at such-and-such a price.

A worker (center) moves the end of the hose suspended from the boom of a concrete pump truck (not visible) to fill the form for a 6-inch deep foundation slab reinforced with 1/2-inch "rebar." The resulting "floating slab" will be given ten days to cure prior to the delivery of the home

This is fair. The last thing any dealer wants is a long wait to get paid because your brother-in-law who was responsible for the foundation forms was out sick for two weeks just before the winter storm season hit.

Working with a general contractor

As a property owner whose land is being prepared for your new home, you want to make sure the project is done in a timely and correct fashion. To do your part in this, you must now walk a fine line between being a closely observant, proactive, three-ring binder carrying landowner and a royal pain in the rear.

Typically, a general contractor has several projects underway at any one time, especially in regions where summertime is the peak building season. The company's foreman will visit each site regularly to check on progress and resolve any questions that arise. It is his or her responsibility to schedule the subcontractors in proper sequence as the site work progresses. You should visit the site daily during periods when work is being done, and be observant.

You will likely have several responsibilities that your general contractor will expect you to cover. These may include ordering electrical, telephone, cable TV, and/or gas services. Most, if not all of these services, may involve burying pipes and wiring. Your contractor will need all these to be correctly placed in the trenches, before backfilling.

You may also need to obtain permits from your local HUD-code enforcement office for any modifications or additions to your home that fall under HUD regulations. For example, if you intend to install a propane gas stove in your living room, you will need a permit and an after-installation inspection. Keep your contractor informed of these activities. He or she will contact the county building department to request inspections when work requiring them is completed. **Note:** Today's manufactured homes are wonderfully safe. But one of the most common causes of fires is the improper installation of after-market wood or propane stoves. There are several ways to screw up. If you're putting in a stove, make sure it's done right.

When disputes with contractors arise—one home buyer's story

No job site is totally immune from Murphy's Law. Stuff happens, mistakes are made. Usually they're the result of a series of small errors by different subcontractors. Most of the time, problems are handled amicably, but occasionally a disagreement needs to be resolved with a little outside help. Here's one home buyer's story:

We had purchased property that already had a septic system installed on it, and the foreman for the general contractor we hired explained that the home needed to be sited high enough so that the sewage from the house would drain properly into the septic tank 100 feet away. For some reason the house ended up being nine inches below the needed elevation.

During a meeting with the foreman, I was puzzled that he seemed unwilling of admitting that a mistake had been made, let alone offer any assurance his company would correct it at their expense. His solution was a vault next to the home containing "a trash pump," or "grinder," that would pump raw sewage up to the septic tank. I wasn't sure if there was a better option but I could imagine how vulnerable such a pump would be to periodic breakdowns due to jammed impeller blades.

Before the next meeting I talked to a few knowledgeable people, all who said the best solution was to put in a second septic tank next to the house and place in the outflow chamber, which doesn't contain solids, an effluent pump that would send the sewage up to the first tank. When next we met I told the foreman what I had learned. He seemed miffed. At length, he said 'OK, but the septic tank goes in no more than eight feet from the house, and you pay for the revised permit. If you want the tank any further away, you pay that cost.'

Putting the tank eight feet out from the house would have placed it directly beneath a soon-to-be-constructed deck. I said it made more sense for the tank to be eight feet away from the end of the house, for easy access. I asked him to keep me posted on developments.

Several days passed with no progress report. My calls were not returned. When I finally reached him by phone, he sounded highly irritated, at one point blurting out 'Look, we're the installers. We know better than you do about these systems. We're getting it done, that's all you need to know.'

That did it. I called the president of his company and asked for a meeting. I was promptly given an appointment for 8 a.m. the next morning. When I arrived I invited the foreman to be present. He declined to sit down, instead stood leaning in the doorway. After I explained my situation, I concluded, "Look, you guys are doing a great job and I understand things can happen, but it's not my responsibility to pay for those mistakes. What I'd really appreciate hearing from you is 'Hey, we made a mistake, we're sorry, it's our responsibility to fix it at our expense.' And I'd also like to see a more cordial, professional attitude from your guy here."

The company president thanked me, said almost word for word what I had hoped to hear, then went further, offering to put in the second septic tank anywhere I wanted, even to remove the first if I wished, all at their expense. After the meeting, he even walked me out to my car.

From then on everything went beautifully. The foreman was courteous and professional, and the job was finished on time. Moral: If something doesn't feel right on your project, or issues are not being resolved, speak up. If you don't, it could cost you. You're the customer and these people are working for you. You should not be, nor do you deserve to be, intimidated. If need be, seek help from your dealer and/or your banker.

As the site preparation proceeds, you will likely want to make a few minor changes—for example, add an additional garden faucet or slightly alter the driveway. Arrange to meet with your contractor, or foreman, at the site to discuss the details, including the cost.

As for monitoring the work in progress, don't hesitate to call the contractor's office on a regular basis to ask for updates. Your active interest in staying on top of things may be more than they are accustomed to seeing, but your doing so may prevent minor screw-ups from becoming major headaches. Example: After the building inspector signs off on a trench in which has been laid the water pipe and the electrical wire, the trench may have been backfilled and compacted. Still to be laid in that trench are the phone and TV cable, but the site crew never got the word. You notice this on your daily inspection and alert your contractor. The trench is re-opened the next morning before the phone and TV service technicians arrive. Conversely, if you failed to inform your GC that you ordered some kind of service that involves a buried line or pipe, you may be asked to pay the cost of reopening the trench.

Manufactured home foundations

Constructing the foundation on which your home will be placed is a major task of site preparation. There are five basic types that fall into two categories: those to which the home is permanently affixed and those that are not, but you may have little choice in the matter. Increasingly lenders (especially Fannie Mae and Freddie Mac) are specifying which foundation type must be built as part of the loan qualifications. Other manufacturers reduce their warranty coverage on homes that are not permanently affixed to their foundations (and which are considered less stable). Many county building codes spell out minimum foundation requirements. The weather in your region can also be a major consideration. Here's the run down. **Note**: Permanent = permanently affixed to foundation; Non-permanent = not permanently affixed.

Surface set (or piers and pads). Non-permanent. The topsoil is removed and the exposed dirt is leveled. Cinder blocks are placed at intervals beneath the steel I-beams and along the marriage line (if a multi-section home). Often a plastic ground tarp is laid on top of the dirt before the cinder blocks are placed. Statistically the most popular and least expensive, the surface set foundation works best in mild climates where the ground does not freeze and remains dry, even during rainy weather. Pros: Inexpensive, can be built in less than a day. Cons: Blocks settle over time, causing the home to shift, the sheetrock to crack, doors to go out of plumb (which most manufacturer warranties won't cover); very likely to need yearly re-leveling—a long-term expense; since home is not tied down (anchored) to foundation, it is vulnerable to being blown off its foundation by high winds (which explains why storm-tossed manufactured homes routinely show up in post-hurricane and tornado news footage).

Pier set, or block and footing. Non-permanent. Identical to the surface set except the cinder blocks are placed on shallow concrete piers or footings (either precast or poured in place), each at least six inches thick and 12 inches or more on a side. Pros: Significantly more stable than a surface set. Reasonable cost ($1,200 to $1,800 on average). Cons: Long-term settling can still occur; susceptible to ground movement because of frost and ground water saturation; unanchored, vulnerable to high winds and earthquakes; many lenders, especially government agencies, prohibit this type in their loan requirements. To meet these lending standards, a variation: Post holes 18" in diameter and 3' to 4' deep (down to the frost line) filled with concrete to serve as footings. A frost wall perimeter is constructed and dirt is backfilled against it. Home is anchored securely to footings. Considered a permanent foundation.

Floating slab. Permanent. The topsoil is removed and the ground is leveled. A concrete slab at least six inches thick, containing steel reinforcement bar (rebar) is constructed. Along the slab's perimeter, usually at eight-foot intervals, six-inch diameter openings through the slab are made, exposing a length of re-bar which will serve as an anchor point. Alternative anchor points: J-bolts inserted in the concrete just after the pour. When the slab is cured (7 to 10 days), the home is rolled on and positioned. Steel, pyramid-shaped, adjustable support piers (similar to jack stands) are used for blocking. At intervals along the home's perimeter, strips of inch-wide steel straps, called tie-down straps, are wrapped around the I-beam and secured to the anchor points in the concrete. (Some industry wages call tie-down straps "banker's knots" because they can always be unfastened if the home is repossessed and moved.) This type is called a floating slab because it keeps the house and the foundation slab tied together, allowing both to move vertically, and without harm, when the ground freezes.

The result is a foundation at grade level that allows a transport truck to drive (or back) the home sections directly onto the slab and spot them within a foot or so of their final destination. Pros: very secure, stable, permanent foundation and tie-down qualifies for interest-rate conventional home loans; almost impervious to frost heave; provides a clean crawl space. Cons: more expensive than the first two alternatives (cost range: $5,000-$7,000), needs a 14-day window for construction (including cure time); the large number of piers (one every four feet along each I-beam) makes the crawl space cramped, some areas hard to access.

Pit-set foundation. Permanent. Identical to a floating slab above except a shallow pit 12 to 18 inches deep is first excavated and leveled. A perimeter wall of split block masonry or treated wood is constructed around the edge of the slab, creating a dirt-free crawl space. Dirt is backfilled against the exterior of the perimeter wall. This is a popular choice in many regions.

A note on crawl space and creepers: To save money on concrete costs, some home buyers opt for a foundation slab comprised of concrete runners, each four to seven feet wide running the length of the footprint and connected at their ends by a two-foot wide runner spanning the width of the slab. The support piers are placed on the runners while the open areas between the runners are backfilled with dirt to the level of the concrete. While this option will save a few hundred dollars in concrete costs, the downside is when you need to move around in the crawl space underneath your home (which averages around 18 inches in height) you will literally be crawling on your back in the dirt—a major hassle.

Recommendation: Spend the extra dollars and pour a monolithic slab which will provide a smooth, clean surface beneath your home. From an auto parts supply store, buy a "creeper," a backboard with a foam headrest on universal wheels that mechanics lie on when working under cars. You can usually get an inexpensive model for around $25.

Leave this handy device under the house by the entry well for those times that you need to get in there to make inspections or to string phone, TV cable or other connections. Not only will zipping around your crawl space be a breeze, but you won't have any dirt to worry about. **Note**: Make sure your installer leaves the foundation clean of debris and any leftover materials (nuts and bolts) so that you have easy "creeping."

Roll-on Foundation. Permanent. More a means of placement than a distinct foundation type, this is identical to a pit-set except the pit is recessed, often four to five feet below grade, preventing the home from being pulled or backed onto the foundation. This option is often used to position the floor of a manufactured home at grade level (as opposed to two feet or greater above it) so that the home blends in architecturally with the other homes in a neighborhood.

Other instances in which a roll-on placement is the solution are when the foundation is totally enclosed by a perimeter wall, or hilly terrain requires constructing a foundation that can't be driven on. In these cases the perimeter wall consists of 6-inch thick reinforced concrete and performs a support function. Still, as with pit-set homes, support piers are arrayed along the marriage line and the I-beams.

With a roller system, the home is delivered alongside the length of the foundation. Using a low-tech but ingenious technique, the contractor builds a pair of temporary tracks on large wood or metal beams on which are placed special two-way rollers. Each section of the home is then raised using hydraulic jacks, allowing the removal of the hitch, wheels and running gear.

The tracks and rollers are placed under the home which is subsequently lowered onto the rollers. The section is then rolled sideways onto the foundation perimeter walls, then blocked and supported with piers from beneath. The same procedure is followed with the second section, following which the tracks are removed and the set-up process continues the same as with a pit-set placement.

A roll-on placement can add $2,000 to $3,000 or more to the set-up cost of a home, but there is some advantage gained: storage space. Some home buyers pay extra to have a monolithic concrete slab poured (instead of just runners) so that the resulting crawl space beneath the home becomes a sealed, ventilated, dirt-free, rodent-free mini-basement in which one can move while stooped over. Pros: Solid, strong, perimeter support (if present) adds resistance to seismic damage, much larger crawl space, easy access. Cons: More expensive than standard pit-set; some manufacturer's warranties may be partially voided if foundation requirements are not followed (e.g., elevation too high above ground).

Basement foundation. Permanent.

Especially popular in the Midwest and throughout the Northeast where basements in single-family homes are common. Many home models come with inside basement access

One minute it's an empty slab in a field, and the next it disappears under two sections of a 1,500 sq. ft. home. This delivery was a cake-walk for these drivers. They positioned the two halves evenly, with less than four inches clearance down the middle, and were gone within 45 minutes.

doors. A local building permit is required. Design and construction can vary widely but usually consist of two long I-beams and floor trusses laid across the top of the basement perimeter walls. A crane is often employed to set the home, a section at a time, onto this foundation.

If a basement is in your budget, you will doubtless be hiring a contractor with expertise in basement construction and home placement. **Note**: almost all manufactured homes can be successfully moved with an ordinary 80 to 100 ton crane which on average costs about $4,000 to $7,000. But the cost can be much more. Your contractor will need to determine the precise weight of each home section.

The factory can weigh each section just before transport. Pros: The strongest, most durable foundation; great strength against wind and earthquake; provides a basement area free of support piers that can be finished, wired, plumbed and heated as additional living space. Cons: The most expensive foundation option, construction time delays placement of home.

The delivery

Before the site preparation got underway, your dealer or salesperson will have visited the property to check for any problems that may complicate the delivery of your home and its placement on the foundation. In fact, such an inspection will likely have been done prior to your inking the purchase contract since your dealer's delivery and set-up budget is calculated using the standard drive-on placement of the home sections. Had delivery involved a roll-on placement, for example, the extra cost involved would have been factored into the purchase price.

Most dealers request—and many require—their customers to be present at the time their home is delivered to its site. Don't miss it. The delivery procession from the factory is an impressive sight: a pilot car, usually a truck, followed by two big diesel tractors (in the case of a double-wide home), each hitched to a section of the home, and often followed by a rear

Transport tales from the trenches

For the record, accidents rarely happen while a manufactured home is being transported. There are companies that specialize in this transport niche. Chances are you won't have a chance to chat with the transport drivers (typically they finish positioning their sections in under an hour and are back on the road), but most are amazingly skilled—and most all of them can tell wonderful war stories.

One such veteran is Doug Eacrett, now retired and living in Port Angeles, Washington. Eacrett's driving career began in 1965, delivering 10' x 50' single-wides to logging communities all over the Pacific Northwest.

"It was a lot more casual back then. I'd show up with a two-bedroom, furnished single-wide with an oil heater and the loggers would be there with chain saws to cut rounds as needed for the foundation. Building permits cost a dollar. The whole house delivered came to just under four thousand dollars."

Eacrett has been through it all. For instance: nearly losing control on a terrifying downhill run towing a single-wide hideously overloaded with canned food; being bitten by a family's lovable Saint

Bernard who somehow sensed his home was about to be moved; and having a hitch break off while traveling at highway speed and watching in the rear-view mirror as his load, sparks flying, plowed up yards of asphalt as it screeched to a halt (the V-hitch had not been properly bolted on at the factory). Here are a couple of small gems from an adventurous career spanning more than three decades:

"One afternoon I arrived to do a relocation move for a couple who owned a single-wide. I had heard that they were heavy drinkers and when I arrived they were inside, both drunk and yelling and cussing each other out. Their home was ready to move but as I hitched up my rig and repeatedly asked them to leave, they refused. Just kept on fighting at the top of their lungs.

Finally I gave up and just locked them in, attaching clips to prevent the door from opening outward. The trip took about an hour along a very curvy road. When I got there and unhitched I opened the door to look in. There they were, sitting next to each other on the living room couch, gentle as lambs—and looking kind of sheepish."

"A few years ago a story made the rounds about a transport guy who delivered a home to property that had a driveway that curved around a bank. The couple who owned the property was there to see the delivery. The back end of the home was dragging for some reason, but the real problem was the driver was too close to the bank. Instead of stopping to check for clearances, the guy kept going. The back end of the house slammed into the bank and the whole section literally broke in two.

The driver got out cursing and complaining. When the couple protested that he had failed to make sure of enough clearance, the driver shouted that no way was it his fault. He told them, "You should have bought a better house!" At that point the husband showed him the camcorder he was holding and replied 'Would you like to see the video we just shot?'"

Big house, tight fit? Call for a robo-cat.

Increasingly in many regions, homes are being placed on lots with difficult access. When the task looks all but impossible, builders often call for a robo-cat. This one, made by Remote Trax of Oregon, is an 8,000 lb. radio-controlled "cat" that, controlled by a skilled operator, does an amazing job moving even the heaviest sections. Land-lease communities also use them for moving homes in and out of very narrow home sites. Prices vary but figure around $350 for 1-4 hours.

vehicle with flashing lights warning of a wide load ahead. State laws vary, but most require all vehicles be in radio contact with each other, with travel restricted to daylight hours.

After all the weeks and months you have invested in creating your new home, understandably you will be thrilled the moment the procession finally arrives at the site—and you lay your eyes on your home sweet home. Hardly before you get used to the sight—an hour or less in most cases—the transport procession departs, leaving behind what appears pretty close to an instant home. **Note**: If you video the delivery, you'll have something neat—and, perish the thought, powerful evidence should something go amiss.

In some regions of the country, as the local inventory of easily accessible property dwindles, manufactured home placements increasingly require the construction or widening of access lanes (tree removal, wider curves and shoulders) and the use of bulldozers to pull the home sections onto the site and foundation. In this challenging environment, remotely operated heavy equipment has been able to perform astonishing feats (see sidebar, Robo-Cats).

The set-up (or installation)

From the moment your home is placed on its foundation, you can be looking at as little as a week to ten days before move-in—if your home doesn't require an extensive trim-out (e.g., full tape and texture) and if the site work is minimal. If you're developing raw property, anywhere from three to six weeks will likely pass before you move in. While your general contractor proceeds with installing power, water, septic systems and/or building porches, decks, or perhaps a garage, an installation (or set-up) crew working for your dealer will set up the house itself. With this task there is technically nothing required of you, and if your dealer is reputable, the setup contractor will be reliable. But it doesn't hurt to get to know the set-up contractor, make regular visits to the site and become familiar with the installation manual that came with your home. You may spot problems that can or should be addressed.

Manufactured Home Installation Inspection Checklist for Washington State (slightly abridged)

Washington State has one of the strongest oversight programs in the country for manufactured housing. The below checklist was developed by its HUD State Administrative Agency. It's a good checklist for an installation in any state. Don't hesitate to stick close to the person conducting the final inspecting of your home to make sure he or she covers all the bases. This is where the building inspector can really be your best friend.

Installer Certification

If present during inspection, has the supervising installer shown proof of certification?
Is the state "Installer tag" or jurisdiction's equivalent completed?

Site Preparation

Is the home site properly graded and sloped to prevent water from collecting under the home? (e.g. 1/2-inch per foot for minimum of 10 feet around home)
If home is pit-set and/or on a sloping site, is natural drainage adequately diverted to prevent water from collecting under home?

Installation Instructions

Are the manufacturer's installation instructions, instructions of an engineer or architect, or instructions for relocated homes available for use during inspection?

Foundation & Support Piers

Do clearances under the home meet the requirements? (18 inches beneath at least 75% of the lowest member of the main frame and no less than 12 inches anywhere under the home.)
If applicable, are pre-poured concrete runners or full slabs placed to the minimum thickness required by: 1. home manufacturer's instructions, 2. instructions of an engineer or architect or 3. current instructions for relocated homes?
Do footings (individual pads, runners, or slabs) meet the local frost-depth requirements?
Are foundation pier pads and support piers sized and placed according to the specifications set forth in the: 1. home manufacturer's instructions, 2. instructions of an engineer or architect or 3. instructions for relocated homes?
If prefabricated piers are used, are the piers installed according to the pier manufacturer's instructions? Has engineering documentation been provided?
Are concrete piers shimmed and wedged so all piers make equal contact with the home? Or, are metal piers adjusted and connected so all piers make equal contact with the home? Is the home level?
If an engineered full foundation system is installed, is the installation according to the system manufacturer's instructions? Has engineering data been supplied?

Anchoring

Are anchors spaced according to: 1. home manufacturer's installation instructions, 2. the instructions of an engineer or architect, 3. instructions for relocated homes; and   are they installed according to the equipment manufacturer's instructions?

If an earthquake resistant bracing system is installed, is the installation according to the equipment manufacturer's instructions? Has engineering data been supplied? (The requirement to use earthquake resistant bracing systems is set by the local jurisdiction.)

Skirting

Are skirting vents installed according to the home manufacturer's instructions? Or, do vents have a net area of not less than one square foot for each 150 square feet of under floor area? (For homes sited in flood plains: your local jurisdictions determine venting requirements.)

Is skirting made of materials suitable for ground contact?

Is skirting recessed behind the siding or trim?

Is an access opening of not less than 18 x 24-inches located so that all areas under the home are available for inspection? Is it covered with a sufficient access cover?

Other

Is a ground cover installed? (Minimum 6 mil. black polyethylene or equivalent not required for full concrete slab with minimum thickness of three and one-half inches.)

Are the structural connections of the sections made per the manufacturer's instructions?

Is the heating crossover duct connected properly?

Is the heating crossover duct supported off the ground?

Are the plumbing water and waste crossovers connected properly?

Is the drain pipe supported according to the manufacturer's installation instructions?

If under floor plumbing was shipped-loose, is it installed according to the instructions provided by the home manufacturer?

Note: Any deviation from the home manufacturer's original design and instructions is considered an alteration to be permitted and inspected by Department of Labor and Industries and must be completed by a certified plumber.

If jurisdiction completes electrical inspection, is the electrical crossover connected properly?

Are all holes and tears in the belly fabric patched in an approved manner?

If required, where a wood or pellet stove is installed, is it blocked? Is the combustion air vented to the crawl space or exterior of the home?

Is the dryer vented to the exterior and 1. Does it comply with the dryer manufacturer's specifications; or 2. Is metal with smooth interior surfaces used?

Has the testing of water lines, waste lines, and gas lines been verified with the installer?

Are heat pump and air conditioning condensation lines extended to home's exterior?

Is the water heater pressure relief valve terminated to the exterior and then down?

Is water piping protected against freezing per the home manufacturer's instructions?

Or is a heat tape listed for use with manufactured homes installed per the tape manufacturer's instructions?

****

A set-up, or installation contractor, brings special expertise to this task, and in many states a license is required. But many states currently have no such requirement. Thirteen states have no program at all (this is about to change—see below). Hence the importance of a reputable dealer in selecting the right installer for the job. Aside from vulnerability to serious injury, an inexperienced or untrained crew can cause major damage to a home by rough handling, dropping sections, improper leveling, forcing components together, incorrect anchoring to the foundation and leaving gaps where water and moisture can penetrate (this alone can promote mold and fungi that can render a home toxic and uninhabitable).

In sum, the installation is a crucial element of a successful home placement. It is during this process that more than 100 HUD code requirements must be fulfilled before the home is officially complete, but keep in mind that the actual on-site installation of a manufactured home is not regulated by HUD.

This final stage of on-site assembly can generate many problems if not done correctly. Consumers Union, in a nationwide survey conducted in the 1990s, found that six out of every ten "mobile homeowners" reported major problems with their homes. A good percentage of these were due to faulty installation. A second report, this one in 2002, focusing on Texas, found a similar percentage (see next chapter).

Your new best friend—the building inspector

Fortunately, hope is on the horizon. In 2000 Congress passed legislation that requires all states to train and license installers and to inspect all manufactured home installations to ensure they are fully up to HUD code. The deadline was December, 2005 but don't hold your breath. In the meantime, in those states that currently require licensed installers and inspections, your local building inspector needs to become your new best friend. He or she will visit your site after various steps in the process have been done, and sign off on the work completed; only then can the next phase of the job be undertaken.

If there is no such requirement currently in effect in your state, consider adapting to your needs the state of Washington's excellent installation inspection check list (see sidebar). Here again, being a proactive home buyer can turn out to be your best insurance.

A rear sun deck with bench seats is an ideal way to greatly enlarge the living area of this home. Ordered as options were two sliding glass doors, one from the dining area, the other from the den, to provide more light and greater ease of access during warm weather.

Left, a 1,000 gal. septic tank shortly after placement. Center, a dry well lined with plastic sheets and filled with rock aggregate. Rainwater from the downspouts of the home and garage rain gutters is directed here, preventing ground saturation that could undermine the home's foundation. Right, a pressure tank (this one in the garage) that pressurizes the well water for delivery to the home. Tip: If tank and water pipes will be subject to extended below-freezing temperatures, build a cabinet around them lined with rigid foam insulation and include a low wattage light bulb activated by a temperature activated switch (about $15 at home improvement stores) to keep the cabinet interior above freezing.

Keep in mind that manufacturers will do their darndest not to accept responsibility for problems caused by installers, but ultimately they are indeed responsible, to a meaningful degree. Regrettably, it may take a persistent, informed effort (and sometimes legal recourse) to force them to take appropriate corrective action. Usually, when aggrieved homeowners reach the end of their patience, they end up suing all parties involved: the installer, the dealer and the manufacturer.

Installation sequence

In the case of a pit-set double-wide home, here is an installer's typical task sequence:

- Spot the home (i.e., precisely position home on the foundation). With manual hydraulic jacks, raise the first section off its wheels, remove axles, wheels and hitch (collectively called the running gear). Lower section onto rollers and use

Once the home is leveled on jack stands, tie downs (diagonal steel ribbons) are anchored to foundation.

Detail of rain water drain. This riser will link to a downspout.

Tip: Plug that 1-inch clearance with lengths of foam pipe insulation to ensure protection from rodents.

The finished home 30 days after completion. The ground immediately around the home has been gently sloped to drain run-off water away from the home. The detached 2-car garage was built with matching roof pitch, shingling, and exterior color. Among the options ordered for this home were four double-glazed skylights to maximize interior light during darker winter months. Time from the date home was delivered on site to the move-in: 43 days—a major advantage over a site-built dwelling.

hand lever winches ("come-alongs") to move section into precise final position. Raise section and lower onto support piers placed beneath the bottom flange of the steel I-beams. Remove the temporary plastic sheeting covering the section's open side (for protection during shipping). Repeat this process with the second section, winching it to precise position where it matches the first section.

- Set and level the home. Make height adjustments to support piers as needed to level the home. Precisely align floor, roof and all intersecting walls, then use manufacturer's provided fasteners to permanently secure ("marry") the sections together. Anchor home to foundation with tie-downs according to specified instructions.

- Make all needed crossover connections between the two sections (electrical, plumbing), connect heating and ventilation ducting to registers.

- Complete inside drywall and finish trim, including cosmetic covering of marriage line along ceiling and floor.

- Tape and texture. Using masking tape (hence the term) and plastic sheeting, tape over all trim, windows and surfaces that will not be textured and painted. Texture the interior surfaces using rollers that give the drying paint an attractive rough texture appearance, then spray on a second coat.

- Once water and power are provided, pressure test the water system and perform a power check. Test all appliances.

- Install (or finish installing) the carpeting. **Note**: In the eastern US most of the carpeting is installed at the factory, leaving only those portions that will cover the marriage line. This is cheap and quick but leaves the laid carpet vulnerable to soiling during set-up. In the western region rolls of carpeting and padding are put in the home as it leaves the factory, with complete installation to be done during set-up.
- Clean completely the interior of home, including windows (exteriors, too).

Tip for protecting the crawl space from rodents: Most skirting around a manufactured home serves no support function, even if it's comprised of several courses of cinder blocks resting on a concrete foundation. Whether the skirting is cinder block, treated plywood, or vinyl, there will often be a small gap—an inch or so—between the top of the skirting and the house. The gap is usually covered by a "belly band," typically 1 x 6-inch siding that is nailed to the exterior walls. However, this can still leave gaps large enough to permit mice, and other critters to gain access to the crawl space where the results can be damage to wiring and insulation (not to mention hornet's nests). To close those gaps, push lengths of foam pipe insulation into the gap before the belly band is attached (see photo). To close other small openings, use expanding insulating foam sealant, available at most hardware stores. These preventive measures, costing less than $50 in materials, are easy for the do-it-yourselfer, and are well worth the extra effort.

Final touches

For many days, more likely several weeks, your home site, with trenches and mounds of dirt everywhere, will have the chaotic look of a typical home project. Then, finally the day arrives when the finishing touches are applied: trenches are backfilled and smoothed over and the area around your home is sculpted into gentle contours with a bulldozer. Crushed rock and gravel, if used instead of concrete or asphalt, are laid on the driveway and compacted neatly, and all construction debris and equipment is removed.

At last, your new home is ready for you.

Chapter 12

The Walk-through Inspection, Warranty Service and Long Term care

In 2005 the Manufactured Housing Institute, the industry's largest trade organization, convened a meeting in Memphis, Tennessee to hear a report from Roper & Associates, the well-known consumer research firm that MHI had hired the previous year to assess the public's perception of manufactured housing and the views of homeowners who had recently purchased manufactured homes. The Roper folks interviewed 700 people who had purchased a manufactured home in the past three years, another 600 who had bought comparable site-built homes, and another 1,000 members of the general public.

The Roper Report's "catastrophic" findings

To absolutely no one's surprise, except some old-line industry die-hards frozen in denial, David Roper, who personally delivered the results, revealed that:

A. Manufactured homes, in general, are well-built, attractive, and offer a terrific price advantage over site-built homes on a cost per square foot comparison, and,

B. The industry comes up way short on literally everything else: its sales methods, financing, installation, warranty service, customer satisfaction—and public perception.

Consider this key finding: Of the 700 owners who had recently purchased a new MH, a whopping 39% said they had experienced "a major problem" with their home during the warranty period. That percentage is about 10 times what is considered acceptable for most other industries that track customer satisfaction. It doesn't matter what the problem was. If they thought it was major, it was major. It's hard to imagine any product with that kind of track record not being recalled, let alone surviving as a viable consumer offering.

As bad as that statistic is, it gets worse: Of the 39% who reported major problems, only 22% reported their problem was corrected to their satisfaction. Which is to say, *78% reported their major problem was never corrected.*

Do the math and that means, out of 700 owners polled, 213, or just over 30%, fell into the major problem never-fixed category. That's close to one out of every three new homeowners. When Roper disclosed this tidbit before his hushed audience of industry big wigs, he characterized the finding as "catastrophic." Considering he was addressing the folks who had just paid him $250,000, he was most assuredly being diplomatic.

Similar levels of dissatisfaction have in recent years been reported by Consumer's Union (Southwest regional office) and the AARP. CU's findings indicated the cheaper the home, the greater the incidence of major problems.

On the plus side, other surveys, including one by Foremost Insurance, a major insurer of manufactured homes, showed that 88 percent of homeowners were either very satisfied or somewhat satisfied by their homes. But there's no denying that poor warranty service is a major problem, especially with low end homes.

In theory, if the owner of a manufactured home with a major problem is at loggerheads with the dealer, he or she can turn to the home's manufacturer, the State Administrative Agency (which administers the HUD code) and often a division of the state consumer affairs agency that specializes in complaints involving manufactured home owners and tenants. However, the enforcement of the federal and state regulations to protect you varies widely from state to state. For example, judging by the November, 2002 report that Consumers Union issued on homeowner complaints in Texas (see sidebar), that state's program flunks its responsibilities across the board.

The fact of the matter is, many of the positions of the state agencies created to oversee HUD-code enforcement are bought and paid for by industry political action committees whose campaign contributions (usually to the governor), ensure that no trouble-makers are appointed to staff positions.

There are a few exceptions—Maine's SAA comes to mind—but on the whole, they behave, as Consumers Union characterized the Texas Manufactured Housing Division, "as a service agency for the industry rather than a protector of home buyers."

Nor is Consumers Union thrilled by the responsiveness of HUD's manufactured housing division in Washington, D.C. A Consumers Union request for records of warnings and enforcement actions against builders, submitted under the Freedom of Information Act, took 18 months to process. This is not a good sign of an agency committed to protecting the interests of consumers.

If you are fortunate enough to have a consumer oriented HUD-code administrator in your state, that agency can be your strongest ally. There are HUD offices in 37 states, called SAAs (State Administrative Agencies) that are responsible for monitoring and enforcing the HUD regulations for manufactured homes. Many have individuals who function as ombudsmen. (See the Appendix for the current listing and toll-free numbers). SAAs can often help consumers cut through the occasional finger-pointing and other hassles.

In many states the Attorney General's office has a person on staff who handles complaints as well. But, on the whole, if your state has a state HUD-code regulator, that should be the first place you go to if your problem is not being resolved.

Nipping warranty problems in the bud

There is also no such thing as a perfect home, no matter how well it's built, or to what code. Moreover, you can expect to find certain quality differences between a home costing $45,000 and one that sells for $150,000. But even the best built abodes will have minor blemishes that need fixing, if only a few hairline cracks in the paint, and the sheetrock beneath, as the home settles over time. These items, along with all other shortcomings big and small, fall in the category of warranty work that your home's manufacturer may cover at no charge.

Warranty coverage, sometimes mandated by state law, lasts at least one year (a HUD-code minimum). Bear in mind that the home itself is warrantied by the manufacturer and the site work, including foundation, is (or should be) warrantied by your dealer or contractor

Texas flunks again—this time it's final inspections and warranty enforcement

In November, 2002, less than a year after it released a scathing report on dealer fraud and misrepresentation in the sale of manufactured homes in Texas (see sidebar, p. 50), the Southwest Regional Office of Consumers Union issued a second report, this one analyzing complaints involving home installation, warranty service and repairs. The picture CU painted not only reflects poorly on the industry, it slams Texas state regulators for doing a miserable job of protecting the owners of new manufactured homes. CU concluded: "Poor service and worse enforcement leave manufactured home owners in the lurch." Here are the report's main points:

• CU examined the outcomes of 1,786 "warranty" complaints for the period 1998-2002 to the Texas department of Housing and Community Affairs Manufactured Housing Division, the agency responsible for enforcing federal and state laws. A "remarkable 36 percent" (CU's words) were rejected without any investigation, mostly because the consumer failed to prove they had notified the manufacturer and retailer in writing about their problems during the warranty period. (Most consumers phoned in their complaints.)

• A "stunning 79 percent" (again, CU's words) of new owners indicated that they had experienced problems with their homes, even if they were generally satisfied.

• While manufactured homes have improved structurally, CU found that many components of these homes still trouble consumers: "...poor quality plumbing fixtures, trim and floor covering poorly affixed, transportation damage and faulty installation leave consumers with less home than they thought they purchased."

• Many consumers reported extensive trouble getting final installation and repairs completed under their warranty contracts. Limited duration, coverage limits, blame shifting among parties, and poor service left many consumers unsatisfied. Nearly three out of ten (28 percent) of consumer with problems were 'completely dissatisfied' with the warranty work on their home."

• Only a third of homeowners surveyed (36 percent) were more satisfied than dissatisfied with their new homes, with 17 percent of new homeowners completely dissatisfied.

• Arbitration agreements in purchase contracts block access to the courts, leaving regulatory relief the only option for some consumers.

• Owners of manufactured homes performed major repairs on their plumbing fixtures at a rate 57% higher than site-built homeowners.

• CU explained "To make certain (that) manufacturers could control the dealer relationship, we limited our calculations to new homes only," adding: "Although retailers may be legally responsible for some...complaints, manufacturers have the ability to select those retailers through whom they market their product. Manufacturers can refuse to sell through retailers with a history of problems."

More information, including the full text of the report, Paper Tiger, Missing Dragon, in PDF format, and a new tips brochure for buyers developed with the information in the CU report, is available at **www.consumersunion.org/mh/**

responsible for that work. Most reputable installers warranty their work for a year.

Most of these problems should be detected during installation (if a good inspection system is in place) or during your walk-through inspection prior to taking possession of the home. The key is making sure such inspections take place. Hence this rule:

A thorough objective installation inspection prior to taking possession of the home is the single most effective way to detect and to document problems with your home.

In many states a local inspector is required by law to make such an inspection. If not, don't hesitate to insist that such an inspection be scheduled—doing so could be the most important action you take to protect you and the safety of your home.

If any problem is serious enough that the bank (in the case of a construction loan) won't pay off the dealer until it is corrected, you likely won't be permitted to move in until repairs have been completed, but this will be a small price to pay. In short, it's all about the cash. Problems have a way of getting fixed with amazing speed when there's money on the line. Hence, another rule:

Regardless of who controls the purse strings (you or your lender), make sure that the dealer does not get paid the last remaining amount of the purchase contract until the completion of the walk-through inspection and the correction of significant problems (to your satisfaction).

The walk-through inspection

Typically, the moment you take possession of your home occurs the day you meet with your dealer's representative to conduct a walk-through inspection of your home following the completion of installation. If a construction loan is involved, someone from your lender may attend as well, especially if the bank requires a satisfactory inspection prior to releasing the final funds. This is almost always a happy milestone, certainly an exciting moment for you. Walk-throughs usually take less than an hour, but this is a time you need to be observant, take notes, flip a lot of switches, and ask questions. You will also be instructed how various appliances operate. Take your time. Resist any pressure to complete the walk-through at faster pace than you feel comfortable doing. Should any issue arise in the future around warranty service, this moment is an important legal milestone when you can identify and document any problems.

Some new homeowners may be shy or intimidated by the thought of bringing up shortcomings during the inspection. If you think you may feel this way, call on your personal advocate for one last trip into the trenches (promise them a congratulatory lunch or dinner afterwards—they will certainly have earned it).

This is absolutely the time to bring up any shortcomings and get them officially recorded. Voicing them later makes much more difficult the task of establishing they were there at the time of inspection.

Look for cuts, scratches, abrasions, scrapes, dents, stains, chips, etc., on any surface: walls, vinyl flooring, appliances, mirrors, glass, woodwork, sheetrock, counters, fixtures, carpet, draperies, hardware—everywhere.

Your home's manufacturer may provide you with a check-off list to help with your inspection. If so, have it with you.

The checklist

Here's a recommended check list for inspecting your home:

Exterior:

- All exterior grading around home makes water flow away from the house. Give this a careful look. You don't want to be surprised on the first day of rain.
- Metal manufacturer's certification tag (commonly, called a "HUD tag," albeit mistakenly) attached and readable on each section of the house. Tags are normally red in color and located near the bottom corner at the end of each section. **Important**: Don't ever remove, alter or paint over these tags. A missing or unreadable tag (carrying your home's HUD number, which is different from the manufacturer's serial number) can literally prevent your home from being sold or refinanced. Obtaining a replacement tag can be a time-consuming, costly, bureaucratic nightmare.
- No loose shingles or other construction materials left on roof. No exposed nails or staples ("shiners"). These should all be covered with asphalt roofing cement. No discrepancies in roofing, including roof cap, flashing, ventilation stacks, etc.
- Gutters and downspouts properly installed—and discharging water away from the house.
- Exterior surfaces, particularly siding, free of defects, properly joined.
- Skirting correctly done. Entry well (or access door) to the crawl space suitably weather protected.
- Crawl space. If you have a monolithic slab foundation: it should be clean and free of any debris that could impede use of a "creeper" to move around in there.
- Exterior light fixtures properly installed.
- Front and rear entry doors, and all sliding doors, and their locks, operate smoothly, with appropriate weather stripping in place. Same with exterior screen doors.

Interior:

Living room, dining room, general interior

- Carpet snugly in place throughout, free of lumps, waves or discoloration.
- Baseboard installed, door and window moldings properly joined.
- No cracks or seams in walls or ceilings. No bulge lines in sheetrock seams.
- Ordered options correctly installed, such as windows, skylights, ceiling fan and chandelier outlets.
- Blinds operate easily. All light switches operable.
- All interior doors, windows open and shut smoothly, latches and locks work properly.

Kitchen and utility room

- No cuts, lumps or discoloration in the linoleum
- Drawers, cabinets open and close smoothly
- Appliances as ordered. Stove, counter tops level (use a small bubble level or

place a ball on counter top).
- Floors level. No squeaks or creaking sounds when walked on. Walk around a bit to test for these.
- Refrigerator on and cold. If installed, drinking water dispenser works OK.
- Hot and cold water OK. Water pressure satisfactory on both.
- Central heating / AC (if in utility room) operating, filters installed.
- Ceiling fan in utility room (for auto air circulation) operating properly.

Bathrooms
- Sinks, tubs free of scratches, irregularities.
- Toilets flush properly.
- Caulking seams (or grout) clean, complete with no irregularities.
- No cuts, lumps or discoloration in linoleum.
- Shower door(s)) properly aligned, open and close properly, providing adequate seal.
- Drawers, cabinets operate properly. Exhaust fan works.

Manuals and documentation

Ideally, at the time of your inspection, the central heating (or air conditioning, if installed) is running so that you can verify its operation by altering the thermostat setting. **Tip**: Ask your dealer's rep to turn on the system before your arrival. Doing so will also allow you to check for proper air flow from the room registers.

In addition to the house master keys, your dealer's rep will hand you one or more large envelopes containing manuals, specification sheets, registration cards, diagrams, warnings, regulations, resource guides and operating instructions for everything from the smoke detector and the front doorbell to the central heating / air conditioning system and major kitchen appliances. **Note**: if you're not given them, ask for them, and make sure you get them. Don't lose them. Besides providing helpful operating instructions, the documents explain how to obtain warranty and repair service for your home's appliances and its heating and air conditioning system. For example, if your wall thermostat malfunctions, your dealer may instruct you to call the manufacturer's toll-free number to obtain the warranty service provider in your area.

The honeymoon—and after

At last, when they're finally all gone—the dealers, the bankers, the contractors, the phone service techs, the building inspectors, every last one of them—there's nothing quite like the feeling of being in your new home. Kick back and enjoy it. You deserve it. Whether your home is on your own land or in a park community or on a rented piece of your uncle's north 40, you have successfully acquired one of the best quality options for family shelter anywhere in the known world, and very likely at a price significantly less than that of a comparable site-built home.

Doubtless, next on your immediate agenda is moving in and making your house a true home. Still, in the weeks and months that follow, you will discover things that need fixing or adjusting. Most will be easily handled by a simple service call. **Important**: Keep a list of them and contact your dealer as needed to schedule repair visits. Planning ahead, make a note of the expiration date of your home's warranty (one year is common) and a month or six weeks before that date, conduct a thorough inspection of the home, similar to the walk-through, and deliver your final list of needed fixes to your dealer.

Here again is where a reputable dealer can really make a world of difference. As described in Chapter 8, dealerships handle warranty service on their homes in different ways. The best dealerships have one or more employees on staff to handle warranty service calls on behalf of the manufacturer (who is billed for the warranty work).

Some dealerships, even factory-owned sales centers, perform no warranty work, instead leaving the task to the manufacturer who employs its own service providers. This can work fine if the manufacturer stays on top of things and the service area is not too large. Presumably, you were given assurances to that effect before you purchased your home.

Note: One of the most common flaws in any new home is small cracks in the drywall that appear as the home settles during the first year on its foundation. Yes, these are almost always covered by your warranty, but before you push for action, consider this: fixing drywall cracks is a messy, fundamentally dirty business that will require time, a lot of furniture moving, extensive cleaning and inconvenience. Unless these cracks really bother you, maybe you're better off just letting them go untouched. In time you won't even notice them. Visitors to your home likely won't either.

The warranty system most susceptible to headaches is when a manufacturer contracts with factory representatives who cover specified territories, sometimes for more than one manufacturer. This arrangement can be very frustrating for homeowners in relatively distant areas. Contract service reps typically wait until they accumulate enough service calls to warrant a trip to more remote regions. Not only does this mean you may wait many weeks before a factory technician shows up at your door, but it's not uncommon that the repair can't be made during the visit because the needed part is the wrong size, or it's not in the truck, or "They didn't tell me you had a Series E gizmo" or some such miscommunication. Result: You end up waiting many more weeks for the next scheduled visit.

Regardless of the arrangement, the warranty on your home is ultimately only as good as the manufacturer behind it. Reputations vary. For example, in the category Unclear on the Concept, some short-sighted manufacturers, to control costs, offer year-end bonuses to their service division chiefs based on how much warranty work they *don't* authorize.

Good dealerships will go to bat for you. In some cases, if a manufacturer determines that your claim is not covered, good dealers will make the repairs at their expense, because they know that happy customers are their best advertising.

When problems arise

When a problem crops up that is obviously a warranty issue, you can give yourself a leg up on getting the help you need if you're polite to all concerned. Any show of hostility is bound to be counterproductive. It's OK to be persistent, even to be a squeaky wheel, but be a persistently polite squeaky wheel.

If possible, find the right contact person at your dealership or the manufacturer and stick with him or her. Otherwise, you can waste a lot of time telling your story over and over.

Take notes, keeping a list of phone numbers. Where possible, don't let a phone conversation end without getting a good idea of what will happen next, and when, and at which point you should call back if *when* comes and goes without action.

If resolving your problem requires a letter, be sure to keep a copy in your files to document action you have taken.

Important tip: Today, virtually every manufacturer's factory has a service center and every service center has an email address. So does most every dealer. Ask for both email addresses at the time you take possession of your home. When you have any problem, email your dealer, and send a copy to the factory. Your dealer can then easily cut and paste your email and send it on to the factory. This way you document your actions with legally admissible correspondence.

Recommendation: Should you conclude that, for some unknown reason, you are being stalled or stonewalled, send a copy of your letter to a third party that may have an interest. For example, one homeowner unable to get her dealer to repair a roof leak that appeared after the first rain, wrote a letter to the dealer, reviewing in a business-like manner the months of delay she had encountered. She concluded with yet another request to have the leak repaired. She mailed a copy of the letter to the manufacturer, indicating this in her letter to the dealer. Within a week, a crew showed up and repaired the roof.

And then, of course, there is the HUD-code housing agency in your state (if it has one). Absent that, you might also consider the assistance available from your local Better Business Bureau, or the State Attorney General's office.

Maintenance for the long haul

Despite the perception of the misinformed, your new home is not an RV. It's not even a mobile home (although the term is used universally by industry folk, even though the politically correct types regularly admonish them not to). RVs, even the most expensive motor coaches, depreciate in value as the years pass. In contrast, your home, especially if it's legally tied to the land you own, will in all likelihood appreciate in value as would a conventional single family home—all the more so if you take good care of your home and the property.

As with any home, yours will require care and routine maintenance, however, you will be amazed how little attention your home actually needs. Once again, cutting edge building products, superior adhesives, factory construction, great quality control and excellent engineering and design all combine to give today's quality manufactured home the same life span as a site-built home.

Don't forget those warranty cards

After you come up for air after moving into your home, browse the heavy package of instructions and manuals you were handed the day of your walk-through inspection. Do the following:

• Make notes on the maintenance needs of your home, its appliances and its heating/ventilation/air conditioning system (HVAC in the trade).

• Have a calendar handy and make notes by dates when to perform routine maintenance such as changing furnace filters, putting new batteries in the smoke detectors and flushing out the water heater.

• Last, and this is important, don't skip filling out and mailing all the registration and warranty cards, particularly to your home's manufacturer. In the case of registering your home, three cards are involved. Your dealer sends one to the manufacturer, leaving two in your manual. Fill out and mail in the second card and keep the third for your records. This way if there is any kind of recall, the manufacturer knows where to find you. If possible, make photocopies before mailing warranty cards. If you contact a manufacturer about a problem, things go much more smoothly if they can quickly bring up your warranty registration information on their screen. Otherwise, you may face the time-consuming task of authenticating your purchase.

It all starts with a reputable dealer

As with so many other aspects of a manufactured home purchase, the quality of warranty service depends so much on the quality of the people involved, starting with finding a reputable dealer. This fact explains why this guide devotes so much attention to strategies to help you find the right professionals in whom to place your trust. The good news is they are out there waiting for you, and you can find them.

For its part, the manufactured home industry is still young and still evolving. As the afterword that follows this chapter explains, the coming years promise to be very eventful as a colorful, highly competitive, rough-and-tumble, distinctly American industry matures. As events unfold, may you follow them while enjoying the comfort and many pleasures of your new manufactured home.

Afterword

The Future of American Housing's Best Kept Secret

Three years ago, as I finished work on the first edition of this guide, I wrote an Afterword that amounted to a pretty harsh indictment of the manufactured home industry. Although I attempted to balance my criticism with suggested fixes and pointed to the tremendous potential of factory-built homes, I didn't hold out much hope that the industry had the collective will to reform itself any time soon. Certainly, if you've read this far, you already know many of the problems this industry faces. A few recent events, however, have given me reason to be more hopeful.

In the aftermath of the 2005 industry meeting described at the beginning of the last chapter (during which Roper & Associates disclosed survey findings that placed the industry in a terrible light, particularly on customer satisfaction issues), the Manufactured Housing Institute convened in Chicago a group of 47 industry movers and shakers for a closed-door meeting to grapple with the issues. The atmosphere was at times tense and tempers flared, but over a period of several days "The Chicago 47" confronted the issues and forged something that approached a consensus, notably on the key issue of customer satisfaction. The gist: the best way to improve customer satisfaction is to hire an independent third party such as J. D. Power & Associates to conduct consumer satisfaction surveys. For the first two years or so the results would be shared only with the participating manufacturers, but not the home buying public, to give those builders with low scores a chance to improve. Presumably, thereafter, the Consumer Satisfaction Index (CSI) for every builder would be made available to the public, much the way J.D. Power survey results are provided for the auto industry. Early in 2006, the MHI announced it was contracting with J. D. Power & Associates to begin customer survey.

Some key issues

Customer satisfaction surveys are a start, especially if the results are eventually made known to the public. Another promising development is the pending implementation of much stronger installation requirements for set-up contractors (mandated by Congress in 2000) and current HUD-led effort to craft an industry wide dispute resolution process that is fair to all parties. Yet, other significant issues remain, and because they are largely cultural in nature, may be less tractable. Here is a brief look:

Public perception of the industry

No getting around it, the term "manufactured home" has yet to supplant "mobile home" in the public's mind, if indeed mobile home has ever fully supplanted "house trailer." The public perception is that the industry is a provider of poorly constructed, unattractive "mobile homes" that are sold like cars, that don't appreciate in value, and when placed in neighborhoods of site-built homes, contribute to lower property values. The truth is, in many regions of the country, particularly the Southeast and South Central U.S., the evidence overwhelmingly supports the public's perception. This was my conclusion after a year interviewing and researching all 79 HUD-code builders in the US and phantom shopping many dealerships for the *Rating's Guide*. The fact is, there are many HUD-code builders who put out dreary, boxy, cookie cutter homes with poor quality construction—how else to make them affordable?—and hundreds of dealerships selling them, many who see no reason to drop the phrase "mobile home" from their names. Why? Because the demand is there, from consumers whose need for basic housing trumps appearance, quality construction and asset appreciation.

The industry's image of itself

Despite the promotional brochures and public pronouncements, the industry remains stuck in a street dealer mentality. It still sees its primary market as the low income buyer with flawed credit and in need of affordable housing. Strangely, at a time when almost every industry in recent decades has undergone great transformation, little within the manufactured home sector, apart from terrific engineering innovations, has changed in 30 years. The factories remain focused on sell, ship and collect, their management knowing little about how other housing businesses operate, or the opportunities those businesses represent for the industry. At the dealerships the stress remains on closing deals, taking care of customers, following up contacts, and fighting over "ups."

A herd mentality prevails. In a very real sense the industry itself has been primarily responsible for keeping manufactured housing the best-kept secret in American housing.

The heart of the dilemma

These issues are in many ways inter-related. So, too, it appears, are the possible solutions. Considering the larger picture, here is what appears to be at the heart of the industry's dilemma:

Over the past quarter century there have been tremendous strides in the design, engineering, and construction of manufactured homes, so much so that today's higher end manufactured home is now equal to, and in many cases, superior to comparable mainstream site-built homes. Yet the way the industry markets these homes has remained largely unchanged. With very few exceptions, it's been street dealers or nothing. It would not be a stretch to say the industry is using yesterday's sales techniques to sell yesterday's product to yesterday's home buyer. This anachronistic approach is not only stymieing efforts to introduce a great product to the mainstream home buyer, but mires the industry in the street dealer image it is trying so earnestly to shed.

By contrast, within the larger housing industry, innovative business models for selling new homes continue to appear, taking advantage of new financial products, developer and real estate partnerships, spec builders, architects, and local lenders. Building of new entry level homes has been at a record pace for two years and these homes are being snapped up by many of the same buyers who would be excellent prospects for manufactured homes, if only the industry could interest them.

Two strategies

No single panacea exists to resolve the this dilemma, but here are two strategies that appear worth considering:

1. Design and build homes that look like site-built homes

Face it, the hallmark of a manufactured home is a shallow roof, no second story, no eves on one side, and a boring boxy shape. No wonder mainstream home buyers are turned off. The choice is obvious here: either the industry continues business as usual, losing market share and playing it safe as a provider of low end affordable housing, or it can get off its rear and start making great looking homes that appeal to mainstream home buyers.

There is nothing in the HUD code that prevents builders from creating homes with a higher roof pitch, articulated exterior walls that feature indentations, pop-outs and second stories, just like site-built homes. Some builders have started doing precisely this, but on the whole, and especially during times of great contraction, the industry becomes its own worst enemy—it hunkers down and clings to its affordable housing customer base, stripping its models of their value in order to survive in a world of cutthroat street dealer price wars. Once again, the self-fulfilling prophecy.

2. Create and implement new business models that successfully appeal to mainstream buyers.

One such model that appears to hold real promise: attractive home centers located away from dealer row and which specialize in turnkey homes. The price includes everything: the house, installation, site preparation, garage, porch, decks, driveway, and landscaping.

The advantages to this business model: the dealer's turnkey package provides an additional profit center; the customer base is less problematic, being comprised of move-up and first-time site-built buyers able to obtain conventional home loans; the buyers are freed from the hassle and responsibility of hiring a contractor and other developer tasks; and the dealer acquires the stature of a traditional mainstream site-built home developer. Lastly, when the home is finished, those who see it won't think "That's a very nice manufactured home." They'll think "That's a very nice home."

Enterprising dealers might take this model a step further and develop an inventory of home sites, either through options with property owners, outright purchase, or other arrangements. True, all this requires greater start-up capital, higher liquidity, a more sophisticated management and sales staff, and the velocity of the transaction cycle will slow down. But the sales commissions will be higher and the revenue stream more diversified and stable. As important, this business model enables the dealer to go toe to toe with the site-built developers, tapping into the larger mainstream home buyer market by offering a quality home package at a very competitive price.

There is a subtle, but potentially powerful consequence that one can foresee with the above marketing scenario: because their appearance will be all but indistinguishable from conventional site built homes, the fact that these homes are manufactured homes will be regarded as more of a technicality than a stigma. They will fall within the rubric "factory-built," along with modular homes, and thus merge quietly into the mainstream image of a conventional home. At that point the bias that has dogged manufactured housing, and the industry's self-esteem, will begin to vanish as well.

The foregoing is only one possible alternative to the street dealership model. Other variations doubtless will emerge—one in particular involves introducing modular homes into the dealer's product mix. What's important is that, with the industry recovered from its latest near-collapse, for those dealerships that survived, the timing is ideal to develop new marketing modalities and invest the resources needed to make them happen. And maybe, just maybe, the manufacturers will see the great opportunity that awaits them as well.

Ethical standards

This is a big one—and a big test of the leadership. On this score the industry doesn't need more round tables; it needs a posse. Strong collective leadership must emerge to crack down meaningfully on the sleaze balls and the predators everywhere within its domain. Until then—and there is no easy way to express this—the public, right or wrong, will continue to believe this industry is riddled with crooks, and that perception can kill future prospects. Moreover, that perception will continue to drive away a lot of very sharp, educated young professionals looking for careers in an industry they can be proud of. And this industry sorely needs new blood.

To its credit, the Manufactured Home Institute has launched a campaign called Lending Best Practices to prevent abuses, but the program, while well-intentioned, is voluntary. If the industry is truly serious about cleaning up its act, it will promptly single out these bad actors—and cut them off. The same holds for dealerships. What is sorely needed is Retailing Best Practices to rid the marketplace of fraud, high pressure sales tactics and other abuses.

Other industries and professions (real estate and banking among them) have devised and put in force proven strategies for tough effective self-regulation, many of them easily adaptable to the manufactured housing sector. Whatever means are chosen, it is time to act. Any further delay of these needed fundamental reforms imperils the industry's potential as a major player in the nation's home building sector.

The path ahead

The manufactured home industry is still young, and in some ways, still immature. Its first generation pioneers are beginning to hand over the torch to a new generation who, one hopes, will answer the challenges facing the industry. Great opportunities exist, and the future holds much promise. The next decade should be especially eventful. What is not in dispute, especially to all those who have discovered the secret, is that the pioneers have created, and now bequeath to their successors, a truly wonderful, peculiarly American innovation in housing that will be around for generations to come.

Appendix

Manufactured Housing and Standards: State Administrative Agencies (SAAs)
How and where to File a Complaint

Technically HUD state administrators are not consumer advocates (they're regulators), but many peform that function, using their regulatory authority and clout on behalf of the home owner. Some SAAs are more aggressive than others. Some are stacked with industry approved appointees and are all but useless to consumers and home owners.

The following states currently have no HUD State Administrative Agency (but will be required to have one established by December 2005): Vermont, New Hampshire, Massachusetts, Rhode Island, Connecticut, New Jersey, Delaware, Maryland, Montana, North Dakota, Oklahoma, Wyoming, Nebraska, Rhode Island, and Ohio.
For complaints in these states, contact:

The Manufactured Housing and Standards Division
Office of Consumer and Regulatory Affairs,
US Department of Housing & Urban Development
451 Seventh Street, SW, Room 9152
Washington, DC 20410-8000
Telephone: (202) 708-6423 or 1-800-927-2891.   FAX: (202) 708-4213

The below information, quoted verbatim, can be found online on the U.S. Department of Housing and Urban Development's Homes and Communities Web site at www.hud.gov: 80/offices/hsg/sfh/mhs/mhssaa.cfm.

All residential manufactured homes (mobile homes) must comply with the Federal Manufactured Home Construction and Safety Standards. Since June 15, 1976, manufacturers have confirmed compliance with the Standards by attaching a red label to the back of each transportable section of a home produced.

The extent to which HUD can help a homeowner resolve a complaint depends on the seriousness of the problem. In cases where safety-related defects in homes create an unreasonable risk of injury or death to the occupants, manufacturers must correct the defect in a short period. HUD cannot require correction unless the defects were introduced into the home during the manufacturing process. The on-site installation of a manufactured home is not regulated by HUD.

If a problem arises with a manufactured home, the first contact should be the retailer. Most problems can be eliminated quickly. If the retailer cannot help, the second contact should be the manufacturer. Manufacturers, for the most part, are quick to respond.

It is important to put a complaint in writing. Also, make a copy to keep with your records. The letter should include the serial number of the home with a list of the problems. List any known factors that contributed to the problem. Also list any secondary issues related to the problem.

If the retailer and the manufacturer do not resolve your concerns, there are offices within most state governments with staff that are knowledgeable about manufactured housing construction and related issues. There are 37 States participating with HUD in a State and Federal partnership to regulate and enforce the Federal manufactured housing program in their state. Many state governments regulate all, or part, of the manufactured housing industry in the state. Some areas that may be regulated in your state are retailers, transporters and installers.

ALABAMA
Mr. Jim Sloan, Administrator
Alabama Manufactured Housing Commission
350 S. Decatur Street
Montgomery, AL 36104-4306
PH: 334-242-4036 ext 22 or 25
FAX: 334-240-3178

ARIZONA
Mr. N. Eric Borg, Director
Department of Building & Fire Safety
Office of Manufactured Housing
99 East Virginia, Suite #100
Phoenix, AZ 85004-1108
PH: 602-255-4072, ext. 244
FAX: 602-255-4962

ARKANSAS
Mr. Whit Waller, Director
Arkansas Manufactured Home Commission
523 South Louisiana Street Suite 500
Little Rock, AR 72201-5705
PH: 501-324-9032 FAX: 501-324-9034

CALIFORNIA
Mr. Richard Weinert, AdAdministrator
Dept. of Housing & Community Development
Manufactured Housing Section
P.O. Box 31
Sacramento, CA 95812-0031
PH: 916-445-3338
DD: 916-327-2838 FAX: 916-327-4712

COLORADO
Mr. Tom Hart, Director
Housing Division, Dept of Local Affairs
1313 Sherman Street, #518
Denver, CO 80203-2244
PH: 303-866-2033 FAX: 303-866-4077

FLORIDA
Mr. Edward D. Broyles, Bureau Chief
Bureau of Mobile Homes & RV
Division of Motor Vehicles
2900 Apalachee Parkway Room A-129
Tallahassee, FL 32399-0640
PH: 850-488-8600 FAX: 850-488-7053
Designee: Chuck Smith, Program Manager

GEORGIA
Mr. Chris Stephens, Asst. State Fire Marshal
Manufactured Housing Division
State Fire Marshal's Office
#2 Martin Luther King Jr. Dr, #620 West Tower
Atlanta, GA 30334
PH: 404-656-3687 or 404-656-9498
FAX: 404-657-6971
Designee: Joe Hall (IPIA)

IDAHO
Mr. Dave Munroe, Administrator
Division of Building SafetyBuilding Bureau
P.O. Box 83720
Meridian, ID 83720-0060
PH: 208-334-3896 FAX: 208-334-2683
Designee: Tom Rodgers

ILLINOIS
Mr. John D. Reilly Jr.
Illinois Department of Public Health
General Engineering Section
Division of Environmental Health
525-535 W. Jefferson Street
Springfield, IL 62761
PH: 217-782-5830

INDIANA
Ms. Richelle (Shelly) Wakefield, CBO
Administrator. Codes Enforcement Division
Indiana Government Center South
402 W. Washington, Street
Room W-246
Indianapolis, IN 46204
PH: 317-232-1407 FAX: 317-232-0146

IOWA
Mr. Jeff Quigle, State Administrator
Department of Public Safety
Iowa Fire Marshal Office
215 East 7th Street
Des Moines, IA 50319-0001
PH: 515-281-5132 FAX: 515-242-6299

KENTUCKY
Mr. Harry Rucker, Chief
Manufactured Housing Division
Department of Housing, Building, and Construction
1049 US 127 South, Bay 5
Frankfort, KY 40601-4322
PH: 502-564-4018 FAX: 502-564-8275

LOUISIANA
Sammy J. Hoover, Administrator
Manufactured Housing State Administrative Agency
Louisiana Manufactured Housing Commission
PO Box 4249
Baton Rouge, LA 70821
PH: 225-342-5919

MAINE
Mr. Robert LeClair, Executive Director
Manufactured Housing Board
Office of Licensing and Regulation
35 State House Station
Augusta, ME 04333-0035
PH: 207-624-8633 FAX: 207-624-8637

MARYLAND
Mr. James Hanna, Director
Dept. of Housing & Community Development
Maryland Code Administration
100 Community Place
Crownsville, MD 21032-2023
PH: 410-514-7220 FAX: 410-987-8902
Designee: Kanti Patel or Charles Cook

MICHIGAN
Mr. Richard A. VanderMolen
Director, Manufactured Housing
and Land Development Division
P.O. Box 30703
Lansing, MI 48909-8203
PH: 517-241-6300 FAX: 517-241-6301
Designee: Kevin DeGroat

MINNESOTA
Mr. Thomas Joachim, Director
MN Building Codes & Standards Division
Dept. of Administration
Manufactured Structures Section
121 7th Place E., Suite 408
St. Paul, MN 55101-2181
PH: 651-296-4639 FAX: 651-297-1973
Designee: Randy Vogt PH: 651-296-9927

MISSISSIPPI
Mr. Millard Mackey, Chief Deputy
Manufactured Housing Division
State Fire Marshal's Office
P.O. Box 79
Jackson, MS 39205-0079
PH: 601-359-1061 FAX: 601-359-1076
Designee: Gene Humphrey, Dep. Fire Marshal

MISSOURI
Mr. Steve Jungmeyer, Director
Dept. of Manufactured Housing
and Modular Units
Missouri Public Service Commission
P.O. Box 360
200 Madison Street, Suite 600
Jefferson City, MO 65102
PH: 573-751-7119 or 1-800-819-3180
FAX: 573-522-2509
Designee: Wess Henderson, Adminstrator

NEBRASKA
Mr. Mark Luttich, Department Director
Nebraska Public Service Commission
Housing & Recreational Vehicle Department
P.O. Box 94927
300 The Atrium; 1200 N Street
Lincoln, NE 68509-4927
PH: 402-471-0518 FAX: 402-471-7709
Designee: Kent Priby
PH: 402-471-0514

NEVADA
Ms. Renee Diamond, Administrator
Department of Business & Industry
Manufactured Housing Division
2501 E. Sahara Avenue, Suite 204
Las Vegas, NV 89104-4137
PH: 702-486-4135
DD: 702-486-4278   FAX: 702-486-4309
Designee: Gary Childers

NEW JERSEY
Mr. Paul Sachdeva, Manager
New Jersey Division of Codes and Standards
Dept. of Community Affairs
P.O. Box 816
101 S. Broad Street
Trenton, NJ 08625-0816
PH: 609-984-7974
FAX: 609-984-7952

NEW MEXICO
Mr. Robert M. Unthank, Program Manager
Manufactured Housing Division
Regulation & Licensing Department
725 St. Michael's Drive
Santa Fe, NM 87505-7605
PH: 505-827-7070
DD: 505-827-7028 FAX: 505-827-7074
Designee: John Wilson (SAA)

NEW YORK
Mr. Tim King, Administrator
Manufactured Housing Unit
Department of State
Code Division
41 State Street, 11th Floor
Albany, NY 12231
PH: 518-474-4073
DD: 518-473-8901
FAX: 518-486-4487

NORTH CAROLINA
Mr. C. Patrick Walker, Deputy Commissioner
Manufactured Building Division
Department of Insurance
410 N. Boylan Avenue
Raleigh, NC 27603-1212
PH: 919-733-3901
Consumer Assistant Line: 800-587-2716
FAX: 919-715-9693
Designee: David Goins, Administrator
PH: 252-754-2195
FAX: 252-754-2516

OREGON
Mr. Joseph A. Brewer, III, Administrator
Department of Consumer & Business Services
Building Codes Division
P.O. Box 14470
1535 Edgewater Drive, NW
Salem, OR 97309-0404
PH: 503-378-4133
FAX: 503-378-2322
Designee: Dana Roberts
PH: 503-378-8450
FAX: 503-378-4101

PENNSYLVANIA
Mr. John F. Boyer, Jr.
Chief, Manufactured Housing Division
Community Development & Housing Office
Center for Community Development
4th Florr, Commonwealth Keystone Building
Harrisburg, PA 17120-0225
PH: 717-720-7413
FAX: 717-783-4663
Designee: Mark Conte

RHODE ISLAND
Mr. Joseph Cirillo, Commissioner
Building Code Commission
State of Rhode Island
Department of Administration
One Capitol Hill
Providence, RI 02908-5859
PH: 401-222-3033
FAX: 401-222-2599
Email: elaineg@gw.doa.state.ri.us
dandedentro@doa.state.ri.us
Designee: Richard Mancini
PH: 401-222-6332

SOUTH CAROLINA
Mr. David Bennett, Administrator
SC Dept. of Labor, Licensing & Regulation
Real Estate & Bldg. Code Professions
110 Centerview Dr., Suite 102
Columbia, SC 29211-1329
PH: 803-896-4682
or 803-896-4688
FAX: 803-896-4814

SOUTH DAKOTA
Mr. Daniel R. Carlson, State Fire Marshal
Office of State Fire Marshal
Dept. of Commerce & Regulations
118 West Capitol Avenue
Pierre, SD 57501-5070
PH: 605-773-3562
FAX: 605-773-6631
Designee: Paul Merriman

TENNESSEE
Mr. Joe VanHooser, Director
Codes & Standards, Div. of Fire Prevention
Department of Commerce & Insurance
500 James Robertson Parkway
Nashville, TN 37243-1162
PH: 615-532-5808
FAX: 615-253-3267

TEXAS
Ms. Bobbie Hill, Administrator
Manufactured Housing
TX Dept. of Housing & Community Affairs
P.O. Box 12489
Austin, TX 78711-2489
PH: 512-475-3983
or 800-500-7074
FAX: 512-475-4250
Designee: James Galbreath

UTAH
Mr. Daniel S. Jones, Director
Construction Trades Bureau
Div. of Occupational & Professional Licensing
Department of Commerce
P.O. Box 146741
160 E. 300 South
Salt Lake City, UT 84111-6741
PH: 801-530-6720
DD: 801-530-6720
FAX: 801-530-6511
Designee: Ed Short

VIRGINIA
Mr. Curtis McIver, Associate Director
State Building Code Administration Office
Dept. of Housing & Community Development
Jackson Center, 501 N. Second Street
Richmond, VA 23219-1321
PH: 804-371-7160
FAX: 804-371-7092
Designee: Lorenzo Dyer

WASHINGTON
Ms. Teri Ramsauer, Manager
Office of Manufactured Housing
Washington State Office of Community
Development
906 Columbia St. SW
Olympia, WA 98504-8350
PH: 360-725-2960 or 1-800-964-0852
FAX: 360-586-5880

WEST VIRGINIA
Ms. Fran Cook, Deputy Commissioner
West Virginia Division of Labor
Building 6, 8749
Capitol Complex
Charleston, WV 25305
PH: 304-558-7890
FAX: 304-558-3797

WISCONSIN
Mr. Ken Fiedler, Administrator
Manufactured Homes,
Safety & Building Division
Department of Commerce
P.O. Box 2538
Madison, WI 53701-2538
PH: 608-266-8577
FAX: 608-267-9723

Acknowledgements

A great many people helped make this guide possible. Foremost among them is Steve Hullibarger, head of The Home Team, the Fair Oaks, California consultancy that advises developers around the U.S. on the use of manufactured homes. Steve is also the author of *Developing With Manufactured Homes*, the definitive reference book for construction professionals, and the first print resource I turned to when I began my own research. He not only shared with me his Rolo-Dex, photographs, and invaluable insights gained from decades of experience in the home building industry, but he somehow found time to review drafts in progress and suggest revisions. I am forever in his debt.

I am most grateful to the following for graciously agreeing to review the final draft: Gub Mix, Director of the Idaho-Nevada-Utah Manufactured Housing Associations; John Boyer, Chief of Manufactured Housing, Pennsylvania Department of Community and Economic Development; Jeff Wick, President, Wick Building Systems; Doug Gorman, owner of the Home Mart dealership in Tulsa, Oklahoma; attorney Martin Lavin of the Mobile Home Lending Corp.; Teri Ramsauer, Manager, Office of Manufactured Housing, Washington State Office of Community Development Housing Division; Grayson Schwepfinger of Salesmaker Associates; Wayne Beamer, editor of the industry magazine *Manufactured Home Merchandiser*; and real estate broker Richard Catlett of Port Angeles, Washington.

In Fred Townsend, the esteemed Atlanta, Georgia-based industry consultant and columnist, I found a veteran professional willing to share his considerable wisdom and knowledge. Thanks for your faith in this undertaking.

I am most grateful to the following consumer advocates, consultants and non-profit organizations for sharing their resources, in particular the Southeastern Office of Consumers Union in Austin, Texas (Kathy Mitchell and Kevin Jewell); Richard Genz of Housing and Community Insight; the Golden State Mobile Home Owners Association (Steve Gullage), and the Manufactured Home Owners of America (Patricia McGahuey).

Investigative reporter Gordon Oliver of the *Portland Oregonian* (and author of the outstanding 2000 series detailing fraud and abuse in Oregon manufactured home sales) merits special thanks for sharing his contacts and helping frame the issues. Thanks, too, to Don Carlson, editor and publisher of *Automated Builder Magazine* for contributing important background on the manufacturing of factory-built homes.

For sharing their insights on consumer issues in California, thanks to Richard Wienart and George Macias of the State of California's Office of Manufactured Home Consumer Affairs.

The Manufactured Housing Institute—in particular Kami Watson, Bruce Savage, Ann Parman and Erik Jennifer—was most helpful, not only providing essential books and documentation, but supplying ready answers and permissions for the use of photographs and copyrighted materials. Joan Brown, executive director of the Washington Manufactured Housing Association provided invaluable referrals, as did Charlotte Gattis, president of the Georgia Manufactured Housing Association.

In the financial community many professionals shared their expertise: Brett Pierce of Conseco Finance Corporation; Vonnie McKnight and Deon Kapetan of First Federal Savings and Loan, Port Angeles, Washington; Sue Ellen Dumdie of Washington Mutual Bank, Sequim, Washington; Christopher Conway of Standard and Poors' New York Division of Structured Financing; Robert Reyes of Guarantee Residential Lending; Alan Leingang of Seattle Mortgage, and Cathy Rawlins of Peninsula Mortgage. Thank you all.

On matters of real estate and land use law, in addition to broker Richard Catlett, I extend thanks to attorney and Realtor Chuck Marunde as well as broker Ken Laidlaw and Realtor Danni Breen.

For background on retail sales I am grateful to Chris Hansen and Tom Martin for reviewing portions of drafts in progress. Helping with insights into the Southeast market was Kevin Druey of Buddy's Homes, Thomaston, Georgia. Home town professionals lending a hand were Rick Cavenaugh, Melvin Henderson, Chuck Turpin, Doug Eacrett, Vella Tudor, Pat Richardson and John Lugar.

Palm Harbor Homes' David Witherspoon, Director of Marketing, and Howard Broughton, Palm Harbor Homes' Vice President, provided valuable insights from the manufacturer's perspective, as did James R. "Buzz" Mouncer, founder of Homebuilders Northwest (Salem, Oregon) and Craig Fleming, Vice President of Marketing, Silvercrest Homes. I am most grateful to you all.

Thanks, too, to Del Detray, Martin Faveluke, Dennis Wilson, John Murphy, Mike Williams, Colleen Rogers, Gary Schneider, Stan Sullins, and Cory and Maryann Startup.

Last, I am profoundly thankful for the steadfast support, love and encouragement of my wife Susan Robinson who from the beginning believed in me and this very special undertaking.

Finally—the first ever consumer ratings guide to every manufactured home builder and their brands, with at-a-glance listings that provide key information home shoppers need to make an informed buying decision.

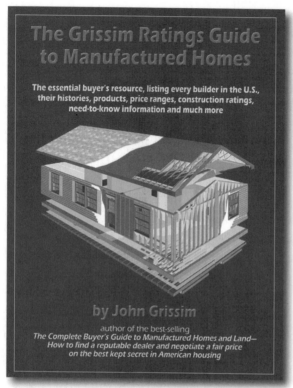

The Grissim Ratings Guide to Manufactured Homes

The essential buyer's resource, listing every builder in the U.S., their histories, products, price ranges, construction ratings, need-to-know information and much more

by John Grissim

author of the best-selling
The Complete Buyer's Guide to Manufactured Homes and Land—
How to find a reputable dealer and negotiate a fair price
on the best kept secret in American housing

Published by Rainshadow Ventures, LLC, 96 pages, 8-1/2" x 11", 1 illustration, 3-page table.
$29.95 + S&H   ISBN 0-9725436-1-9

All 79 U.S. builders evaluated
More than 300 brands and series described,
Plus, an annotated Construction Rating Table
with 56 criteria you can use to evaluate
any home—*before* you buy

If you have *The Grissim Buyer's Guide to Manufactured Homes & Land,* you already know that today's manufactured homes are truly the best-kept secret in American housing. Now, John Grissim has written a companion guide that takes a close look at every manufacturer and the brands they build, providing up-to-date, essential information together with the same authoritative, no-nonsense insights that made *The Grissim Buyer's Guide* the #1 best-selling book on purchasing manufactured homes.

Together, these books are the most comprehensive, up-to-date, authoritative—and trusted—consumer buying guides to manufactured homes and land.

Each manufacturer's listing includes:
• Company background/history
• States where sold
• Principal market niche/target customer
• Retail price range
• Who they compete against
• Construction rating on a 1-10 scale
• Brands and series described

• Description of a popular model
• What distinguishes brand from others
• Number of dealerships
• Warranty structure
• Availability of in-house financing
• Web site rating and evaluation
• Author's comments

To learn much more about the book (excerpts, reviews and a sample listing), please visit **www.grissimguides.com**. You may order a copy online or call toll-free (800) 304-6650. Orders usually ship in one business day. The book may also be ordered from any book store.